Eduard Mörike's Reading and the Reconstruction of his Extant Library

American University Studies

Series III
Comparative Literature

Vol. 8

PETER LANG
New York · Berne · Frankfurt am Main

Hal H. Rennert

Eduard Mörike's Reading and the Reconstruction of his Extant Library

PETER LANG
New York · Berne · Frankfurt am Main

Library of Congress Cataloging in Publication Data

Rennert, Hal H., 1939–
Eduard Mörike's Reading and the Reconstruction of his
Extant Library.

(American University Studies. Series III, Comparative
Literature; vol. 8)
Bibliography: p.
1. Mörike, Eduard Friedrich, 1804–1875 – Books and
reading. 2. Mörike, Eduard Friedrich, 1804–1875 –
Library. I. Title. II. Series: American University
Studies. Series III, Comparative Literature; v. 8.
PT2434.Z5R399   1985   831'.7   83-49184
ISBN 0-8204-0080-7

CIP-Kurztitelaufnahme der Deutschen Bibliothek

Rennert, Hal H.:
Eduard Mörike's Reading and the Reconstruction
of his Extant Library / Hal H. Rennert. –
New York; Berne; Frankfurt/M.:
Lang, 1985.
(American University Studies: Ser. 3,
Comparative Literature; Vol. 8)
ISBN 0-8204-0080-7

NE: American University Studies / 03

ISSN 0724-1445

© Peter Lang Publishing, Inc., New York 1985

Printed by Lang Druck Inc., Liebefeld/Berne (Switzerland)

Contents

Je ne sais comment j'appris à lire:
je ne me souviens que de mes premières
lectures et de leur effect sur moi: c'est
le temps d'où je date sans interruption
la conscience de moi-même.

Jean-Jacques Rousseau, *Les Confessions*

Of one thing, then, we may be certain:
impressions of Bartram's 'inchanting little
Isle of Palms' were among the sleeping
images in Coleridge's unconscious memory at
the time when 'Kubla Khan' emerged from
it . . . Those images of Tartary, and Florida,
and Abyssinia, and Egypt, and Cashmere —
had certainly become (in Coleridge's own
words) 'as difficult to separate as two dew-
drops blended together on the bossom of a
new-blown Rose.'

Sir John Livingston Lowes, *The Road to Xanadu*

Manchmal rufe ich in einer waghalsigen
Szene Gestalten aus Büchern zusammen, die
sich, von unterschiedlichen Geistern erfunden, nicht treffen dürften, aber sich nun
begegnen in einer kleinen, phantastischen
Abendgesellschaft.

Peter Härtling, "Mein Europa" in *Meine Lektüre*

Preface

No doubt the reason why we see in so many photo-portraits of the 1860's the subject holding a book is because a book must have appeared to be as innocuous an object as could be held onto by self-conscious hands in those heady days of the birth of photography. In Eduard Mörike's case, in almost all of the daguerreotypes we have of him, it was a matter of supreme preference to be seen holding a book; he relished reading. He preferred to read even when surrounded by his family and relatives in the setting of a sunny summer's day next to a fountain in a garden.

How does a supremely gifted poet who — as one devotee once put it hyperbolically — had suddenly appeared on the scene like Athena sprung from the brow of Zeus without model or antecedent, how does such a poet read? That question became an immensely pleasurable task for me as a professional reader to explore, and is the subject of this book. I approached the question from two directions. My interest in the problem of Mörike's reading was triggered by his lyric poetry, specifically by the resonance or rather the shine of "Auf eine Lampe" and its apparent equipoise as a text between the Classical and the Romantic tradition. This is one direction I took with the aid of some aspects of the theoretical groundwork laid by reader-oriented ciriticism. The other direction I took is through a reconstruction of a kind of protocol or case history that Mörike left behind in the form of marginalia, notes, *Lesefrüchte*, and books in his personal possession as well as in his all-important letters. This led me to the ongoing attempt at the reconstruction of his extant library. In this latter task the editorial apparatus compiled for the critical-historical edition of Mörike's works in progress at the *Mörike Archiv* of the *Schiller-Nationalmuseum* and *Deutsches Literaturarchiv* in Marbach has been essential.

It is this institution, its director, Bernhard Zeller, and its librarians and researchers, especially Walter Scheffler and Hans-Ulrich Simon, whom I wish to thank for unstinting assistance in that special perusal which must be devoted to original sources, as well as for the permission to publish heretofore unpublished materials and notations. I also thank the *Nationale Forschungs- und Gedenkstätten der klassischen deutschen Literatur in Weimar,* in particular the staff of the *Goethe-Schiller Archiv,* for the use of and permission to cite from the Mörike *Teilnachlaß.* Also my thanks go to the *Stadtarchiv Stuttgart* for the use and selective citations from the Fritz Kauffmann collection of Mörike manuscripts and memorabilia. To the *Deutscher Akademischer Austauschdienst* I express my gratitude for generous financial assistance on two occasions which allowed me to pursue my research in Germany. For encouragement and constructive exchange of ideas I thank my mentors and colleagues Raymond Immerwahr, Ernst Behler and Frank Jones at the University of Washington as well as Mary Crichton at the University of Michigan and Gregory Ulmer at my home institution, the University of Florida. My special thanks for occasions of Mörike homage go to Ulrich Hötzer, Tübingen. Finally I wish to thank my wife Sarah for her support and understanding.

Gainesville, Florida   H.H.R.
July 1983

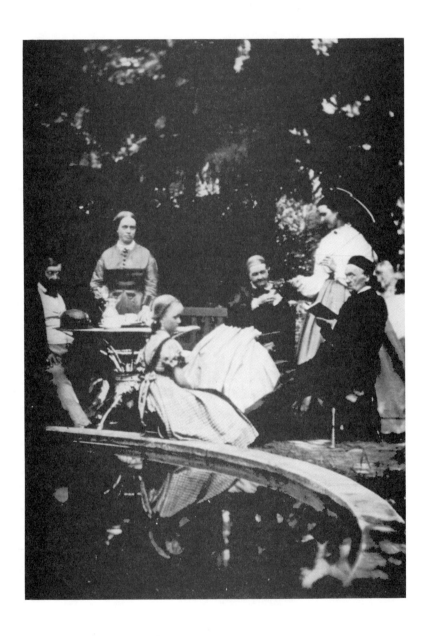

Chapter I

Main Currents of Restrospective Influence: Mörike's Reading of Shakespeare, Goethe, and Lichtenberg

The pleas of David Friedrich Strauß and Friedrich Theodor Vischer to Mörike for more philosophically and historically-based works and Mörike's replies surely belong to the most celebrated exchanges of crossfertilization of the philosopher/aesthetician with the poet in the literature of nineteenth century Germany.[1] This exchange is based on a fundamental misreading not of the poem "Das Märchen vom sichern Mann" which had in part triggered it, but of a misreading of Mörike's intentions of his creative processes. The key replies by Mörike are: "Was ich nicht aus mir selbst und etwa aus dem Leben nehmen kann, hat keinen Reiz für mich," and "indessen weißt Du ja, mein Lieber, wie sich ein Mythus im Lauf der Zeit bald besser, bald schlechter formiert."[2]

The year was 1838, when Mörike was approaching the pinnacle of midcareer with the first edition of his collection of poems in press and laying plans for other works such as the *Classische Blumenlese*. Thus, characteristically before the publication of a major work, Mörike had sought eleventh-hour advice and indirectly had enlisted help for reviews of his work from the best minds among his friends. A less well-known anticipatory disclaimer by Mörike is a postscript he wrote a few days prior to the previously cited one to Strauß: "Noch eins: Ich brauche ein Motto aus Shakespeare im Originaltext und kann denselben hier unten nicht wohl kriegen: tu mir daher doch den Gefallen, die Stelle gelegentlich auszuschreiben. Sie steht im Romeo Act 3. Sc. 3, wo Romeo die Trostgründe Lorenzos verwirft: 'An den Galgen mit der Philosophie, wenn Philosophie nicht eine Julia schaffen kann.'" (Mörike quotes from memory; the correct version in the Schlegel-Tieck translation is: "Hängt die Philosophie / kann sie nicht schaffen eine Julia.")[4]

This postscript is remarkable in several respects, because it puts several lines of discussion below in perspective: 1. It indicates a repeated attempt by Mörike to locate his place aesthetically-artistically in a rich literary tradition and vis-à-vis his contemporaries. 2. It indicates the still fragmentary picture we have of Mörike based on outdated and incomplete editions and other documentary evidence. 3. It indicates Mörike's deep knowledge and active devotion to Shakespeare to the extent that he considers a key passage of the creative imagination as the muse-motto for his collection of poems about to be published. 4. It indicates his limiting circumstances caused by conditions of near poverty and of rural isolation. The first three aspects, then, form a major part of the background to this study.

In exploring Mörike's reading I was giuded by serveral unanswered questions. None of these questions, which are recognized as genuine problems by serious students of Mörike, had been fully answered in the scholarship. First I wanted to know what and how widely Mörike had read; what pervasive influences existed in his work; who were his favorite authors; which were his favorite works. How did Mörike read? And, from a cross-cultural point of view, what modern languages and which works of European literature did he know? Answer to these questions, as well as the process of answering them by accounting for lacunae in the documentary evidence also form the main endeavor of this chapter. There is an emphasis throughout this study on the period before the appearance of Mörike's first edition of this collected poems (1838).

The need to answer questions about Mörike's reading arises from his growing recognition as one of Germany's major poets. His work and life without this clarification cannot be fully understood. As S.S. Prawer puts it in the first comprehensive *Wirkungsgeschichte* ever written about Mörike: "Noch ist es zu früh, ihn der Weltliteratur zuzurechnen. Wenn aber nicht alle Zeichen trügen, so ist Mörike jetzt endlich auf dem Wege, sich einen gebührenden Platz neben anderen Lyrikern zu sichern deren Stimme auch außerhalb ihres eigenen Landes gehört wird; einen Platz neben Puschkin, neben Leopardi und neben Baudelaire."[5] Mörike, with the attention received on an international level and attracting some of the best scholars in Germany after World War II (F. Sengle, B. v. Wiese and E. Staiger), was beginning to be recognized as a major lyric poet.

A shift in critical perspective during the last twenty-five years paved the way for an inquiry into Mörike's reading. In several ways F. Sengle's study in 1951, "Mörike-Probleme," summarized the research surrounding Mörike best with its recommendations for the future.[6] Basing his conclusions on a wide range of older works on Mörike, he pointed out that inquiries into Mörike's "Gedankenwelt," philosophy and religion have remained fruitless. Secondly, citing E. Staiger's view that Mörike lacked "ein bestimmtes eigenes Dasein"[7] he warns that such a view could lead to studies of purely artistic, technical-literary aspects of Mörike's work.[8] Sengle felt that pure *explication de texte* would also be fruitless because "zur reinen Artistik fehlt Mörike die Kälte, die handwerkliche Ausdauer."[9] In the process of asking what, if not the philosophical and the artistic sphere, does sustain Mörike's art, Sengle points to Mörike's myth-building, his humor and his pervasive playfulness. Finally, with regard to Benno v. Wiese's major study on Mörike,[10] which Sengle finds to be the best to date, he nevertheless warns against Wiese's totally ahistorical perspective and urges a return to historical, bio-graphical inquiry into "Wechselspiel von Leben und Werk."[11]

But Sengle's appeals some twenty-five years ago have born fruit after a fifteen- to twenty-year span of "modern criticism" or *imma-nente Literaturkritik*. There is, for example, a lengthy discussion of the influence of Goethe's *Wahlverwandtschaften* on Mörike's *Maler Nolten* in J. Kolbe's study *Goethes Wahlverwandtschaften und der Roman des 19. Jahrhunderts*.[12] S.S. Prawer, in turn, explores Goe-the's influence on Mörike's "anti-Meister" novel *Maler Nolten* in his study "Mignon's Revenge."[13] Even more recent is G. Rückert's fruitful re-exploration of the older area of the scholarship, Mörike as classicist, *Mörike und Horaz*.[14] Most recently M. Koschlig makes a valuable contribution in this field of the history of ideas with "Die Barock-Rezeption bei Mörike" which covers a dozen poems starting with the early one "der junge Dichter" and concludes with "Denk es, o Seele!"[15] A more limited number of poems, namely "Venedig. Nach Sannazar's Epigramm" and "Crux Fidelix" are, in turn, ex-plored by H.H. Krummacher in terms of Mörike's skills of "Nach-dichtung" which also presupposes his reading and schooling, in this case in the 16th and 17th century humanistic-literary tradition.[16]

The first study dealing with a specific reading by Mörike is by M. Enzinger, who concentrates on one specific poem: "Mörikes Gedicht 'Auf eine Lampe,'"[17] Precisely because "Die Deutungen bleiben vielfach immanent,"[18] Enzinger tried to probe deeper, urged on by the extraordinary critical attention to this poem which began with the Staiger-Heidegger Briefwechsel in 1951.[19] This critical debate stimulated at least seven major articles during the following decade.[20] Enzinger is able to trace Mörike's extensive reading of Homer; of the Greek Anthology, an important formative factor in the poem; and familiarity with German classicism, represented by Goethe and Schiller.[21] It goes without saying that Mörike's own translations of classical poets from Theocritus to Catullus deepened and informed his "Lampe" poem as well as his other *Dinggedichte*. Most challenging is Enzinger's suggestion that the poem was influenced by Mörike's perusal of the Goethe-Schiller correspondence and by Goethe's *Italienische Reise*, specifically the description of his visit to Herculaneum and Pompeii on March 18, 1787.[22] Enzinger's analysis goes deeper than previous explications, because he effectively combines literary analysis with relevant facts about Mörike's reading, at the point where scholars were at a loss to explain the origin of the mysterious and classical lamp in this poem.

Sengle's call for expanded exploration of "Wechselspiel von Leben und Werk" was most comprehensively taken up by Renate von Heydebrand's concentration on Mörike's poetry in which she explores Mörike's "Sprechsituationen" and "Formenvielfalt" — based on a much wider selection of Mörike's poems than had ever been done before.[23] Most penetrating and stimulating for the focus of this study of Mörike's reading is von Heydebrand's conclusion of Mörike's view of the therapeutic effect of art as well as the "Grundmotiv" of all of Mörike's literary-critical views (including those he made in regard to his reading): the necessary link of "Kunst und Harmonie."[24]

Indeed, though Mörike's raw life may have been lacking in content from which to draw for his artistic output, he led a rich, bookish life by immersing himself in the works of other writers. In other words, reading became a transference of past experience onto the plane of the present for Mörike.

In line with the work of Kolbe, Enzinger, and von Heydebrand, this study intends to increase our awareness of the role of Mörike's reading, and in particular of his knowledge and use of Shakespeare. Although reading is not assumed to be synonymous with influence, both aspects are pursued in their interrelationship throughout this study. As we shall see, for example, the Schiller-Goethe Correspondence as well as Lichtenberg's "Sudelbücher"-turned aphorisms were powerful precursors for the artistic training ground of Mörike's own writing style in his letters and of self-awareness as artist.

The traditional view, of which Mörike's first important editor and biographer Harry Maync was the major representative, was to claim almost total autonomy for his art.[25] Perhaps the greatest overstatement of this was made by the avid Mörike collector F. Kauffmann, when he observed: "Eigentliche Vorläufer, vollends Vorbilder hat Eduard Mörike nicht gehabt. So wie die aus dem Haupt des Zeus entsprungene Athene war er in seiner unverwechselbaren dichterischen Eigenart auf einmal da."[26] On the contrary, precisely some of those works which have come to be viewed as Mörike's greatest achievements, such as the poems "Um Mitternacht," "Gesang zu zweien in der Nacht," "Auf eine Lampe," some of the "folksongs" which by some magic on Mörike's part are not folksongs at all, such as "Denk es, o Seele!" "Das verlassene Mägdlein", and "Erstes Liebeslied eines Mädchens," the playet "Der letzte König von Orplid" in the context of *Maler Nolten* and the novella *Mozart auf der Reise nach Prag*, are pieces of creative divergence and completion of Mörike's poetic imagination, elements of what Harold Bloom calls "Tessera."[27] Precisely the combination of native poetic genius, poetic affinity for the "strong poets" Shakespeare, Goethe, Horace, and Lichtenberg and the folksong tradition, as well as his assimilative reading have produced such fine literary creations. In other words, the very tension generated between his own sensibility and outside influence has contributed significantly to his creations. This dialectic, from which Mörike undoubtedly also suffered was perhaps the key meaning of his exhortation "Laß, o Welt, o laß mich sein!" Throughout his poems and letters are scattered suggestions of the threat of powerful individuals. He knew the world could consume him and he studiously avoided personally meeting such overpowering figures as

Lenau, Thieck, and Hebbel.[28] Through the intermediary medium of art the world could be endured.

In a review of Kenzo Miyashita's biographical study, *Mörikes Verhältnis zu seine Zeitgenossen*[29] is the comment by L.B. Jennings: "Mörike's position is unusual in that the late blossoming of his reputation exposed a certain dearth of positivistic underpinnings."[30] Jennings was prompted to make his statement after warmly welcoming Miyashita's compilation of Mörike's relationship to his contemporaries and after wondering why such a study had not appeared before. Jennings' answer to his own question hints at problems of the scholarship dealing with Mörike, and it deserves further clarification. Specifically, the lack of a definitive edition of Mörike's works, and especially of a reliable and accessible edition of the letters has resulted in an almost total absence of studies solely devoted to Mörike's sources. Thus the view of Mörike as a poet lacking *Dasein* may have come about partially as the result of having been denied *Dasein* by the all-too-slowly grinding wheels of philological-textual foundations. With the appearance of the first of nine planned volumes of Mörike's letters, a major revision of our view of Mörike can begin to take place.[31] And, though urged by several critics, most recently by H.H. Holthusen, who points to the lack of a study "Mörike als Leser," there is no comprehensive study of Mörike's reading.[32]

Miyashita's study with its "positivistic underpinning" is based almost entirely on Mörike's letters. But a study based exclusively on letters contained, as they are at present, in a score of incomplete, obscure and unscholarly collections and editions, runs the risk of distorting the picture we have of Mörike, or rather of perpetuating a distorted picture. I refer to arbitrary exclusions and omissions in the two most comprehensive collections available in the two F. Seebaß volumes and the later G. Baumann volume.[33] Curiously, the most common omissions are those letters and passages in which Mörike comments on his reading. The new volume of letters, *Briefe, 1811–1828*, now contributes significantly to a clearer and more comprehensive picture of Mörike as a reader of literature outside his own national and cultural boundaries; a significantly revised picture of Mörike as literary critic, as translator, as teacher, as a restless, discontented and impoverished country curate is emerging.

This restoration of Mörike's correspondence is also of key importance to Mörike's view of himself, because he prized letters above any other form of writing, feeling that they contained the highest degree of sincerity a writer is capable of. A few examples of the previous omissions, which have now been restored, with particular relevance to the problem of reading, will suffice.

In the fall of 1828 Mörike decided to try to live solely by his writings rather than continue in the position of Pfarrverweser, which he found odious. First he looked for a position as librarian, an occupation he always longed and repeatedly applied for.[34] Together with his friend Mährlen he also tried to get a position at the publishing house of Cotta in Stuttgart or Augsburg. He also planned to edit a literary almanac, *Barbara Bavaria*, together with Mährlen.[35] Finally, he signed a contract with the publisher Franck in Stuttgart to write articles, only to break it a few weeks later because of an inability to work with short deadlines. Many letters from that time (1827−1828) help us to date his poems, but also give us insights into his resourcefulness, his plight and frustration, his assessment of his own talents, and especially of his writing and reading. In a letter to Mährlen dated Sept. 20, 1828, which also contained his poem "Am frischgeschnittnen Wanderstab," Mörike espresses second thoughts about a job, working as a translator for Kolb at Cotta: "Wenn er aber glaubt, einen französischen Übersetzer in mir zu finden, so hat er sich verrechnet; für d. Eilfertigkeit, womit solche Berichte geliefert werden müssen, reicht weder mein Wortschatz noch ganz meine *Syntaxis* hin. Wollen sehen, ob sich nicht insofern e. Änderung im Plan machen läßt."[36]

This letter and several others during that time − though crucial to our understanding of aspects of Mörike's life and work − are not included in the Seebass collections and now too are restored. In a letter dated June 21, 1828 to G. Schwab, who was undoubtedly in a position to further Mörike's writing career as the editor of the Cotta *Morgenblatt*, one of the few outlets open to the budding poet at the time, the following passage was eliminated in Seebaß and Baumann and is now restored:

Ich hatte die Lieder- und Romancen-Gattung lange ganz bei Seite gelegt; darf ich Ihnen aber sagen, daß Ihr über allen Ausdruck schönes (in der Schwäb Alb enthaltenes) Gedicht: "Die Feyen des Ursulenberges" mich neulich wieder schnell dahin berauschte? Sie werden mir dieses Geständnis nicht als eine einfältige *captatio benevolentiae* auslegen; weder schmeichelt man so grob, noch kann Ihnen ein Wort von mir schmeicheln.[37]

At least three important matters come to light in this passage. Mörike had put aside writing and reading lyric poetry in an attempt to write a successful play. Secondly, he was trying to impresss Schwab not with flattery, but instead with his critical discernment: out of the many poems by Schwab he lauded one in particular. And thirdly the passage reveals more accurately Mörike's very selective love of works by the "Swabian Romantics," G. Schwab, J. Kerner and L. Uhland. Mörike must indeed have admired Schwab's poem very much because it is one of very few by the Swabian poets which he copied and retained in his *Abschriften* SNM.[38] In fact in a second copy Mörike prefaced the poem:

> *Aus dem Gedächtnis in Pürkelgut geschrieben als ein dicker Nebel die Gegend vor meinem Fenster bedeckte d. 13. Dezbr. 1850 abends 3 1/2 Uhr*
>
> *(Abschriften* GSA)

Being able to copy the poem from memory twenty-two years after first praising it should be ample proof of no undue flattery.

The new volume of letters includes a number of previously unknown and completely unpublished ones as for example a letter to Cotta, dated March 21, 1828 in which Mörike applies for a job with the publisher.[39] There are also several letters and many passages of letters with reference to reading and literary plans, which are still contained in rare, small and specialized exchanges of letters. The limited correspondences between Vischer and Möriker and between Kurz and Mörike are particularly noteworthy, because Mörike's plans and his somewhat rare ciritical views are expressed here. Again, both Seebaß volumes and the recent Baumann collection exclude some of the most crucial passages in which Mörike reveals his reading and ventures forth to express ciritical views. Two of such letters, one to

Vischer, dated May 23, 1832 is discussed below in Chapter III and the other to Kurz, dated June 30, 1837 is discussed in Chapter II. Perhaps the greatest problem with omissions that contain references to reading and critical views exists in the collection of letters to Hartlaub edited by Renz.[40] *Beilagen* and *Lesefrüchte*, too numerous to mention were eliminated and will have to be restored by the remaining eight letter volumes of the critical-historical edition.

Besides the heretofore unpublished and neglected letters there are Mörike's notations in his extant library, his *Abschriften* and a set of unpublished calendars containing important clues as to intensity and concentration of his reading. Though the notes in the calendars cannot be reproduced in detail in this study, I would like to cite two entries, which qualify both as new facts and as notes of interest from a crosscultural point of view. In his "Sack und Schreib-Kalender," 1825, under *d. 28* [October] Mörike wrote: *Abends bei Gelegenheit des Werner v. Byron — den Gedanken zu einer Trag.πχ gefasst / Je m'encourage.*[41] It should give us pause that Maync said of this time that Mörike's friends, Waiblinger and Lohbauer sought adventure and experience, or that others composed songs to the Greeks in response to Byron's devotion to the Greek cause, but that "von Mörike wissen wir nichts derart."[42] It seems to me that when it comes to Mörike's reading and sources of inspiration, we have not looked carefully enough. In one of his other calendars for the year 1837 Mörike noted under the months January to March:

> *Ich las in kurzer Zeit folgende W. Scottsche Romane, Invanhoe, Guy Mannering, dazwischen Bauers Alexander d. G., Redgauntlet, Altherthümler, Quentin Durward, Waverley, Kloster Abt., Herz von Midlothian, die Schwärmer, St. Ronans Brunnen.*[43]

Although Mörike's reading of Scott's novels has probably not left a discernible, permanent mark on his thinking and writing the possibility exists. As is true for many other names included in lists of Mörike's "Lektüre" in short discussions in secondary literature, it has never been determined for Mörike, exactly which works he read and when, and which of these works occupied him most. But *how* Mörike read and how this reading left its mark on him is intimately bound up with the question of *what* occupied him most. Judging from Mörike's works, letters, notations in his extant library, *Abschriften*, translations, editorial-critical notes for fellow poets and calendars, I believe the three authors most dominant in his thinking and writing are Shakespeare, Goethe and Lichtenberg. In the following discussion an attempt is made to delineate Mörike's preoccupation with these authors.

Mörike's preoccupation with Shakespeare occurs in all major phases of his work and life and therefore falls into four categories' 1. Most intense and sustained period of identification and intersubjectivity (letters, lyric poems, Orplid, *Maler Nolten*) through 1832; 2. Criticalaesthetic phase (correspondence with Vischer, Strauß and Kurz) mainly through 1850, but also later; 3. Shakespeare as "Volksdichter" and tradition (occasional verse and commonly shared allusions) cutting across all periodes but mostly post-1850s; 4. Pedagogical, public phase (teaching, lecturing and translating in Stuttgart) through 1867. Let us here specifically turn to the latter three phases (phase one is the main topic of Chapters II and II below).

The only friends or associates with whom Mörike could share his interest in Shakespeare on a sustained and critical level were Vischer and Kurz. Vischer, for example, reveals his sensitivity to Mörike's poetry and his solid, critical grasp of Shakespeare when he observes in a letter about Mörike's image of the ghostly prince in the poem "Die traurige Krönung:" "Das nickende trippelnde freundliche Kind ist ganz Shakespearisch angeschaut."[44] Without probing deeper into a specific parallel, Vischer was quite right in his observation. The scene described in "Die traurige Krönung," without Mörike's explicit intention, resembles the ghostly closing scenes of *Richard III*, with the specters of Richard's murdered victims gathering to haunt his dreams.

Kurz, in turn, was translating Shakespeare in the late 1830s, specifically *Cymbeline*. He helped Mörike finish the libretto "Die Regenbrüder" (1839), which evokes the merry, dreamy and supernatural interaction of lovers, tradesmen and fairies in Shakespeare's *A Midsummer Night's Dream* and the aura of mysterious and dominating winds of *The Tempest*.

20

In regard to the third phase outlined, this is part of the rich Shakespeare tradition in Germany that had reached its pinnacle with the Schlegel-Tieck translation. In summarizing this tradition and its aftermath throughout the early nineteenth century (including Heinrich Heine, but not Mörike), L.M. Price points out: "Like Goethe, the Stürmer and Dränger, and Otto Ludwig Heine found in Shakespeare what was in himself."[45]

There are at least three direct allusions to Shakespeare in Mörike's poems. Such direct allusions to figures in literary tradition are reserved for Mörike's light occasional verse. Because of the open allusions to Shakespeare we cannot speak of influence. Rather, certain Shakespearean figures and metaphors had become "Volkseigentum." in the first of these poems, "Die Visite" (1838), the allusion presupposes a common knowledge of one of the most widely known pranksters of Shakespeare, an almost public figure, Puck in *A Midsummer Night's Dream*. In this poem Mörike himself plays Puck. The following are the first two stanzas of this four-stanza poem:

Philister kommen angezogen:
Man sucht im Garten mich und Haus;
Doch war der Vogel ausgeflogen,
Zu dem geliebten Wald hinaus.
Sie kommen, mich auch da zu stören:
Es ruft, und ruft im Widerhall −
Gleich laß ich mich als Kuckuck hören,
Bin nirgends und bin überall.

So führt ich sie, nur wie im Traume
Als Puck im ganzen Wald herum;
Ich pfiff und sang von jedem Baume,
Sie sehn sich fast die Hälse krumm.
Nun schalten sie: Verfluchte Possen!
Der Sonderling! Der Grobian! −
Da komm' ich grunzend angeschossen,
Ein Eber mit gefletschtem Zahn.[46]

In the much later poem, "An Fräulein Elise v. Grävenitz" (1854), the "occasion" is more specific, but also more restricted in intention and in applicability. Again the direct reference to Shakespeare is to the popular, by then almost native dramatist. The context is again characterized by humor and levity. Let it suffice to cite Mörike's explanatory note, which he added below the title: "Aus Anlass einer Maskerade, bei der sie in Gestalt einer Distel erschien, zugleich mit ihr die Maske des verwandelten Zettel, Weber, im *Sommernachtstraum*" (I, 843). It should be observed in this connection, that Mörike excluded most of such occasional verse from the final authorized edition of his poems in 1867; but both of these poems — as one further indication of Mörike's love for Shakespeare — were included.

A third poem, "Nach einer schläfrigen Vorlesung von 'Romeo und Julia'," (written 1846, published in *Salon: Unterhaltungsblatt zur Frauen-Zeitung*, 1858) was not included in the final authorized edition of the poems. Again, the allusion to Shakespeare is overt, and characterized by levity and humor. Also, as in the case of Puck the two famous lovers are taken from their "literary" context, as if they have become common cultural property. The five lines are entirely couched in dialogue:

> Guten Morgen, Romeo;
> Wie geschlafen?
>
>   Ach so so.
> Und du, süße, Julia?
> Ebenfalls so so la la.   (II, 387)

Many of Mörike's later occasional poems share this lack of pretentiousness. They are almost purely aimed to please, as the medium of this poem's publication suggests.

Still another major aspect of Mörike's preoccupation with Shakespeare consists of his use of Shakespeare for his private lectures, alongside of his teaching duties at the Katherinenstift in Stuttgart during the years 1851 to 1866. Prior to accepting the teaching position Mörike was, as always, in dire need of supplemental income, for he was about to be married. In reply to his inquiry into possibilities for journalistic work in Stuttgart, Vischer had answered him: "Wenn ich doch nur auch eine Quelle lukrativer Tätigkeit für Dich wüßte . . . Einen Gedanken, woraus etwas werden könnte habe ich früher schon jemand an die Hand gegeben: ein vernünftig kastrierter Shakespeare. Man sagte natürlich zum voraus, daß man sehr wohl wisse, was es sei um die Kastration, aber es gebe und müsse geben neben dem objektiven Standpunkt den pädagogischen, insbesondere fürs weibliche Geschlecht."[47] Coldly calculating though Vischer's attitude might have been, he was also trying to help his friend by this suggestion. (Cf. Mörike's "self-censorship" in connection with item No. 45 of Annotated Bibliography, Chapter V.)

Maync, who also refers to Vischer's suggestion, dismisses it with the comment: "doch abgesehen davon, daß Mörike das Englische in keiner Weise beherrschte, tat ihm das 'blutige Geschäft' selbst leid."[48] Mörike's translation skills in English and his rekindled interest in Shakespeare require further clarification, however.

Kurz reported in his letter to Mörike, dated Jan. 9, 1839, that to his great surprise the Bibliographical Institute was seeking Mörike as a translator of English.[49] Kurz was surprised, because Mörike had earlier, in a memorable phrase, commented on his skill in English when he had sent a song from *Twelfth Night* to Kurz: "Wenn ich Ihnen, einem Sprachkundigen, diese Strophen englisch zitiere, so folgt daraus nicht, daß ich Englisch verstehe. Ich schmecke den Sinn nur heraus."[50] To trust his instincts and to "taste" the sense in order to produce poetic and meaningful translations must have been Mörike's method in several extant translations of passages from Shakespearean plays in the *Abschriften* GSA.[51] Mörike could help himself quite nicely as a poet by comparing several translations of Shakespeare, notably Eschenburg's and Schlegel's and by applying his own interpolating genius to whatever English he knew to arrive at a superior translation. Similarly, in his translations of Greek and Latin poets in *Classische Blumenlese* (1840), in *Theokrit* (1855) and in *Anakreon und die sogenannten Anakreontischen Lieder* (1864) Mörike used existing translation extensively, even though his knowledge of Greek and Latin was excellent. In exploring Mörike's sources Ulrich Hötzer in his discussions "Bearbeitungsanalysen" and "Hinweise zur Quellenbenutzung" characterizes Mörike's translation method as "anlehnendes Übersetzungsverfahren."[52] Among the many translations and reference works used for these purposes was an excerpt from an English version, Thomas Moore's *Odes of Anacreon*.[53]

23

The Shakespeare translations in the *Abschriften* GSA do not, however, seem to have left a permanent mark on Mörike's poetry, because most of them undoubtedly came into existence in connection with his lectures to the reading society of the Stuttgart Bürgermuseum. His applicable calendar, "Königlich Württembergischer Landeskalender für 1892," lists a total of sixteen lectures between January 3 and April 17, 1852.[54] Under the date 3. Jan. Mörike noted: *Erste Damenvorlesung im Museum (Hamlet, Einleitung, Akt 1).* The next fourteen lectures are taken up with *Hamlet, Dreikönigsabend (Twelfth Night), Macbeth* and *Romeo and Juliet.* The final lecture on April 17 was taken up with an *Auswahl deutscher Gedichte.*[55] An excerpt from one of Mörike's translations may serve to demonstrate his use of Eschenburg and Schlegel to take the best from both and to arrive at a smoother more condensed and more readable translation: In Act IV, ii of *Macbeth* Ross tries to calm Lady Macduff, who is very anxious about her husband's departure, leaving her vulnerable to Macbeth and his henchmen. Mörike retranslates her reply to Ross' calming words (11. 6–14) as follows:

> *Lady.*   *Klugheit? Im Stich zu lassen Weib und Kinder,*
>   *Sein Haus u. seine Würden, an dem Ort*
>   *Aus dem er selber flieht! Er liebt uns ō!*   [ō = nicht]
>   *Es fehlt ihm das natürliche Gefühl.*
>   *Denn, der Zaunkönig selbst der kleinste Vogel*
>   *Verficht ((doch wider)) gegen die Eule doch sein Nest. –*
>   *Die Furcht ((thut)) ist bei ihm alles, nichts die Liebe.*
>   (*Abschriften,* GSA)

In comparison, Schlegel's version in this instance is somewhat less readable. In his attempt to translate all of Lady Macduff's statements he obscures the thrust of her emotion in the last two lines of her reply. Mörike's solution for "natural emotion" (das natürliche Gefühl) also seems more felicitous than Schlegel's "Naturgefühl:"

> Lady Macduff.   Weisheit! Sein Weib, die kleinen Kinder lassen,
>   Haushalt wie seine Würden, an dem Ort,
>   Von dem er selbst entflieht? Er liebt uns nicht,
>   Ihm fehlt Naturgefühl. Bekämpft der schwache

Zaunkönig, dieses kleinste Vögelchen,
Die Eule doch für seine Brut im Nest.
Bei ihm ist alles Furcht, und Liebe nichts;
Nicht größer ist die Weisheit, wo die Flucht
So gegen die Vernunft rennt.[56]

Eschenburg's version, in prose, is even more faithful to the original and even less dramatic than Schlegel's because the thythmic formality of metered speech is lacking and because the wordiness deflates the anxious and derisive tone of Lady Macduff's reply:

> Lady. Klugheit! – Sein Weib zu verlassen, seine unmündigen
> Kinder, seinen Landsitz und seine Titel an einem Orte
> zu lassen, von dem er selbst entflieht! – Er liebt
> uns nicht; er hat kein Naturgefühl! Denn der
> armselige Zaunkönig, der allerkleinste unter den Vögeln,
> wird für seine Jungen, die er im Neste hat wider die
> Eule kämpfen. Seine Furcht ist bei ihm alles, seine
> Liebe nichts, und eben so wenig bedeutet da die Klugheit,
> wo die Flucht so gegen alle Vernunft anrennt.[57]

Mörike's translation is almost entirely based on Schlegel's but its diction also reveals a reading of Eschenburg. Mörike chose "Klugheit" over "Weisheit" and, as his corrections reveal, he wisely rejected Eschenburg's aurally ambiguous "wider" for "gegen." It is also noteworthy, in turn, that Schlegel's last line is almost an exact echo of Eschenburg's.

Mörike's other translated passages from *Twelfth Nigth* and *Romeo and Juliet* also serve the function of easier readability. In *Romeo and Juliet* Mörike also took pains to circumvent some of the bawdiness in the Nurse's speech. Besides being the basis for a series of lectures, Mörike undoubtdely recited passages aloud, because certain single, double and triple underlinings of single words seem to represent stress marks.

In summary we observe that although Mörike expended a great deal of engery on his Shakespeare lectures, there is no discernible effect on his late poetry of the Stuttgart years. But, in a sense, the translations reveal Shakespearean influence in retrospect. How and to what extent Shakespeare had an impact on Mörike's poetry, especially in the years 1818 to 1833, are the central problems dealt with in Chapters II and III of this study.

Perhaps the only work in Mörike's final period (1851 to 1875) that contains a hint of his pervasive preoccupation with Shakespeare, aside from occasional poems, is *Mozart auf der Reise nach Prag*. As Maync pointed out, a very early reviewer of the novella detected what he thought were parallels between Mörike's episode of having Mozart recall scenes from his trip to the Gulf of Naples in Italy and scenes from Shakespeare's *Antony and Cleopatra*.[58]

Although there are occasional references throughout Mörike's letters to other British authors in translations, none of these seems to have left a permanent mark on Mörike's work or occupied him extensively. In the 1820s Mörike had read, for example, Oliver Goldsmith's *The Vicar of Wakefield*, Byron's poetry (including "Werner"), James McPherson's "Ossian" poems, Edward Young's "Night Thoughts" and Owen's "Epigrams." In the 1830s he read several of Sir Walter Scott's novels (as previously cited), Kurz's translation of Byron's "Prisoner of Chillon," Swift's "Märchen von der Tonne," Bulwer's novel *Paul Clifford* and an "Erzählung" by (the American author) Washington Irving. Except for Byron, the English Romantic poets seemed to have been unknown to Mörike.

The remarkable similarities between Mörike's "Auf eine Lampe" (1847) and John Keat's "Ode on a Grecian Urn" (1821) are coincidental, if that word can be used to describe similarities based on the mutual but independently shared tradition of classical Greek and Roman art and poetry. Thus, equally remarkable are the numerous morphological, stylistic studies that are based on these similarities. The most recent of these by Helmut Jochems uses the effective concept of "partielle Isomorphie" to explicate the multiple affinities between Mörike's "Lampe" and Keats's Urn.[59]

Judging from the frequency of reference in letters and from the extensive notations in his extant library, no other author occupied Mörike as much as Goethe. To assess accurately Mörike's reading of Goethe or to assess Mörike's literary debt to Goethe is beyond the scope of this study and requires a special treatment. I want to restrict myself here to the Goethe-Schiller correspondence and to several aspects of Mörike's most extensive notations in this Goethe edition as recorded in Chapter V below.

Mörike's favorite reading was autobiographical writing, such as diaries, travelogues, *Lebenserinnerungen* and especially letters in which he could see his own experience and creative processes reflected as in an "Abgrund der Betrachtung." It is therefore not surprising that one of the young Mörike's favorite works was Goethe's *Dichtung und Wahrheit*. Mörike had apparently received the first two volumes from Waiblinger, who out of deep admiration for Goethe had entitled his diaries, "Hugo Thorwald's Lehrjahre."[60] Mörike had replied to Waiblinger: "Die beyden ersten Baende v. Dichtung und Wahrheit hab ich nunmehr gelesen. Sie hatten eine wunderbare anmuthige Wirkung für mich. Es thut einem wohl, den Grossen so menschlich zu sehn, man meint keine Ursache zur Schüchternheit vor ihm zu haben, fühlt sich ihm naeher gebracht, wenn man hier liest, wie er so umgänglich und menschlich war, – an jedem aus seiner Umgebung findet er etwas Gutes."[61]

Although Mörike's enthusiastic response to his reading was not to remain later as naively worshipful as in 1821, when the poet was seventeen years old, his way of seeing the human being behind the towering stature of the poet (also true of Shakespeare, as we shall see below) was characteristic for almost all of his critical commentary. It is interesting that with Goethe this human level has to do with the creative process. In this sense Mörike's reading is a recreating experience of the creative act. The passage to Waiblinger goes on to describe Goethe's "Anschaun": "Heut sagte einer der das Buch vor sich hatte, zu mir, er wisse nicht, das Ding sey eigentlich doch ein Saich! Nicht wahr, der hatte wohl v. dem Ahndungsvollen nichts verspürt, wovon das Gemüth bei Schilderung des alterthümlichen Vaterhause oder der Empfindungen die der Knabe beym Anschaun von den ehrwürdigen Dingen hatte, – eingenommen wird?"[62] As the passive voice syntax of this passage indicates, there is here a total identification of Goethe-as-boy with the Mörike-as-boy reading. Additionally, in the historical context, Mörike's attitude toward great poets and great men (e.g. Napoleon) should be seen as a measure of his sensitivity, but also as a characteristic stance of the entire Biedermeier period (1815–1848), with its tendency toward miniaturization and its preference for the small idyllic of life. As F. Sengle puts it: "Die Neigung zum Kleinen, Nahen und Konkreten hat sich nicht nur bei den Künstlerischen, sondern auch bei den soziologischen Formen ausgewirkt."[63] Mörike's special attention and devotion to aspects of "der Grosse," as elements to which he could more easily relate than to the monumental literary creations (especially during his formative years) reflect one of the prevailing tendencies of his epoch.

As we see in Mörike's repeated reading of the *Goethe-Schiller Briefwechsel* and of the other Goethe volumes in his possession, the search for the very human qualities, this probing at the innermost circles of the great artist in the setting of his workshop gave Mörike insights into the minutiae of the artist's everyday life and into the creative process in general. Because of the human or autobiographical dimension, but also because ideas in it were discussed against the backdrop of what he sees as a harmonious, congenial and conciliatory friendship, the *Goethe-Schiller Briefwechsel* was Mörike's most favorite reading. It is interesting how high a value Mörike places on what he sees as Goethe's conciliatory nature, not only toward Schiller himself, but also in regard to Schiller's numerous literary quarrels. This can be seen in the minutely detailed commentary in Mörike's personal copies of the letter exchange, in which he recorded Goethe's attempt at smoothing things over (see Chapter V, item No. 2 of the Annotated Bibliography).

In his own letters Mörike again and again comments on his reading of the Goethe-Schiller correspondence. His initial response in 1829 was to the first two volumes of the six volume set which Cotta published in 1828-1829. One of his first readings is cast into its own literary form as a magical event or as a kind of epiphany:

Da zeigte mir der Satan einen Band des Briefwechsels auf dem Tisch. Ich griff so unentschieden darnach, als wollt ich nur den Überschlag beiläufig mustern; es war der Zweite Band. Das tolle Büchlein klebte aber in meinen Händen fest — seine Blätter flogen eilig, wie besessen von der Rechten zur Linken, ich stand bald mitten in heiliger classischer Atmosphäre, las endlich sachte und sachter, ja ich hielt den Atem an, die ruhige, tiefe Fläche nicht zu stören, in deren Abgrund ich nun senkrecht meinen Blick hinunter liess, als dürfte ich die Seele der Kunst anschauen. Einmal blick' ich auf

und verliere mich in eigenem Nachdenken. Das Licht war tief herabge-
brannt; ich putzte es nicht. Mein Kopf war aufs äußerste angespannt –
meine Gedanken liefen gleichsam auf den Zehenspitzen, ich lag wie über
mich selbst hinausgerückt und fühlte mich neben aller Feierlichkeit doch
unaussprechlich vergnügt. Statt mich niederzuschlagen, hatte der Geist
dieser beiden Männer eher die andere Wirkung auf mich. Gar manche
Idee – das darf ich Dir wohl gestehen – erkannte ich als mein selbst er-
worbenes Eigentum wieder, und ich schauderte oft vor Freuden über
seine Begrüssung.[64]

When Mörike refers to his own ideas which he recognized in these
letters, he was not so much thinking of literary ideas which are con-
cretely represented in his own works, as of a set of beliefs and
attitudes which he shared with the two great masters. One set of
ideas of this nature certainly concerns the creative process. On the
endpaper of his personal copy of the second volume of the letters,
Mörike had noted: *Über das Bewusstlose der künstlerischen Production S. 338.*[65] Although Mörike did not express himself formally
about his views on the creative act, his notation refers essentially to
ideas dealing with this problem in Schiller's letters to Goethe dated
March 27, 1801, and Goethe's reply of April 3, 1801. When Goethe,
in this discussion for example, speaks of his "Glaubensbekenntnis,"
Mörike must have felt he was looking at the "soul of art."[66] The
high quality of both form and content of Mörike's own letters can be
attributed to Mörike's love for the *Goethe-Schiller* letters. The act of
reading is recast as a creative act itself. This is why our understanding
of Mörike as poet must include the letters as part of his large Poem:
the totality of his work.

This love or self-reflection Mörike shows in several letters at various times. To Mährlein, in a letter dated Febr. 11, 1830 he writtes of
the letters: "Sie sind unerschöpflich an Belehrung . . . Ich brenne vor
Begierde, bis Du die folgenden schickst."[67] Then, again to Mährlen,
on Sept. 20, 1830, Mörike reports: "Die neue Folge von Briefen
schlang ich gleich in einem *haustus* hinunter."[68] And on Sept. 27,
1830 he writes: "Es hat wohl kaum einen redlicheren und dankbare-
ren Leser der Schiller- und Goethe-Correspondenz gegeben, wie mich,
was einigermaßen daraus erhellt, daß ich sie wirklich [*wirklich*=
Swabian for *jetzt*] zum fünftenmal durchmache."[69] In this tone of

elation and joy Mörike also recommends the correspondence to his friend Hartlaub in letters dated Sept. 14, 1831 and again, much later, on Nov. 14, 1845.[70] Also later, in his personal Goethe edition of 1840 (see Chapter V, item No. 12 of the Annotated Bibliography) Mörike leaves many reading marks in the letters in which Goethe describes his trip to Switzerland (1797) through Ludwigsburg, Stuttgart and Tübingen in his letters to Schiller. Leaving aside that he was not born until 1804, this is the closest Mörike ever came to actual contact with Goethe; and Goethe's descriptions of his activities and contacts in Mörike's birthplace and home towns probably was one additional reason for his love of the *Goethe-Schiller* letters.

In connection with Mörike's preoccupation with Goethe let us now consider additional aspects of his notations in the Goethe edition of 1840. As is the case for the *Goethe-Schiller* letters, Mörike tried to create for himself a definitive text with his many corrections and notations. But the notations are not as calligraphic as in the *Goethe-Schiller* letters and seem to have been written from more of a critical than an editorial perspective. Their limitations should also be kept in mind. They represent a concrete set of reading notes in a concrete set of books; they are not synonymous with Mörike's knowledge of Goethe. But not the least remarkable aspect of these notations is that they indicate repeated perusal of all of Goethe's writings in forty volumes sometime after 1840. This suggests another instance of influence in retrospect. That is to say, the notations surely indicate rereading of Goethe, who exerted his influence much earlier in Mörike's career.

Though his reading of Goethe generally seemed to be more assimilative than ciritical, in these notations – some were written as late as 1866 – Mörike's perspective is more complex than in his earlier views of Goethe, as the various categories indicate under which he systematized his comments. Among his critical notations one category concerns a special attention to words. Mörike loved unusual words. He had a keen eye for peculiarities of Goethe's diction. The headings he gave to this category are Goethe's *Eigenheiten* and *grata negligentia*.

An especially interesting fact is that Mörike's overall heading for this category is *Grimm*. He seemed to have listed many of Goethe's coinages with the intention of submitting them to the compilations of the Grimm *Wörterbuch*, which was in the planning stages in the late 1840's and early 1850's. Some examples of Goethe's coinages which Mörike noted were, "geklirrlos," "glimmern," "ermüdigt," "vorbewußt," "schweighaft," "erläugt" and "Wohngewinn." There ist, however, no evidence of Mörike's submission of his findings to the staff of editors of the Grimm *Wörterbuch*.[71] R. Steig in his article, "Mörikes Verehrung im Grimmschen Kreise," also makes no mention of Mörike's study of Goethe's diction.[72] Although there are no letters extant of a correspondence between Jacob Grimm and Mörike, in a letter dated July 13, 1847, to L. Uhland, Grimm recommends Mörike for the Tiedge poetry prize, which Mörike received later that year.[73] Mörike, in turn, was an avid reader and admirer of the first volumes of the *Wörterbuch*, when they came out in 1854. Among the *Abschriften* SNM are lists of vocabulary copied by Mörike from the *Wörterbuch*, as well as from the Joh.Chr. Schmid. *Schwäbisches Wörterbuch*, published earlier, in 1831. The direct benefit of Mörike's etymological and lexical studies can ultimately be seen in the unusual — often dialectal — diction in his five stories "Lucie Gelmeroth," "Der Bauer und sein Sohn" "Der Schatz," "Die Hand der Jezerte" and "Das Stuttgarter Hutzelmännlein." With these stories and the love for words suggested in them, Mörike carries on the great tradition of reinvigorating the language which had received such a powerful impetus by Goethe.

Another aspect of Mörike's notations is his interest in Goethe's characterizations. A comment he made in connection with his reading of Goethe's *Die Wahlverwandtschaften* is particularly noteworthy. Ottilie, in a speech in which she acknowledges the power of destiny in her life, demonstrates considerable self-understanding. Mörike observes in reference to this speech, in Part one, paragraph 16 of chapter 14: ex. *Beispiel der eigentlichen psycholog. Erscheinung, die ich u. einer meiner Freunde . . . "Identitätsmomente" nennen . . . Es müssen ō immer bedeutende Augenblicke sein.* Aside from the curios hide-and-seek attitude expressed toward a potential reader of his comment, Mörike implies that Goethe is borrowing an idea from somewhere or that Goethe simply shared a commonplace of psychology with Mörike and his friend. Just as likely is that Mörike's knowledge of this psychological idea originates with Goethe. Who Mörike's friend might be is an intriguing question (Vischer comes to mind), but this is of less importance than the overall point made of the concept of self-awareness of insight. Here, again, another version of influence in retrospect is operative.

There are several such moments of heightened self-understanding by characters and personae in Mörike's work. *Identitätsmomente* are often preceded by intensely visual experiences in the larger process of sight leading to insight. In "Der letzte König von Orplid," for example, Silpelit holds up a mirror to Ulmon just before his destiny ushers him hence. He sees his image and his past go by in a flash. The moment of recognition of the meeting of self and destiny occurs and he can peacefully die. These moments seem to be Mörike's way of symbolizing the momentary awareness by the individual of the individual's will colliding with his destiny. At the collision of the two the *Identitätsmoment* occurs. In one of Mörike's late poems, "Erinna an Sappho" (1863), Erinna, while facing herself in the mirror, thinks of her friend Sappho. Somehow a dual sense of transitoriness takes hold of her and she has premonitions of death:

Als ich am Putztisch jetzo die Flechten löste,
Dann mit nardeduftendem Kamm vor der Stirn den Haar-
Schleier teilte — seltsam betraf mich im Spiegel Blick in Blick.

Augen, sagt ich, ihr Augen, was wollt ihr?
Du, mein Geist, heute noch sicher behaust da drinne,
Lebendigen Sinnen traulich vermählt,
Wie mit fremdenden Ernst, lächelnd halb, ein Dämon,
Nickst du mich an, Tod weisagend!
— Ha, da mit eins durchzuckt' es mich
Wie Wetterschein! Wie wenn schwarzgefiedert ein tödlicher Pfeil
Streifte die Schläfe hart vorbei.
Dass ich, die Hände gedeckt aufs Antlitz, lange
Staunend blieb, in die nachtschaurige Kluft schwindelnd
hinab. (I, 736)

It is in such a rare moment that one comes face to face with destiny. Besides mirrors, Mörike often speaks of an abyss (Abgrund) in this connection. This abyss seems to represent the dark and unknowable element of one's identity as well as the sum of one's life in the past.

32

As deterministic and as dark as these moments can be, they are not necessarily linked with death, but they always seem to include the meeting of selfawareness with awareeess of destiny. But as Mörike points out, such a moment does not need to be *bedeutend*; it can occur while one glances into a mirror.

Mörike's view of time, the extended moment of identity, is indeed a central part of what makes up the identity of the lyric voice, the narrators in *Maler Nolten* and *Mozart auf der Reise nach Prag*, as well as the consciousness of the characters in these major prose works. Wolfgang F. Taraba, in connection with illustrating the underlying unity of the various "Einschiebsel" in *Maler Nolten* puts it this way: "Orplid ist für Mörikes Leben die Umformung der realen Erinnerung in eine von der Zeit des eigenen Daseins abgelöste 'Zeit' göttlichen Ursprungs und damit Fixierungsversuch. Dies ist es, was auch Larkens mit 'meiner Insel' meint: die Schöpfung einer eigenen Welt, die örtlich fixiert und damit dem Zerfließenden bloßer Phantasie entrückt ist, die aber zugleich auch, dem Vergehen physikalisch-meßbarer Zeit entnommen, auf einer Stufe ewiger, weil göttlicher Gleichzeitigkeit ruht."[74]

In summary of the general impact of Goethe on Mörike, we note that although Mörike seems to have read essentially all of Goethe's works several times, the geatest impact was from Goethe's more autobiographical writing, such as the letters and especially those to Schiller. *Wilhelm Meisters Lehrjahre* and *Die Wahlverwandtschaften* occupied Mörike deeply and left their mark on *Maler Nolten*.[75] Mörike also indicates a thorough familiarity with Goethe's other major works, especially *Faust*. In one of his letters to Mährlen he seems to represent the mixed reaction of his time to Goethe's "Helena-act." The letter is dated March 14, 1828: "Den Bogen aus dem neuen *Faustus* hab ich mit grossem Interesse gelesen. Ein kuriöses, aber nicht unkräftiges Schattenspiel. Doch will sich der griechische Faust dem deutschen schlecht *amalgamiren*. — Ein Minister Poieseos aber ist zu allem Möglichen privilegirt."[76] The only work about which Mörike expressed negative criticism is *Wilhelm Meisters Wanderjahre*. He comments in his notations: *Zusammengestoppelte Fetzen und höchst willkürl. Erzählungsform* . . . (Cf. Chapter V, item No. 12 of the Annotated Bibliography of Mörike's Extant Library). There can also be little doubt of Mörike's thorough familiarity with Goethe's epic and lyric poetry, as the many smaller references in letters and *Abschriften* demonstrate.

In several other respects Mörike can be shown to be both an appreciative-critical reader and an heir to Goethe. Thus, for example, Mörike's debt to and affinity for Shakespeare surely was in part only possible because of Goethe's life-long role of an intermediary between Shakespeare and the Shakespeare tradition in Germany during the latter part of the eighteenth and the early nineteenth century. But an exhaustive study of Mörike's knowledge of and debts to Goethe is still lacking, and may well remain so in the absense of a completed definitive edition of Mörike's poetry and letters. With this study I want so shed some additional light on the scope of Mörike's life-long preoccupation with Goethe. A minor methodological aim is to open the possibility for discussions of actual influence and Mörike's attempts to escape that influence.

In the past Mörike was often seen as the "son" of Goethe with the suggestion that whatever relationship existed between the two poets was too deep (in line with the genetic metaphor) to be accounted for by means of the concept of influence. Gottfried Keller saw in Mörike a poet "von einer unvergleichlichen Feinheit und Anmut; er ist gerade, wie wenn er der Sohn des Horaz und einer feinen Schwäbin wäre."[77] But preceding this famous pronouncement by several years, the not-so-well-known Rudolf Lohbauer observed in an even more memorable phrase: "Mörike ist, als wäre er ein Sohn Goethes, geistig, aus geheimnisvoller wilder Ehe."[78] But, memorably though the genetic metaphor was applied in the nineteenth century, it has drawn the following comment from K. Miyashita: "Die innere Beeinflussung durch Goethe ermöglichte es Mörike, seine Individualität mit dem klassischen Gut des Weimarer Dichters vollends zu verschmelzen . . . Goethes Einwirkung auf Mörike vollzog sich in einer so tiefen, wesentlichen Schicht, daß sie sich in einem äußeren Vergleich und dem bloßen Parallelismus der Werke beider Dichter nicht feststellen läßt."[79] This view ist not persuasive. Although there is in Mörike's response to Goethe that deeper level which Mörike sought, a *Mensch* to *Mensch* and *Geist* to *Geist* relationship, it should not be assumed that the possibility of actual literary debt to Goethe diminishes Mörike's artistic stature. In the light of modern views of the artist as conscious craftsman, Mörike's discernment and critical assimilation make up for a loss of "original genius."

Another favorite author of Mörike whom he called beloved, is Georg Christoph Lichtenberg (1742–1799). If there exists an elemental-mythopoeic attraction to Shakespeare and a spiritual-intellectual and cultural kinship to Goethe, it is the playful, satiric impulse and what L.B. Jennings called "grotesquery"[80] as well as the empathy for a fellow hypochondriac that ties Mörike to Lichtenberg. Again as in the case of Shakespeare and Goethe, Mörike frequently refers to the author in his letters, but he also had read and worked with Lichtenberg's various editions carefully and repeatedly (see Chapter V, item No. 27 of the Annotated Bibliography of Mörike's Extant Library).

During his own time Lichtenberg became well known as the editor and main contributor, for twenty years, of the *Göttinger Taschenkalender*, for which he wrote such diverse essays as "Von der Äolusharfe," "Vom Recht der Hagestolze bei Deutschen, Römern und Griechen" and "Eine kleine Aufgabe für die Übersetzer des Ovid in Deutschland." This latter essay Mörike quoted almost in its entirely with his poem "Eine Vers-Tändelei," and we will have occasion to return to it. Perhaps Lichtenberg's most important work, a work in which he emerged as an important intermediary between England and Germany, was his series of essays, "Ausführliche Erklärungen der Hogarthischen Kupferstiche," (1794 ff). But Lichtenberg's later fame throughout the nineteenth century to the present, and Mörike's attraction to him is based on his aphorisms. Modeled on what he called the British habit of keeping a "waste-book," Lichtenberg labeled his diaries "Sudelbücher." Selections from his "Sudelbücher," which contained diverse insights from his immediate experiences and readings were subsequently published as aphorisms. Thus Lichtenberg turns out to be one of the early innovators of a lesser known genre in Germany before its effective use by Novalis, Fr. Schlegel, Schopenhauer and Nietzsche. In fact, according to F.H. Mautner, it was Nietzsche's ironic praise of Lichtenberg that gave a powerful boost to his reputation in the twentieth century.[81]

Again we note in Mörike's concentration on the aphorisms and letters, the attempt at probing for the human dimension behind the various literary and public postures. As in the case of Shakespeare and Goethe this way of reading was the way to find himself. Perhaps this search for the human/poet role model is what Sengle means, when he refers to Lichtenberg as "den genialen Anthropologen" in the context of his discussion "Mörikes Bildungsgeschichte," and, without further explanation, views Mörike's study of Lichtenberg as "von allergrößter Wichtigkeit."[82] And it was probably again through his friend Waiblinger that Mörike was first introduced to Lichtenberg's writing. Waiblinger recorded his reading of Lichtenberg as early as Nov. 1823.[83] Besides having read the various volumes of Waiblinger's diary, the young Mörike was very much under the sway of the brilliant, Shelley-like Waiblinger who at this time was ahead of Mörike as a published writer.

Of all the interests he seems to share with Lichtenberg, such as dreams and the theory of dreams, psychology, belief in innocent superstitions, belief in the efficacy of "Sympathie," humorous and unusual habits and words, classical Greek and Roman literature, and the modern British stage and its most famous actor, Garrick, none emerges more clearly than the love of language. Of the many and lengthy references to Lichtenberg in Mörike's correspondence this recurring aspect along with Lichtenberg's rhetorical power dominates Mörike's concentration. Lichtenberg's style, reminiscent of Samuel Johnson in the British tradition, in the sense of saying things not for the first time, but better than ever before, lent itself very well to long quotes in letters to friends, as if the views expressed were proverbs or the wisdom of sententious maxims. Furthermore, it should be noted that Lichtenberg was an important intermediary for Mörike's knowledge of England as well as of English literature and culture.

In one of his many carefully composed letters addressed to Hartlaub, dated March/April, 1826, Mörike indulges in a lengthy description of a recently discovered picture by Reynolds. (Such picture descriptions are frequent in Mörike's as well as Goethe's prose.) He concludes with specific details of a female figure:

Diese steht unbeweglich, der Kopf etwas gesenkt, das Auge lauschend, freundlich bescheiden, fast etwas besorglich . . . Es ist unerträglich, wenn das Wort Anmut (gewiß eines der schönsten, das wir haben!) mißbraucht wird; aber ich bin überzeugt, daß Einer, dessen treffende Wortwählung wir kennen, dieses hier brauchen würde – Lichtenberg.[84]

It is Lichtenberg who comes to Mörike's mind in his search for just the right word. Not only did Mörike have a deep appreciation for Lichtenberg's careful use of language, but with his use of the word *Anmut* Mörike half intentionally evokes the beloved Rococo period of the previous century, which was fond of such a word as *Anmut*. Furthermore, it may have been Lichtenberg's use of the word *Anmut* in his *Erklärungen* of Hogarth which Mörike remembered and alluded to here. An additional element here may be attributable to an association of ideas. That is to say, the English painter Reynolds made Mörike think of Lichtenberg.

It would not be an overstatement in this connection to note that a good measure of Mörike's knowledge of England was assimilated from Lichtenberg's numerous reports abroad. Unfortunately, but understandably, this knowledge turned out to be too limited for Mörike. That is to say, Mörike's knowledge of England through Lichtenberg may very well explain why he used English names and an English setting for the first version of his story "Lucie Gelmeroth" (1839) which in the original was entitled "Miss Jenny Harrower" (1834) [dated a full year ahead], in the literary magazine, *Urania*. Aside from his own imaginative island of "Orplid" the only other countries and contemporary setting Mörike seems to be familiar with were Goethe's Italy and Lichtenberg's England. But it may very well have been a negative review with which "Miss Jenny Harrower" was greeted that made Mörike change his mind about the English setting. Vischer had reported the negative reaction to Mörike in a letter dated Dez. 29, 1833: "In den Blättern für literarische Unterhaltung kam eine sehr ungünstige Rezension über Deine Erzählung in der Urania . . . Besonders werden die Schnitzer in der Beschreibung einer englischen Jury getadelt."[85] In the later version of the story Mörike provided a short note as part of the subtitle, but did not explain the change with: "deutschen Verhältnissen angeeignet." By also changing all the personal names from English to

German, he seems to indicate that his knowledge of English society and circumstances was indeed inadequate. But again, let us not overlook Mörike's sly use of his heroine's original last name: in both versions she is an instigator of murder – harrowing indeed.

There is another interesting indication here of Mörike's knowledge and admiration of Lichtenberg. They story, "Miss Jenny Harrower" was originally planned to be part of a larger philosophical-psychological novel. Mörike never finished it. Since Maync's first publication of it this fragment is now generally known as "Bruchstück eines Romans" in subsequent editions. There is Mary, the mysterious main character, daughter of Baron and Lady von Leithem; there is Master Thomas, "der britische Hausfreund" there is the servant Gunnefield or Gonnefield; and there is Professor Killford, the uncle of the narrator; and there is City, the daughter of Killford. The characerization of Professor Killford seems to be based on Lichtenberg! The parallels are indeed striking. The narrator states: "Er hatte vordem an der Universität G** als ordentlicher Lehrer der klassischen Literatur gestanden . . . Sein eigentliches Fach waren die Naturwissenschaften gewesen." (I, 623). Lichtenberg, before becoming a man of letters was a Professor of Physics at the University of Göttingen. Killford's English name, in turn, naturally arises in Mörike's association of Lichtenberg with English and England in general. Mörike even alludes to Lichtenberg's playful use of language on a later occasion, when Killford makes an analogy between the mysterious Mary and logogriphs: "Nun, ja, geht mir's doch selber mit dem Mädchen, wie einem zuweilen mit Logogryphen geschieht: kaum glaubt man einen Teil des Wortes glücklich wegzuhaben, so stößt man auf neue Merkmale, welche nicht stimmen und man wird so vom Hundertsten aufs Tausendste geführt." (I, 626) It is our loss not to have a fully developed Killford, especially in view of Mörike's masterful portrait of Mozart, a contemporary of Lichtenberg. But perhaps the reason why Mörike never finished the novel was the lack of opportunity to acquaint himself more fully with the English language and with the contemporary culture of England.

A few years before his work on "Lucie Gelmeroth" and the unfinished novel Mörike included lengthy excerpts from Lichtenberg's views on religion and love in letters to his fiancée, Luise Rau. Lichtenberg's views on love and friendship must have interested Mörike very much, because he had been wrestling with these problems for several years. In his letter to Luise, dated Dez. 28, 1829, Mörike included a quote by Lichtenberg to augment his own view on the subject for Luise:

Apropos, weil wir ohnehin an der Lektüre sind, so will ich Dir doch eine Stelle hersetzen, die mir neulich in meinem über alles werten Lichtenberg begegnete. Was hältst Du davon? 'Was die Freundschaft, und noch mehr das glückliche Band der Liebe so entzückend macht, ist die Erweiterung seines Ichs und zwar über ein Feld hinaus, das sich im einzelnen Menschen durch keine Kunst schaffen läßt. Zwei Seelen, die sich vereinigen, vereinigen sich doch nie so ganz, daß nicht immer noch der beiden so vorteilhafte Unterschied bliebe, der die Mitteilung so angenehm macht.'[86]

For such rhetorical clarity and simplicity Mörike repeatedly turned to the enlightened and enlightening Lichtenberg. Lichtenberg's views also interested him because of his preoccupation with love in terms of oneness and twoness. Mörike seemed to be haunted by the fear that a full harmonious unity may not be possible through human love alone. In the process of seeking an answer he had also turned to Shakespeare again and again. But this point is taken up in greater detail in Chapter II.

Another indication of Mörike sharing with Lichtenberg a love of language and a life-long interest in problems of translation has found an echo in Mörike's couplet "Eine Vers-Tändelei." This small couplet should, of course, be seen as a tribute to Lichtenberg rather than as evidence of a literary debt. In a lengthy prose preface to his couplet Mörike recounts Lichtenberg's acceptance of a challenge by John Dryden. Dryden, according to Lichtenberg, had once challenged his contemporaries with two lines of Ovid, of which he had said, that they could not be translated into English with only two lines. Mörike then includes Ovid's original with the two attempts by Dryden:

Si, nisi quae forma poterit te digna videri
Nulla futura tua est, nulla futura tua est.

If but to one, that's equally divine,
None you'll incline to, you'll to none incline.

If, save whose charms with equal lustre shine,
None ever thine can be, none ever can be thine.   (II, 373)

Then Mörike continues to quote Lichtenberg, who had challenged the poet G.A. Bürger to produce a German translation. According to Lichtenberg the results were very unsatisfactory and Bürger's versions remained unknown to Mörike. Finally, Mörike presents his version:

Wisse nur, daß, wenn, ohne durch Schönheit dich zu verdienen,
Keine die deinige wird, – keine die deinige wird.

(II, 374)

Though not a poet himself, but rather an acute critic and reader, Lichtenberg effectively transmitted the poet's delight in word-play to Mörike. And playing with words ultimately seems to be the root of Mörike's affinity for Lichtenberg, who, after Shakespeare and Goethe, is Mörike's favorite author and also one of the most important sources of his humanism and humor.[87]

Notes – Chapter I

1 For the most lucid summary and analysis of this exchange with implications for Mörike's poetics, cf. Dagmar Barnouw, *Entzückte Anschauung; Sprache und Realität in der Lyrik Eduard Mörikes* (München: Fink, 1971), pp. 17–33.

2 Letter to Strauss, Febr. 12, 1938. *Eduard Mörike: Sämtliche Werke.* vol. III: *Briefe*, ed. Gerhart Baumann and Siegfried Grosse (Stuttgart: Cotta, 1959), p. 427. Hereafter referred to as Baumann, *Letters*.

3 Karl Walter, "Ungedruckte Briefe Mörikes an David Friedrich Strauss," *Das literarische Echo*, vol. 24 (1921–22), p. 594.

4 William Shakespeare, *Shakespeares Werke*, transl. A.W. Schlegel and L. Tieck. 4 vols. (Berlin: Paul Franke, no date), vol. I, p. 69. Hereafter all references to the Schlegel/Tieck translation of Shakespeare are to this edition.

5 *Mörike und seine Leser* (Stuttgart: Ernst Klett, 1960), p. 114.

6 "Mörike-Probleme," *Germanisch-Romanische Monatsschrift*, N.F., vol. XXXIII (Oct. 1951), pp. 36–47.

7 *Die Kunst der Interpretation* (Zürich: Atlantis, 1955), p. 184.

8 Hans Egon Holthusen, more recently, also vigorously rejects the "fatale Ideologisierung des Erlebnis-Begriffs" which has led to an unfortunate "Kanonisierung" of the Goethe Model. Cf. *Eduard Mörike in Selbstzeugnissen und Bilddokumenten* (Hamburg: Rowohlt, 1971), p. 150.

9 "Mörike-Probleme," p. 41.

10 *Eduard Mörike. Ein romantischer Dichter*. Tübingen: Wunderlich, 1950 (rpt. 1978).

11 "Mörike-Probleme," p. 46.

12 Stuttgart, 1968, pp. 56–85.

13 *Publications of the English Goethe Society*, vol. XXV (1956), pp. 63–85.

14 Nürnberg: Hans Karl, 1970.

15 In *Daphnis: Zeitschrift für Mittlere Deutsche Literatur*, vol. 7, Heft 1–2 (1978), pp. 341–359.

16 "Sannazaro und Venantius Fortunatus in Nachdichtungen Mörikes," *Mannheimer Hefte*, Heft 2 (1978), pp. 73–83. Krummacher also indicates his skepticism (with which I concur) that there is a "barocker Grundton" according to Koschlig in Mörike's poetry. Krummacher characterizes Mörike's Barock-Rezeption rather as a kind of "punktuelle Begegnung."

17 *Österreichische Akademie der Wissenschaften*, 245. Band, 4. Abh. (Wien, 1965), pp. 1–47.

18 *Ibid.*, p. 13.

19 M. Heidegger and E. Staiger, "Zu einem Vers von Mörike: Ein Briefwechsel mit M. Heidegger," *Trivium*, vol. IX (1951), pp. 1–6.

20 Leo Spitzer, "Wiederum Mörikes Gedicht 'Auf eine Lampe,' " *Trivium*, vol. IX (1951), pp. 133–47; I. Appelbaum-Graham, "Zu Mörikes Gedicht 'Auf eine Lampe,' " *Modern Language Notes*, vol. LXVIII (1953), pp. 328–33.

21 Enzinger, p. 22.

22 Enzinger, p. 38.

23 *Eduard Mörikes Gedichtwerk*. Stuttgart: J.B. Metzler, 1972.

24 *Ibid.*, p. 284ff. The need for *Harmonie* as outlined by von Heydebrand Mörike certainly also sought in relationships with friends and fellow poets. Relationships based on two were guarantors of this. Gerhart von Graevenitz's discussion of the "Dreiergruppen" in Mörike's life in the study, *Eduard Mörike: Die Kunst der Sünde. Zur Geschichte des literarischen Individuums* (Tübingen: Max Niemeyer, 1978), represents an interesting challenge to this notion. In my view, Mörike's writing reflects a characteristic avoidance of the dialectic of *three* as an ever-present potential for conflict. (Cf. below, Chapter II, discussion of the concept of twosomeness.)

25 *Eduard Mörike: Sein Leben und Dichten*, 5th ed. (Stuttgart: Cotta, 1944), p. 314ff.

26 *Eduard Mörike und seine Freunde* (Stuttgart: Turmhaus Druckerei, 1965), p. 12.

27 In his seminal study, *The Anxiety of Influence: A Theory of Poetry* (New York: Oxford University Press, 1973), Bloom breaks down the concept of influence into six psychological/philosophical constructs which are operative in the relationship of the new generation poet, the "ephebe," and his antecedent or the "precursor." One of these concepts is "Tessera," "which is completion and antithesis; I take the word not from mosaic-making, where it is still used, but from the ancient mystery cults, where it meant a token of recognition, the fragment say of a small pot which the other fragments would re-constitute the vessel. A poet antithetically 'completes' his precursor, by so reading the parent-poem as to retain its terms but to mean them in another sense, as though the precursor had failed to go far enough," p. 14.

28 In the summer of 1941 Ludwig Tieck had visited Kerner. They met in Heilbronn. Mörike was specifically invited to meet Tieck. Although at the time living only a few miles from Heilbronn, in Cleversulzbach, Mörike did not come to the meeting. Tieck, who knew of Mörike's reclusive habits and his proverty, subsequently wrote to Kerner in a letter, dated July 3, 1841: "Vielleicht hätte sich Mörike auch weniger geniert, zu Ihnen als nach Heilbronn zu kommen. Der Arme! Und daß ich ihn nicht habe kennen lernen. Ich habe es in meinem Sinn seitdem immer hin und her geworfen, wie ihm zu helfen sein möchte, ich kann aber immer noch kein Mittel, keinen Ankerplatz finden, wo ich einlaufen dürfte." (*Justinus Kerners Briefwechsel mit seinen Freunden*, ed. Theobald Kerner. Stuttgart & Leipzig, 1897, p. 199).

29 Bern and Frankfurt: Herbert Lang, 1971.

30 *The German Quarterly* (Sept., 1974), pp. 160–161.

31 The definitive edition of Mörike's works and letters is in preparation in the Mörike-Archiv of the Schiller-Nationalmuseum (SNM), in Marbach, Germany: *Eduard Mörike: Werke und Briefe, historisch-kritische Gesamtausgabe*, ed. Hans-Henrik Krumacher, Herbert Meyer and Bernhard Zeller, 19 vols., Stuttgart: Klett-Cotta, 1967ff. The first of nine volumes (10 through 19) was published in 1982, with the remaining eight to come out in annual intervals. The first vol. of letters hereafter referred to as *Briefe, 1811–1828*, vol. X.

32 Holthusen, *Eduard Mörike*, p. 127.

33 *Eduard Mörike: Briefe*, ed. Friedrich Seebaß (Tübingen: R. Wunderlich, 1939). Hereafter referred to as Seebaß, *Letters; Eduard Mörike: Unveröffentlichte Briefe*, ed. Friedrich Seebaß (Stuttgart: Cotta, 1945). Hereafter referred to as Seebaß, *Unpubl. Letters*; Baumann, *Letters*.

34 This letter/petition is directly addressed to the King of Württemberg, dated July 9, 1841, SNM 10436. According to Dr. Hans-Ulrich Simon of the Mörike-Archiv, the absence from the letter collections of such letters has the

following reason: "Nach einer älteren Ablageform wurden offizielle Schreiben Mörikes nicht bei den Briefen abgelegt, sondern bei 'Lebenszeugnissen'
oder 'Lebensdokumenten.'"
35 Maync. *Biography*, p. 139.
36 "Eduard Mörike: Briefe aus seiner Sturm- und Drangperiode," ed. Rudolf
Krauss, *Deutsche Rundschau* (Jan., 1895), p. 69.
37 SNM, *Letters*. To represent Mörike's handwritings or unpublished MSS
italics are used throughout this study.
38 Mörike's copies and notes from works by other authors are also kept at the
Mörike-Archiv of the Schiller-Nationalmuseum (SNM), under the headings
"Verschiedenes" and "Abschriften fremder Werke." In Weimar at the
Goethe-Schiller Archiv (GSA), there is also a small collection of *Abschriften*. In order to distinguish hereafter in the citations, these two sources are
cited as *Abschriften* SNM and *Abschriften* GSA: These *Abschriften* consist
of handwritten copies of poems, songs, lists of words and excerpts of plays,
novels, biographies and letters, which Mörike collected. Some of these *Abschriften* Mörike called *Lesefrüchte*; many were sent to his friend Hartlaub.
Whenever I am quoting from *Abschriften*, it is in italics, since it represents
Mörike's handwriting.
39 *Briefe, 1811–1828*, vol. X, p. 202–3.
40 *Freundeslieb' und Treu': 250 Briefe Eduard Mörikes an Wilhelm Hartlaub*,
ed. Gotthilf Renz (Leipzig: L. Klotz, 1938). Hereafter referred to as Renz,
Letters.
41 GSA, II, 9. Mörike wrote intermittently in calendars between 1818 and
1867. Some of these calendars are part of the auxiliary material for the
edition in preparation in SNM.
42 Maync, *Biography*, p. 67.
43 SNM, 2682, "Königlich-Württembergischer Kalender."
44 *Briefwechsel zwischen Eduard Mörike und Friedrich Theodor Vischer*, ed.
Robert Vischer (München: C.H. Beck, 1926), p. 107. Hereafter cited as
Vischer, *Letters*.
45 *The Reception of English Literature in Germany* (Berkeley: University
of California Press, 1932), p. 342.
46 *Eduard Mörike: Sämtliche Werke*, ed. Jost Perfahl and Helga Unger. 2 vols.
(München: Winkler, 1967 and 1970), vol. I, p. 861. Hereafter references to
Mörike's poems are to this edition, cited in the text by volume and page
number.
47 Vischer, *Letters*, p. 195.
48 Maync, *Biography*, p. 421.
49 *Briefwechsel zwischen Hermann Kurz und Eduard Mörike*, ed. Heinz Kindermann (Stuttgart: Strecker & Schröder, 1919), p. 183. Hereafter referred
to as Kurz, *Letters*.
50 Kurz, *Letters*, p. 50. This letter dated June 30, 1837, also contains a long
passage in which Mörike discusses several contemporary poems in which

he had detected parallels to a song in Shakespeare's *Twelfth Night*. This particular passage was exluded in Seebaß, *Letters*.

51 The translations from Shakespeare consist of three excerpts: (1) *Macbeth*, IV, all of scene ii. (2) *Twelfth Night*, I, iii, lines 20–26 and lines 58–84; and I, v, lines 4–28. (3) *Romeo and Juliet*, I, iii, lines 41–58.

52 *Historisch-Kritische Gesamtausgabe, Übersetzungen*, vol. 8, part 1 (1976), and *Übersetzungen. Bearbeitungsanalysen*, vol. 8, part 3 (1981), pp. 11–18. For an older reference on Mörike's use of sources for the classical translation also see Helga Unger, *Mörike Kommentar zu sämtlichen Werken* (München: Winkler, 1970), pp. 151–159.

53 *Abschriften* GSA, II, 7.

54 SNM, Mv 20.

55 *Ibid*. The manuscript for this final lecture is in the Mörike *Nachlass* at GSA.

56 *Shakespeare Werke*, vol. VIII, p. 67.

57 William Shakespeare, *William Shakespeare's Schauspiele*, transl. Johann Joachim Eschenburg. 2nd ed., 11 vols. (Zürich: Orell & Füssli, 1798–1804), vol. V, p. 316.

58 Eduard Mörike, *Mörikes Werke*, ed. Harry Maync. 3 vols. (Leipzig and Wien: Bibliographisches Institut, 1909), vol. III, p. 509.

59 Cf. "Urne und Lampe. Vorüberlegungen zu einem textanalytischen Transformationsbegriff," *Literatur in Wissenschaft und Unterricht*, vol. XIII (1980), pp. 115–123.

60 Wilhelm Waiblinger, *Die Tagbücher: 1821–1826*, ed. Herbert Meyer (Stuttgart: Ernst Klett, 1956), p. 60.

61 *Briefe, 1811–1828*, vol. X, p. 25.

62 *Ibid.*, p. 25.

63 *Biedermeierzeit* (Stuttgart: J.B. Metzler, 1971), vol. I, p. 48.

64 Baumann, *Letters*, p. 139–140. It is interesting that Mörike should cast his experience of reading the Briefwechsel in terms of the temptation scene in the Garden of Eden. Harold Bloom in a persuasive paradigm sees the post Enlightenment poet's philosophical/psychological condition vis-à-vis their precursors in terms of Milton's fallen Satan who turns to his task of rallying "everythink that remains," cf. *The Anxiety of Influence*, p. 21.

65 *Briefwechsel zwischen Schiller und Goethe: in den Jahren 1794 bis 1805*, 2 vols., 2nd ed. (Stuttgart and Augsburg: Cotta, 1856). (See Chapter V, Annotated Bibliography of Mörike's Extant Library, item No. 2). In this second edition of the *Goethe-Schiller Briefwechsel* which Mörike had in his possession Mörike undertook more careful changes and corrections than in any other books he owned. From the kinds of comments he made it is clear that he collated his edition with the original manuscripts which were at the time in the possession of the publisher Cotta in Stuttgart. In his notations Mörike refers to *im Original* and once to a manuscript as being in the *Besitz der Verlagshandlung*. The extremely unusual care which Mörike took in his textual and editorial work suggests that he wanted to create a

definitive edition for himself and that he wanted to contribute to corrected editions in the future. All significant changes of content exist in recent editions of this letter exchange (see *Briefwechsel mit Friedrich Schiller*, ed. Ernst Beutler (Zürich, 1949), Vol. XX.) But not all of Mörike's changes in dates and sequence of letter appear in subsequent editions. For this reason Mörike's notations should be considered significant variants. A careful comparison of original Schiller-Goethe letters with Mörike's notations is in preparation and will be included in the critical-historical edition. *Mörikes Bearbeitungen fremder Werke*, vol. 9. There are no indications in Mörike's letters or in the papers of the Cotta-Archive in Marbach of Mörike's specific participation in the editorial process of the letters. The fact, however, that Mörike had made his changes on the basis of original manuscripts and the care he took to make his changes and "Lesarten" legible suggests that his contributions may well have been considered by Cotta for editions after the second edition of 1856.

66 Johann Wolfgang Goethe, *Briefwechsel mit Friedrich Schiller*, ed. Ernst Beutler (Zürich: Artemis, 1949), vol. XX, pp. 850—856.

67 Baumann, *Letters*, p. 178.

68 Baumann, *Letters*, p. 224.

69 Baumann, *Letters*, p. 228.

70 Renz, *Letters*, pp. 49—50 and 248.

71 In the lenghty list of contributors to the *Wörterbuch* Mörike is not listed.

72 *16. Rechenschaftsbericht des Schwäbischen Schillervereins* (Marbach, 1911/1912), pp. 35-45.

73 *Ludwig Uhland: Eine Gabe für Freunde zum 26. April 1856 . . .* (Stuttgart: Cotta [no date]), p. 338. (See Chapter V, Annotated Bibliography, item No. 52.) Mörike received the Tiedge-prize for the poem "Idylle vom Bodensee oder Fischer Martin," "in sieben Gesängen" (1846).

74 "Die Rolle der 'Zeit' und des 'Schicksals' in Eduard Mörikes *Maler Nolten*," in *Eduard Mörike*, ed. Victor G. Doerksen (Darmstadt: Wissenschaftliche Buchgesellschaft, 1975), p. 143.

75 Vischer, *Letters*, p. 11.

76 *Briefe, 1811—1828*, vol. X, p. 202.

77 Requoted by Gerhard Rückert, *Mörike und Horaz* (Nürnberg: Hans Karl, 1970), p. 10 from A. Frey, *Erinnerungen an Gottfried Keller* (Leipzig, 1919), p. 31.

78 Wilhelm Lang, "Rudolf Lohbauer," *Württembergische Vierteljahrshefte für Landesgeschichte*, Jahrgang V (Stuttgart, 1897), p. 107f. Lang quotes from a letter, dated Sept. 27, 1840, which Lohbauer sent to his fiancée.

79 *Mörikes Verhältnis zu seinen Zeitgenossen* (Bern and Frankfurt: Herbert Lang, 1971), p. 51ff. There are two other studies which deal with the Goethe-Mörike relationship: H. Ilgenstein, *Mörike und Goethe*, Berlin, 1902 and L.F. Barthel, "Mörikes 'Vater Goethe'," in *Goethe Kalender* (1938), p. 101—154. Both studies merely indicate similarity of tone and perspective

in both authors. A statement by Barthel may indicate the kind of impressionistic criticism practiced by both commentators in comparing Goethe and Mörike: "Da wie dort die gleiche, herzerquickende Einfalt, der gleiche, bald unbekümmerte, bald leidumdunkelte Ton zu singen und zu sagen." (p. 141)

80 Cf. Lee B. Jennings, "Mörike's Grotesquery: A Post-Romantic Phenomenon," *Journal of English and Germanic Philology*, vol. LIX, No. 4 (Oct. 1960), pp. 600—16.

81 *Lichtenberg: Geschichte seines Geistes* (Berlin: Walter de Gruyter, 1968), p. 5. Mautner paraphrases Nietzsche: "Lichtenbergs Aphorismen seien eines der drei deutschen Prosawerke, die allein außer Goethes Schriften es verdienten, 'wieder gelesen zu werden'."

82 Cf. Sengle, *Biedermeierzeit*, vol. III, p. 697.

83 Waiblinger, *Die Tagebücher*, p. 242. Also p. 246: "Lichtenbergs Witz ist ungemein treffend, fein und ungezwungen, wie seine ganze Sprache und Darstellungsweise. Seine Briefe über Garrick sind das Interessanteste, was ich irgend über Schauspielkunst gelesen."

84 *Briefe, 1811—1826*, vol. X, p. 124.

85 Vischer, *Letters*, p. 115.

86 *Eduard Mörike: Briefe an seine Braut Luise Rau*, ed. F. Kemp (München: Kösel, 1965), p. 43.

87 Part of the humanism Mörike is heir to includes a good portion of healthy skepticism with which Lichtenberg sees the world, including verisimilitude in the creation of fictional characters. This may even include chipping away at the Olympian Goethe. Thus, for example, Lichtenberg laments Goethe having Werther reading Homer instead of the book of nature. Cf. Bruce Duncan's discussion of the relevant, re-quoted Lichtenberg passages in "'Emilia Galotti lag auf dem Pult aufgeschlagen:' Werther as (Mis-) Reader," in *Goethe-Yearbook*, vol. I (1982) p. 49.

Chapter II

Cult, Oracle and Images of Twosomeness:
Mörike's Reading of Shakespeare with Emphasis on the
Years 1818 to 1828

One aim of this chapter is to assess the impact Shakespeare had on Mörike's sensibility in his first creative period (to approximately 1828), based on letters and on other concrete evidence, such as unpublished copies of songs and passages from Shakespeare's plays as well as letter fragments. A second aim is to pursue this impact of Shakespeare in a number of Mörike's lyric poems, especially "Die Schwestern," "Um Mitternacht" and "Gesang zu zweien in der Nacht." Mörike's encounter with Shakespearean productions through the theater predates his preoccupation as revealed in poems and letters and is explored first. In a subsequent chapter the influence of Shakespeare on Mörike is discussed, primarily with reference to Mörike's use of characterization and setting in the novel *Maler Nolten* and in the playet "Der letzte König von Orplid." In Chapter III I also cite heretofore unknown and unpublished fragments of translations and lecture notes, which are part of a collection of Mörike's *Abschriften*.[1] These *Abschriften* or notes and copies further demonstrate Mörike's fascination as an artist, humanist, literary critic and teacher with the works of Shakespeare. Beyond Mörike's personal preoccupation with Shakespeare, we also find him heir to a vigorous Shakespeare tradition in Germany of the late eighteenth and early nineteenth century. Throughout the following discussion an attempt is made to distinguish between this tradition and Mörike's specific reading and use of Shakespeare.

Since a key part of my endeavor is to identify and assess long neglected, tangible and extant evidence of Mörike's reading and knowledge of Shakespeare, I would like to preface my discussion of the letters and poems with a reference to a set of missing Shakespeare volumes in Mörike's personal library. In an obscure auction catalogue

of 1932, which is now part of the Mörike Archiv in Marbach, is the
following entry:

Shakespeare, Dramatische Werke. Übersetzt von Aug. Wilh. v. Schlegel u.
L. Tieck. Bd. 1, 2, 5, 6 u. 7. Brin. 1825–32 Pbde. "Mörike besaß den
Shakespeare nie vollständig; so bittet er in einem Brief vom 5. Dez. 1851
seinen Freund Hartlaub ihm für seine Vorlesungen (im Bürgermuseum) ein
gutes Lustspiel von Shakespeare vorzuschlagen: 'und, sofern es sich nicht
in meiner defekten Schlegel'schen Übersetzung befinden sollte. . . den
betr. Band zu leihen . . .' Von Mörikes Hand sind die Rückentitel auf sämtlichen Bänden (im ersten Band mit dem Zusatze "Tübingen 1825") sowie
unzählige Anmerkungen, vorwiegend in Band 1 und 6. Die Anmerkungen
(hauptsächlich zu Hamlet und Heinrich IV.) sind Umfassungen einzelner
Sätze der Schlegel'schen Übersetzung in andere Form."[2]

This auction catalogue entry and its annotation by H.W. Rath is the
only evidence we have of Mörike's Shakespeare edition. This entry is
important because it is the only evidence, besides the fragments in
the *Abschriften*, of Mörike's efforts in translating Shakespeare. It is
also important because it quotes from a heretofore unpublished
letter by Mörike. Finally, it is important because we now know that
Mörike had the Schlegel translation in his possession as early as 1825.
Unfortunately, Mörike's Shakespeare volumes and the annotations in
it, which were never recorded in any other form than in the Rath
auction catalogue, have not been located to his day. There has been no
evidence since the auction in 1932 whether these volumes still exist,
in whose possession they are, or whether they were destroyed during
World War II. Hermann Hesse, who was also an avid Mörike collector,
reported in 1953 and 1954 that several other books from Mörike's
library were destroyed during the war.[3]

But the Schlegel-Tieck Shakespeare edition, which was in Mörike's
possession, is only one of many clues for Mörike's life-long preoccupation with Shakespeare. This preoccupation begins with Mörike
attending Shakespearean plays in 1818–1820, and it concludes in
1874 with Mörike crossing in his Goethe edition sundry comments
Goethe made about Shakespeare.[4] Mörike's very first exposure to
Shakespeare was not through a prescribed encounter in school but
by his own choice through the theater in Stuttgart. It should also be

noted in this connection, as is pointed out in Chapter I, that Mörike had very little knowledge of English, French being the only modern language taught on the secondary levels in Germany at that time.

Among some of the very earliest writings by Mörike as an adolescent, I was able to find a diary entry in a notebook of 1818. In this notebook Mörike recorded visits to the Stuttgarter Hoftheater, which occurred in 1818 and perhaps 1819, while he was on vacation from the theological seminary in Urach:

W. Tell, Esslair zum letzten Mal vor seiner Kunstreise /
Julius Caesar. Die Schricknadelen [?] *Schauspiel von*
Kotzebue Abbälino der große Bandit original St. Mehrere
mimische Darstellungen die ihm sehr gelungen.
Sttg. / Vacanz aus Urach
Hamlet Trauersp. nach Shakesp. v.
Don Juan Oper Mus. v. Mozart
Titus der Spieler Schauspiel v. Iffland und
Gastrolle.
Wildfang Braut v. Messina.[5]

Mörike was particularly fascinated by the actor Ferdinand Esslair as Brutus in the 1818 Stuttgart premiere of *Julius Caesar* and in *Hamlet*. We have no other information about Mörike's theater attendance at that time, though in later years Mörike took every opportunity he could to attend the theater in Stuttgart. As late as June, 1874, Mörike delightedly reports reading Eduard Devrient's *Geschichte der deutschen Schauspielkunst*, in which he found a review of his friend, the talented Shaksperean actor Karl Grunert.[6] Mörike also loved to act himself, and we have evidence that he was in at least two plays: in Urach in Molière's *Heurath* [sic] *wider Willen*[7] and in Scheer (1829) in Schiller's *Kabale und Liebe*[8], playing the lead in each.

It should also be observed, in connection with Mörike's 1818–1820 notebook notations, that his recording of a *Hamlet* performance in 1818 or 1819 suggests an interesting revision of the reported staging history of the Stuttgart Hoftheater of that time. E. Stahl in his compendious history of German Shakespeare productions reports performances of only *Julius Caesar* in 1818 and *Macbeth* in 1820 at Stuttgart; in both plays Esslair took leading roles, prior to his permanent departure for München in 1820.[9]

There is also the following unpublished, partially undated letter by Mörike about a *Hamlet* performance:

> *Mit angenehmer Überraschung verehrtester Herr Actor,*
> *empfing ich Ihre gütige Einladung zu dem heutigen*
> *Hamlet. Ich werde gewiß nicht fehlen und danke*
> *vorläufig zum höchsten!*
>
>   *Freundschaftlich grüßend*
>   *3. Apr.*   *ganz ergeben*
>
>   *Mörike.*[10]

E. Ungerer in his booklet also reports about a *Hamlet* performance in Schwäbisch Hall in 1844, which he thinks Mörike almost certainly attended during his stay there in 1844.[11] But Mörike did not arrive in Schwäbisch Hall until the 16th of April, according to his calendar in his *Haushaltungsbuch*.[12] The letter, on the other hand, is dated April 3. According to Ulrich Simon the note refers to a performance in Stuttgart, 1861 and is addressed to Feodor Loewe.[13] Mörike seems to have attended at least three different *Hamlet* performances during his lifetime.

Let us now turn to Shakespeare in Mörike's letters. As already pointed out in Chapter I, the importance of Mörike's letters to a full understanding of Mörike's philosophical and literary orientation and specifically of Mörike's knowledge of Shakespeare cannot be over-emphasized. The Briefwechsel zwischen Schiller und Goethe, an epistolary axchange of ideas about literature mixed with messages of high personal regards, one of Mörike's most cherished books, may very well have served Mörike as a model. (Cf. below, item No. 2 in *Part A* and *B*, Chapter V: Annotated Bibliography of Mörike's Extant Library.) Many scholars, among them Friedrich Sengle, who view letters in general as an important genre of *Biedermeier* literature, have called for much needed study and research of Mörike's letters: "Mörike ist ohne seine Gelegenheitslyrik und seine immer noch zu wenig bekannten Briefe auch als Dichter kaum zu würdigen."[14] Despite the present state of the Mörike letters, they are our best source for our knowledge of his reading of Shakespeare.

The first mention of Shakespeare in Mörike's letters occurs in March, 1822, when he reports to his new friend Wilhelm Waiblinger his reading of Shakespeare upon that friend's recommendation for reading material: "Was die Lektüre des Calderon und Shakespeare betrifft, so hat mich der letztere, soweit er mir zugänglich war – am meisten durch den Hamlet, den Lear und Macbeth entzückt und erschüttert."[15]

Mörike's intensely personal reaction to Shakespeare at this time was by no means exaggerated. Shakespeare for Mörike was much more than interesting reading. Shakespeare's plays were a very important source for Mörike's knowledge of the sepctrum of human behavior. His reaction places Mörike well within the tradition of German Romanticism's view of Shakespeare; that is to say, Shakespeare expressed life and nature directly. Secondly, Shakespeare expressed the wonderful world of dreams to which German romantics were so attuned.[16] The briliant young Waiblinger who was more directly heir to the romantic tradition than Mörike, who was in close touch with the Swabian "school" of romantics, notably Gustav Schwab, and who stimulated Mörike's interest in Shakespeare, also identifies Shakespeare directly with life, when he says in his diary: "Shakespeares Universalleben in Tag und Nacht find ich eher in mir, im Leben selbst – ich könnt ihn eher missen, aber ich möchte nicht seyn ohne zu denken an jene schönen Heldengestalten der unwiderbringlichen Vorwelt [in Homer]."[17] Waiblinger feels that he would be able to generate a Shakespeare-like world in his own literary creations, that Shakespeare could be found within, but that he would have to continue reading and thinking about Homer, because Homer's art was not to be found within his own sensibility. Waiblinger here echoes the kinship that A.W. Schlegel, L. Tieck and, of course, the young Goethe, felt toward Shakespeare, and which we find expressed in Mörike's letters as well.

Mörike also believed Shakespeare expressed raw nature and the reality that one finds by looking into one's own heart, as opposed to the history and artifice with which one finds other great authors veiled, as Waiblinger puts it. Mörike always reports extraodinary reactions to the reading or attending of Shakespeare's plays. His fellow poets and friends corroborate Mörike's reactions. Late in Mörike's life Friedrich Hebbel reports: "Nach dem innigen 'Gott lohn's,' das er mir zurief, hat mein Besuch ihm wohl getan, obgleich er mir erklärte, daß meine Unterhaltung ihn wie ein Bergsturz über-käme, und daß er sich so einem 'ganzen Menschen' wie ich, eben so wenig gewachsen fühle, wie einer Darstellung des Lear, die ihn immer krank mache."[18]

In the only psychiatric study we have on Mörike, this intense reaction to attending *King Lear*, which certainly goes beyond a romantic identification of Shakespeare with life, is also alluded to by A. Müller: "Lebhafter Verkehr schon griff seine Nerven an, und als er den bedeutenden, ihm befreundeten Schauspieler Grunert einmal den Lear hatte spielen sehen, mußte er den ganzen folgenden Tag das Bett hüten."[19] But Mörike's reading of Shakespeare in early life at the theological seminary in Urach and at the University in Tübingen, was intensely personal in several other ways.

Shakespeare was read by the young theology student as so many young Americans read Hermann Hesse in the 1960's and early 70's. Shakespeare was also viewed by Mörike and his friends Waiblinger and Ludwig Bauer as a personal source of wisdom, an alternative reality, and an adventure. Thus, in a letter to Friedrich Kauffmann dated July 20, 1825 Mörike reports from the "Stift" at the university in Tübingen: "Bauer nahm mein Verlangen, den übrigen Abend mit Lesen in Shakespeare's Troilus und Kressida außerhalb dieses Zimmers zubringen, gutwillig an. Also nahm man (die vortreffliche Schweizer-Armbrust u. Pfeile nicht zu vergessen) den Band mit in jenes rosenfarbene Gartenhäuschen, an dem Euer Gefärth bei dem Uhlandischen Garten vorbei gefahren ist."[20] This strikes the reader at first as a report of young people's typical merry-making. But in fact the reported details are carefully chosen by the writer. On the one hand there is an attempt at life imitating art (the young men arming themselves as the warriors do in *Troilus and Cressida*), and on the other hand there is a conscious attempt on the writer's part to polish and enrich his prose. Finally, the reading itself finds subtle reverberations in Mörike's later prose and poetry, in allusions to Shakespeare.

Mörike's reading of *Troilus and Cressida* also led in another direction. It was probably at this time in 1825 that Mörike recorded his ideas on the "Doppelte Seelentätigkeit," an unpublished essay to which Maync affixed the present title.[21] In this much neglected little essay Mörike discusses his concept of "wissende Traumseele," which led him — so Mörike reports — to consult Shakespeare's *Troilus and Cressida* as an oracle. Here Mörike formulates a quasi-theory of subliminal awareness, though he hesitates to take himself too seriously and couches his discussion in an almost frivolous tone. Also, what Mörike does not say here is revealing. He does *not* say that he apparently viewed Shakespeare as a source fo psychic date quite independent of the mysterious promptings of the unconscious. The setting of the occasion for the essay is an animated gathering of friends in the dormitory room in Tübingen. Mörike describes reaching for a volume of Shakespeare:

Halb zum Spaß, halb im Ernst befrug ich das Schicksal um mich . . . indem ich . . . den nächsten besten Teil des deutschen Shakespeare herunternahm, mit dem Daumen hineingriff und hier . . . sogleich auf eine Stelle stieß, die wir als bejahende Antwort nahmen. Frappant, gewissermaßen komisch-frappant, war sie dadurch, daß sie selber den Ausdruck *Orakel*, also die genaueste formale Beziehung auf meine Absicht enthielt. Ich habe in der Folge die Sache kaum jemanden erzählt, weil jedermann sie allzu unwahrscheinlich finden muß und ich mich nicht lächerlich machen wollte. Auch hatte ich seit vielen Jahren ganz und gar vergessen, wo die Worte vorkommen. Im "Troilus" fand ich jedoch unlängst zu meiner Überraschung in den Reden zwischen Achill und dem Hektor, Akt IV, Szene 5, folgendes:

 Ach. − − Antwort, ihr Götter!
 Hekt. Missziemen würd' es heil'gen Göttern −
    Antwort zu geben solcher Frage. Sprich!
    Glaubst du, etc.
 Ach. *Ja, sag' ich dir.*
 Hekt. *Und wärst du, solches kündend,*
    ein Orakel. Nicht glaubt' ich dir.

Das Unterstrichene, was, als Bescheid auf meine Frage angesehen, ganz nach Orakelart ironisch zweideutig wäre, ist ohne Zweifel eben die betreffende Stelle von jener Nacht. Was wäre nun davon zu halten? Entweder ist es purer Zufall, oder kann ich es nur mit meiner alten Hypothese von einer doppelten Seelentätigkeit erklären. In dieser Beziehung, als psychologisches Problem, hat neuerdings der Kasus ein wahres Interesse für mich.

Im allgemeinen ist meine Voraussetzung diese: die Seele strahlt und wirkt von ihrer Nacht- oder Traum-seite aus in das wahre Bewußtsein herüber, indem sie innerhalb der dunklen Region die Anschauung von Dingen hat, die ihr sonst völlig unbekannt blieben. Ihre Vorstellungen in der Tag- und Nacht-sphäre wechseln in unendlichen kleinen, gedrängten Zeitmomenten mit äußerster Schnelligkeit ab, so daß die Stetigkeit des wachen Bewußtseins nicht unterbrochen scheint . . . In dem oben genannten Fall nun hatte die wissende Traumseele den Einfall, das Buch zu befragen, bei mir angeregt und mich im folgenden durchaus geleitet: das heißt ich verhielt mich in dem Augenblick bis auf den entscheidenden Griff meines Fingers hinaus partiell somnambül. So fremd und abenteuerlich das auch aussieht, warum sollte es geradezu unmöglich sein? Und übrigens: 'Eine geradezu falsche Hypothese ist besser als gar keine' sagt Goethe irgendwo in bezug auf seine Farbenlehre.[22]

The significance of this essay goes far beyond its anecdotal appearance as one of several "Vermischte Gelegenheitsschriften," as Maync calls it. On the contrary, I believe that this little essay is of central importance to our understanding of Mörike's preoccupations and literary themes. The essay and its occasion in 1825 seem to mark the beginning of Mörike's reading of Shakespeare for his attempt at assimilating principles of human psychology.

There are at least four characteristic elements of Mörike's work suggested here: first, again, Shakespeare's plays are a concrete source of psychological data, or what we would today think of as literary characterization. There are, for instance, Agnes's insanity in *Maler Nolten* and the grotesquerie of comic characters in the playet "Der letzte König von Orplid." These aspects are taken up below in Chapter III. Secondly, Mörike in this essay formulates a rudimentary theory of the unconscious. The terminology Mörike employs seems to be very accurate in describing the psyche. Mörike's "wissende Traumseele" is a very felicitous epithet. We would think of this "Traumseele" as part of the subconscious mind. Unfortunately Mörike does not explore further what kind of knowledge it is, which is lodged in the "Traumseele," or how this knowledge is acquired. But apparently Mörike felt that the transfer of knowledge occurred in a

54

state of somnambulism or during dreams. He seems to suggest that the "Traumseele" is also related to destiny. Thus "Traumseele" must be be seen to have an external component, linking it to a higher spiritual force. Mörike's term "somnambül" roughly corresponds to today's "subconsciously." Mörike, at that time, was beginning to take an active interest in Justinus Kerner's work on somnambulism and the occult.[23]

We also note, in the formal aspects of the essay, that Mörike's preoccupation with depth psychology was not a momentary whim. There were at least three different times, widely separated, in which Mörike devoted his attention to the composition of this essay. First there was the actual event, probably in 1825, but certainly between 1822 and 1825 while Mörike studied theology in Tübingen. Then there was a later period when Mörike read *Troilus and Cressida* once more, presumably for other reasons than consulting an oracle, when he came across the dialogue of Hector and Achilles, in which the word "oracle" occurs. This time may have been in the late 1820's while he was writing *Maler Nolten*. It was at this time that the first part of the anecdote, without the interpretation of it, was actually recorded: Finally, as Maync rightly indicates in his notes, beginning with the interpretive comment, "Was wäre nun davon zu halten," the manuscript shows a much later handwriting. This third encounter, when Mörike added his interpretation of a "wissende Traumseele" was probably added as late as the 1860's.

A third characteristic preoccupation in Mörike's work, which is alluded to in this essay, is the concept of "Schicksal" or destiny.[24] Throughout Mörike's work there are references to destiny and fate, and to situations in which the individual finds himself in an inevitable clash between individual will and destiny. "Schicksal" is a key word in *Maler Nolten, Mozart auf der Reise nach Prag* and in *Die Regenbrüder*. The dialogue between Hector and Achilles, which Mörike quotes, deals with this problem. Hector and Achilles are flyting; each assails the other with verbal violence. Prior to the lines quoted by Mörike, Achilles demands melodramatically of the gods to tell him where, on his body, he will inflict the mortal wound of Hector:

> Tell me, you heavens, in which part of his body
> Shall I destroy him? . . . Answer me, heavens! (IV, v, 242–246)

Hector replies that to try to force the gods to account to a mortal is impossible and beneath the gods' dignity:

> It would discredit the blessed gods, proud man,
> To answer such a question . . .
> Wert thou an oracle to tell me so,
> I'd not believe thee . . . (IV, v, 246–247, 252–253)

Hector stops short of accusing Achilles of blasphemy. In fact, he fails to see that Achilles' statements are blasphemous. There is a strong note of dramatic irony in the way Hector continues, because he is unaware, that he in turn commits blasphemy by defying Achilles, even if Achilles were an oracle. That is to say, if Achilles were a true oracle or a mouthpiece of the will of the gods, Hector would refuse to believe it. Of course, Hector's speech is as hyperbolical as is Achilles', but the underlying reality of inevitable, imminent combat adds weight to the heroic flyting. There was additional complexity for Mörike in this dialogue, which he calls "nach Orakelart zweideutig." That is to say, Mörike seems fully aware that he cannot force the Shakespearean text to be his personal oracle; and even if that were possible he would still be left with the decision of how much credence he would dare to put in Shakespeare as an oracle. And if Mörike has chosen a slightly frivolous tone throughout the essay, it can be seen as an attempt on his part to moderate or defuse the enormity and awe which surrounds the problem of destiny for the sensitive theology student and poet.

Fourth, this essay is revealing in view of Mörike's life long preoccupation with wonder in general and with supernatural phenomena, extrasensory perception, telepathy, animal magnetism and somnambulism. Stimulated by his reading of Max Perty's work *Die mystischen Erscheinungen der menschlichen Natur*[25] as late as 1861, Mörike published two personal anecdotes, "Aus dem Gebiete der Seelenkunde," in which he discusses two cases of telepathy, one from the year 1833 and the other from the years at Mergentheim 1844–1850.[26] But Mörike's interest in the occult should be distinguished from his interest in psychology, even though he himself obscures this difference at times.

Mörike speaks in the essay of reaching into the Shakespeare volume with his thumb: ". . . mit dem Daumen hineingriff." He was using, it seems, a method of random revelation still used today by certain protestant fundamentalists in Württemberg known as "Däumeln." In this process the Bible, not Shakespeare, is being passed around among a set of readers. Each reader will have his turn opening (thumbing) the Bible at random and will let whatever passage his eyes happen to fall upon be a prophetic revelation, which is then read to the peer group. It seem to have been an easy transference for Mörike, the theology student, to use the Shakespearean text in a similar half awe-struck, half playful way. In the 1820s Shakespeare has similar universal applicability for Mörike to that of the Bible for the devout fundamentalist.

Returning to the letters of the years between 1825 and 1830, we find that Mörike objectified his reading of Shakespeare in several ways. In a letter to his beloved sister Luise in August 1825, he includes a fanciful comparison from *A Midsummer Night's Dream*. He seems so struck with the set of elaborate metaphors that occur in a speech by Helena that he passes it on to his sister as a form of supreme compliment and celebration of her relationship to her friend Lotte. Mörike quotes at length from the Schlegel translation:

> Wie kunstbegabte Götter schufen wir
> Mit unsern Nadeln Eine Blume beide,
> Nach Einem Muster und auf Einem Siz,
> Ein Liedchen wirbelnd, beide in Einem Ton,
> Als wären unsre Hände, Stimmen, Herzen,
> Einander einverleibt. So wuchsen wir
> Zußammen, einer Doppelkirsche gleich, – –
> Zum Schein getrennt, doch in der Trennung Eins,
> Zwei holde Beeren, Einem Stil entwachsen,
> Dem Schein nach zwei Körper, doch Ein Herz!
> Zwei Schildern eines Wapens glichen wir,
> Die friedlich stehn, gekrönt von Einem Helm.[27]

Much later, in the 1840s Mörike wrote down these lines once more. This time he wrote the excerpt: *Clärchen und ihrer Freundin*, the girl friend being Gretchen Speeth, Mörike's wife-to-be. He also added the following lines:

> Die Heimlichkeiten alle, die wir theilten,
> Der Schwestertreu Gelübde, jene Stunden,
> Wo wir den raschen Tritt der Zeit verwünscht,
> Wenn sie uns schied – wirst du sie je vergessen? (Abschriften SNM)

These lines represent, of course, a change from the original Schlegel translation, where the passage, with all metaphors intact, is an angry chastisement by Helena of Hermia. Mörike needed to change the last line of the original passage in order to adapt it: "Wie sie uns schied: o, alles nun vergessen?"[28] But much more important here are thematic and symbolic content for Mörike. Clearly, Mörike is fascinated by the bond implied in the sisterly relationship, and beyond this by the image of twins and its many implications. The idea of twins Mörike envisioned as the highest embodiment of closeness and harmony. Friendship, kinship and love play important roles in his work. The desire for harmony and its concrete reflection in Restoration or Biedermeier literature (1815–1848) has been pointed out recently by Sengle.[29]

Whether Mörike found in Shakespeare's metaphors of the two as one an affirmation of his own preoccupation, or whether Shakespeare's play was the creative germ of that idea which Mörike then assimilated, is impossible to determine. But henceforth we note that the specific idea of intimacy and the idea of sameness captured in the image of twins fascinate Mörike. (The twin lacks, however, the large psychological dimension of the romantic *Doppelgänger*; Mörike's poetic image is much more limited.) Variations on the theme of the lookalike twin, of becoming one with one another and the loss of one another are taken up in several poems. In "Die Schwestern," for example, a poem belonging to a later creative phase, written a decade after his first intensive perusal of *A Midsummer Night's Dream*, the idea of oneness is central:

> Wir Schwestern zwei, wir schönen,
> So gleich von Angesicht,

So gleicht kein Ei dem andern,
Kein Stern dem andern nicht.

Wir Schwestern zwei, wir schönen,
Wir haben lichtbraune Haar,
Und flichst du sie in einen Zopf,
Man kennt sie nicht fürwahr.

Wir Schwestern zwei, wir schönen,
Wir tragen gleich Gewand,
Spazieren auf dem Wiesenplan
Und singen Hand in Hand.

Wir Schwestern zwei, wir schönen,
Wir spinnen in die Wett,
Wir sitzen an einer Kunkel,
Und schlafen in einem Bett.

O Schwestern zwei, ihr schönen,
Wie hat sich das Blättchen gewendt!
Ihr liebet einerlei Liebchen —
Und jetzt hat das Liedel ein End. (I, 507)

Clearly, the metaphors of oneness from *A Midsummer Night's Dream* previously cited reverberate in this poem, and seemed to have stayed permanently in Mörike's creative imagination. Whereas in his personal realm (Clärchen und Gretchen) the Shakespearean metaphors served a dedicatory function, in which the poet celebrates the simplicity of oneness, in his poetry Mörike probes deeper. This poem clearly reflects the everpresent problem of separation. Oneness is built up in four stanzas and countered in a fifth in a simple Volkslied-like pattern. In the first four stanzas each "Wir" becomes an "Ein," but the third person "ihr" destroys this harmonious unity. The only "ein" that follows, precedes, ironically, the word "End." The poem concludes with a bitter-sweet note of separation. Folkssong qualities such as simplicity of diction and rhythm, repetition of the first line and redundancy in line four keep the thought of separation well submerged. The capriciousness of the last live even lends an additional note of levity.

This strikingly simple song is also interesting for the fictitious inception with which Mörike surrounds it. In his letter to Hartlaub, Nov. 7, 1837, Mörike tells an elaborate story of taking a walk in the countryside and of overhearing barely the refrain of this song, sung by three maidens nearby. Upon his return to town he asks a neighbor girl whether she knows the rest of the lines, and lo and behold the girl recites them in full. He then asks his correspondent sheepishly: "Was sagst du zu diesem Geschichtchen."[30] Here Mörike is at his best in what has been often called "fabulieren." Mörike included the same fiction with the poem in his letter to Vischer in Dec. 1837. But aware of Vischer's great sophistication as a literary critic, he concluded the letter as follows: "Doch — per parenthesin— das Liedchen vorhin ist von mir: ich wollte nur, daß Du's mit unbefangenen Augen lesest und mir sagest, ob's für ein Volkslied gelten kann? Es ist morgens im Bett unmittelbar nach einem heiteren Erwachen gleichsam aus dem Stegreif entstanden und war in weniger als acht Minuten beisammen."[31] Besides challenging himself and his friends to crystallize concepts of what constitutes a folksong, Mörike was actually testing those of his friends with intimate knowledge of some of Shakespeare's plays, whether they would detect echoes of Shakespeare in his poem.

But there is, of course, still a good bit of self-deception involved. Without *A Midsummer Night's Dream* and *Twelfth Night; or, What You Will*, in which there is also powerful twin imagery, the poem seems unthinkable. In *Twelfth Night* Antonio expresses his amazement over the look-alikes, Viola and Sebastian:

> How have you made division of yourself?
> An apple, cleft in two, is not more twin
> Than these two creatures . . . (Act V, Scene I, 1. 210–212)

In Schlegel's translation the apple metaphor is changed into an egg metaphor. And Mörike, in turn, uses the egg metaphor in "Die Schwestern" as part of his catalogue of resemblance. In a very real sense Mörike's debt is thus as much to Schlegel's diction as it is to Shakespeare's song. In the following excerpt from the Schlegel translation we find the metaphor of the egg, which is so masterfully turned into a part of an autonomous folksong-like poem by Mörike:

Wie habt Ihr denn Euch von Euch selbst getrennt?
Ein Ei ist ja dem andern nicht so gleich,
Als diese zwei Geschöpfe. (Vol. 4, p. 86)[32]

The moving force about whom these lines are spoken in *Twelfth Night* are, of course, the twins Sebastian and Viola. Viola is furthermore disguised as a man which adds to her striking resemblance to her brother. Again, undoubtedly because the idea of twins, which are not metaphorical twins as in *A Midsummer Night's Dream*, but instead real twins, *Twelfth Night* engaged Mörike more deeply than some other Shakespearean plays. There are several excerpts of other passages of this play in *Abschriften* GSA, which are more closely discussed in Chapter III.[33] Though the passage containing the image of the egg is not among his notes, Mörike copied one of the songs from *Twelfth Night* in both German and English. Thus in indicates that Mörike must have been keenly conscious of the imperfections of translations of some of Shakespeare's lyric language. This is one of the very few times Mörike wrote English and it is also a testimony to Mörike's love for the play *Twelfth Night* and for the songs in Shakespeare's plays:

An old Song.
(*Shakesp. Twelfth Night*)

Come away, come away, death!
  And in jad [sic] *cypress let me be laid;*
Fly away, fly away, breath!
  I am slain by a fair cruel maid.
My shrewd [sic] *of white, stuck all with yew,*
    O, prepare it;
  My part of death no one so true
    Did share it.

Not a flower, not a flower sweet,
  On my black coffin let there be strown;
Not a friend, not a friend greet
  My poor corpse, where my bones shall be thrown!

A thousand thousand sighs to save
Lay me, o! where
True lover never find my grave,
To weep there.   (*Abschriften* GSA)

Except for the addition of "An old" in the title, the spelling in lines 2 and 5, and for the word "sad," which is missing from the beginning of line 15, Mörike's transcription is accurate. Mörike also included a translation into German of this song in his *Abschriften* GSA. Below it he noted (*Eschenburg*). Though he generally resorts to Schlegel translations, here he preferred the earlier German Shakespeare translator, who was also highly esteemed by Schlegel.[34] Mörike's version of the song is in fact an adaption of Eschenburg's translation:

Ein alter Sang

Komm hinweg, komm hinweg, Tod!
In dichte Cypressen verschleuß mich;
Flieh hinweg, flieh hinweg, Hauch!
Ein grausames Mädchen erwürgt mich;
Mein Leichentuch, mit Laub besteckt,
Bereitet!
Die Liebe hat zur Bahre mich
Geleitet.

Keine Blum', o! keine Blum, streu
Je Wohlgeruch über mein Grab hin;
Nicht ein Freund, nicht ein Freund geh
Zu meinem Leichnam und klag ihn!
Begrabt mich, tausendfaches Weh
Zu sparen,
Hin, wo Verliebte nichts von mir
Erfahren!
      (*Abschriften* GSA)

In at least two instances Mörike's changes are definitely for the better.[35] Mörike's version differs from Eschenburg in the following ways. Eschenburg entitled the song merely, "Lied." In line 2 Eschenburg wrote, "Im Trauergewande verbirg mich!" Mörike's "In dichte Cypressen verschleuß mich," even with the somewhat archaic "verschleuß," seems to be the better version, because it retains the original line better and because it is more concrete. In line 10 Eschenburg wrote, "über den Sarg hin!" Here, again, Mörike's "Mein Grab" improves the line with the more determined possessive adjective. In line 12 Eschenburg wrote, "Hin zu meinem Leichnam," and in line 13 he wrote, "tausendfält'gen Schmerz." Mörike changes here are slight. In other respects Mörike's version is identical to Eschenburg's.

It is almost self-evident why Mörike ignored Schlegel's translation except for the use of "Cypressen" in line 2. Unlike Schlegel's masterful translation of dialogue, his translation of the song seems almost tortured. This is true for both stanzas:

> Komm herbei, komm herbei Tod,
> Und versenk' in Cypressen den Leib.
> Lass mich frei, lass mich frei, Not:
> Mich erschlägt ein holdseliges Weib.
> Mit Rosmarin mein Leichenhemd,
>   O bestellt es!
> Ob Lieb' ans Herz mir tödlich kömmt,
>   Treu' hält es!
>
> Keine Blum', keine Blum', süß
> Sei gestreut auf den schwärzlichen Sarg;
> Keine Seel', keine Seel', grüß'
> Mein Gebein, wo die Erd' es verbarg.
> Und Ach und Weh zu wenden ab,
>   Bergt alleine
> Mich, wo kein Treuer wall' ans Grab
>   Und weine.
>   (Vo. 4, p. 35)

Schlegel's line 2, with the impersonal phrase "den Leib," the obscure lines 7—8 and line 13 with its protestant-hymnal inversion "zu wenden ab" seem particularly forced and help explain why Mörike merely improved upon the Eschenburg version.

On the one hand, Mörike's translation and his copy of the original came about because he was dissatisfied with the Schlegel text. On the other hand, at this time, around the year 1837, as we see in Renate von Heydebrand's study, Mörike was developing a "Volkston" in some of his poems.[36] Other examples of poems in which Mörike used this tone are "Die Soldatenbraut," "Ein Stündlein wohl vor Tag," "Das Verlassene Mägdlein" and "Schön-Rohtraut." Mörike was also very actively writing and editing at this time, because he was arranging his poems with the help of H. Kurz for his first edition in 1838. As his active correspondence with Kurz and F.T. Vischer indicates, he was also reading widely in German and world literature at the time. His active writing, editing and especially his reading may have directly contributed to this "Volkston."

Mörike seemed to have thought of Shakespeare's song from *Twelfth Night* as a folksong. In a letter to H. Kurz, dated March 30, 1837, he hints at hearing echoes of this song in Kurz's poem "Das schöne Kind," as well as in Uhland's "Elfenlied" which is also written in the "Volkston":

> In dem alten englischen Lied (das auch bei
> Shakespeare vorkommt) heißt es:
>> 'Not a flower, not a flower sweet
>> On my black coffin let there be strewn,
>> Not a friend, not a friend greet etc.'
>
> . . . Hierauf anklingend, ohne es zu wissen, singt Uhland:
>
>> 'Eine Blüt', eine Blüt mir brich![37]

In this letter Mörike continues his discussion of echoes which he has discovered of Shakespeare's "An old Song" in German poetry, and he cites as another example a poem by the Swabian poet Johann Martin Miller. Probably because he was struck by the folksong-like aspects of Shakespeare's song himself, Mörike added the words "an old" to the title. Though Mörike's particular English edition may have carried the longer title, he is undoubtedly speculating when he claims a prior existence for the song.

Mörike's conjectures point to an ambiguous attitude toward Shakespeare. On the one hand, as in the letter to Kurz, Mörike gently rebukes Kurz, Uhland and Miller for echoing Shakespeare. On the other hand, he thinks of Shakespeare's song as part of an older tradition, and by doing so, feels justified in adapting elements from

Shakespeare's plays and songs for his own use. But what Mörike says of Uhland may also be true for himself: his use of twin images and elements of a folksong-like tone could have come about just as unwittingly, "ohne es zu wissen." Ultimately, we will also have to acknowledge Eschenburg's contribution in addition to Schlegel's to German poetic diction.

Let us return for another brief consideration to aspects of the twin motif in Mörike's poetry. On a secondary level, once removed from direct allusions to twins, this motif also plays a part in the poem "Neue Liebe" and in the "nature poems" "Besuch in Urach" and "Mein Fluß." Though no attempt is made here to explicate these major poems, elements of the motif of unification, which seems to receive its strongest impetus from Mörike's fascination with the twin concept, will be traced. In "Neue Liebe," one of Mörike's few religious poems, the aspect of total harmony in the unification of two human beings is taken up:

Kann auch ein Mensch des andern auf der Erde
Ganz, wie er möchte, sein?
− In langer Nacht bedacht ich mir's, und mußte sagen, nein!

So kann ich niemands heißen auf der Erde,
Und niemand wäre mein?
− Aus Finsternissen heil in mir aufzückt ein Freudenschein:

Sollt ich mit Gott nicht können sein,
So wie ich möchte, mein und dein?
Was hielte mich, daß ich's nicht heute werde?

Ein süßer Schrecken geht durch mein Gebein!
Mich wundert, daß es mir ein Wunder wollte sein,
Gott selbst zu eigen haben auf der Erde!   (I, 771)

The speaker in this poem gives at first a negative answer to his own longing for perfect harmony. Total unification on a human level is not possible. The impossibility of it is underscored by the allusion to the solitude of a long night. The speaker then succeeds in transcending his limitation by seeking unification with God. The qualifying phrase "auf der Erde" anticipates this other-worldly unification. But the speaker is also painfully aware that his impulse to be unified on a human level preceded his revelation of a possibility for spiritual unification. In fact, we may not even be justified to use the term revelation, since the speaker seems to receive the "Freudenschein" entirely from within himself. Thus, the spiritual unification contains overtones of consolation for a more human need. In the very process of findling unification with God, which constitutes the new love which the title postulates, the poet wonders what has kept him from a purely spiritual view of unification all along. He wonders both about and at it. This wonder still leaves behind a note of hesitation about its fulfillment in spiritual terms.

The poems concludes with something of a paradox: the very process of realizing how easy it is to find God's love constitutes a wonder. Thus, in "Neue Liebe," a qualified transcendence of human lack of harmony is achieved. For this reason we can add "Neue Liebe" to a number of other poems by Mörike of which Holthusen says that they are Mörike's unique contribution to German lyric poetry with their "gemischte Stimmung."[38]

In the poems "Besuch in Urach" and "Mein Fluß" the speaker seeks unification with nature, or rather with the spirit which for Mörike's characteristic view of nature resides in nature. In "Besuch in Urach" this unification is sought on at least two levels. On the physical level or perceptual level the poet succeeds in unification:

> Hier wird ein Strauch, ein jeder Halm zur Schlinge,
> Die mich in liebliche Betrachtung fängt;   (I, 687)

But on a spiritual level the human sphere of the speaker is forever separated from the spirit, residing in nature:

> Dir biet ich denn, begier'ge Wassersäule,
> die nackte Brust, ach, ob sie dir sich teile!
> . . .
> Was ist's, das deine Seele von mir trennt?   (I, 687)

On another level, the visit to Urach is also a return to the nature of the visitor's youth. Though the poet on his present return feels he cannot recapture a previous unification with nature, je expresses his deep gratitude for the earlier nurturing which nature gave him:

66

O Tal! du meines Lebens andre Schwelle!
Du meiner tiefsten Kräfte stiller Herd!   (I, 689)

The present memory of this nurturing provides the speaker with deep satisfaction. But the earlier kinship with nature is no longer possible for him. The diction here is revealing: "Schwelle" and "Herd" are part of a house and of domesticity. These terms also connote safety. By applying these terms to nature. Mörike, in a sense, perhaps unwittingly, tries to domesticate nature which in its raw state is threatening. This urge by the speaker is furthermore reinforced when he attributes to nature a kind of guardian angel in the closing line: . . ."und sei dein Engel mein Geleite!" This urge to cloak nature, to render it harmless, further underscores an inability to deal with it in all its raw and threatening aspects.

In the poem "Mein Fluß" the poet's attempt at unification is couched in powerful, passionate and erotic diction:

O Fluß, mein Fluß im Morgenstrahl!
Empfange nun, empfange
Den sehnsuchtsvollen Leib einmal,
Und küsse Brust und Wange!
– Er fühlt mir schon herauf die Brust,
Er kühlt mit Liebesschauerlust
Und jauchzendem Gesange.   (I, 693)

The unification of man and nature sought in the poem is only temporarily possible as the river buoys the swimmer. On a symbolic level swimmer and river become lovers:

Die Woge wieget aus und ein
Die hingegebnen Glieder;
Die Arme hab ich ausgespannt
Sie kommt auf mich herzugerannt,
Sie faßt und läßt mich wieder.   (I, 693)

If the erotic experience were all the speaker sought, as S.S. Prawer would have us believe in his reading of the poem,[39] the temporariness of the union of swimmer and river would not be a problem. But the speaker also gently prods the river by asking: "Du murmelst so, mein Fluß, warum?" In the way the speaker asks the river for its mystery he seems to acknowledge his prior awareness, that the river will not surrender its secret. He is not very insistent. He keeps himself from committing the pitfall of the scientific poet, which Keats in his letters called the poet's "irritable reaching after fact and reason."[40] The speaker in the poem will not force nature as if he knew already that it will not reveal its secret. He is almost too easily content with the rejection he experiences. Thus Mörike achieves a balance; erotic desire is balanced by a deep sense of mystery with regard to nature. As S.S. Prawer puts it, Mörike's poetry is "subtly balanced emotion between sadness and joy, partaking of both without being either."[41] This balance can also be seen in Mörike's contentment with occasional moments of union and communion with nature.

In two other major poems of Mörike's first creative period to 1828, in the poems "Um Mitternacht" and "Gesang zu zweien in der Nacht" there is more direct evidence of his reading and use of Shakespeare than in "Besuch in Urach" and "Mein Fluß." In "Um Mitternacht" and "Gesang" Mörike recreates the atmosphere of some of Shakespeare's poetry.

In one of his many "fabulieren"-letters, which has the appearance of an enclosure, dated Oct. 3, 1827, addressed to his friend Mährlen, Mörike wrote:

> Damit diß Blatt nicht leer bleibt sez ich noch 2 (zum
> Erstaunen getreu übersezte) Verse aus *Shakespeares*
> *Venus* und *Adonis*
>
> Gelassen stieg die Nacht ans Land,
> Hängt träumend an der Berge Wand;
> Ihr Auge sieht die goldne Wage nun
> Der Zeit in gleichen Schaalen stille-ruhn
> Und kecker rauschen die Quellen hervor,
> Sie singen der Nacht, der Mutter, ins Ohr
> Vom Tage
> Vom heute geweßenen Tage!
>
> Das uralt alte Schlummerlied
> Sie achtets nicht, sie ist es müd,

Ihr klingt des Himmels Bläue süßer noch,
Der flüchtgen Stunden gleichgeschwungnes Joch.
    Doch immer behalten die Quellen das Wort
    Es sprechen die Wasser im Schlafe noch fort
        Vom Tage
        Vom heute geweßenen Tage![42]

At first the reader is inclined to think Mörike, who knew little
English, composed an artful joke for Mährlen, who was quite profi-
cient in English. There are no passages in all the 1194 lines of Shakespeare's "Venus and Adonis" that could be seen as a direct translation in this poem, to which Mörike later added the title "Um Mitternacht." Indeed, in her extensive discussion of the poem, von
Heydebrand, who also quotes from the letter in which the poem
first appeared, dismisses Mörike's claim of a translation laconically:
"Davon kann nun keine Rede sein."[43] This is no mere translation,
indeed, but to conclude that the two poems are unrelated or that
Mörike merely made an incongruous joke is, I believe, a mistake.

A closer reading of "Um Mitternacht" reveals several elements
both formal and thematic, which it has in common with Shakespeare's "Venus and Adonis." First of all, meter, rhyme and stanzaic
pattern reveal similarities. In both, iambic pentameter predominates.
"Venus and Adonis" uses iambic meter throughout, but in "Um
Mitternacht" the four dominant lines of iambs are followed by two
lines of dactyls. Except for the added refrain in Mörike's poem, both
poems use a six line stanza. The rhyme scheme in "Venus and Adonis" is ab ab cc and in "Um Mitternacht" a similar pattern of couplet
is used: aa bb cc with a refrain of xx. In both poems we find a
striking duality. This duality in stanza and meter is stronger in
"Um Mitternacht." But with the greater expanse of Shakespeare's
poem this duality pervades throughout the themes, imagery and
narrative.

"Venus and Adonis" deals with male against female, chastity
against lust, night against day, life against death, and many more
sets of opposites. There is Venus, the hot, impassioned, mature
female, versus Adonis, the cool, calm and youthful male, whom
Venus is trying to seduce. The two are opposites in the poem by
means of images such as fire versus water and lust versus love. Venus'

69

own emotions are represented by the dual opposite of hope versus despair in her pursuit of Adonis. Even when she first sees the killer-boar that slashes Adonis this duality is carried out:

> Whose frothy mouth, bepainted all with red,
> Like milk and blood being mingled both together.[44]

This duality is also carried out in "Um Mitternacht." Because of its severe limits of only two stanzas this duality is expressed primarily in the external structure with pairs of couplets, two stanzas and a duality within a double refrain. Having in mind Shakespeare's poem, Mörike seems to have recreated this dual design quite intentionally.

There is also a thematic duality in "Um Mitternacht"; the peace of night against the noise of day and its echoing artesian springs. The scale and yoke images complement each other and imply their own weighty dualities.

The two poems share another striking structural similarity in the division created by the indentation of lines five and six resulting in a quatrain and couplet. In "Venus and Adonis" this division has the structural function of a shift in perspective in some stanzas, allowing the poet to comment in the couplet on what has preceded in the quatrain, similar to the shift in tone from lyric to epigrammatic in Shakespeare's sonnets. Thus in the following stanza, for example, there is a shift of perspective from extended simile to direct description. We should also note her Shakespeare's masterful and empathetic observation of nature which constitutes another important similarity to Mörike's poem:

> Or, as the snail, whose tender horns being hit,
> Shrinks backward in his shelly cave with pain,
> And there, all smother'd up, in shade doth sit,
> Long after fearing to creep forth again;
> > So, at his bloody view, her eyes are fled
> > Into the deep-dark cabins of her head,   (1033–1038)

In a very similar way the quatrains in both stanzas of Mörike's "Um Mitternacht" deal with one set of observations, the personified night,

70

and the following couplet in both stanzas shifts the perspective to the "talking" artesian springs. In no other poem does Mörike use this "Venus and Adonis" stanza.

The content of Mörike's poem, more precisely its images and atmosphere also bear resemblances to "Venus and Adonis." Von Heydebrand in her discussion concedes the difficulty of finding a clear thematic meaning in the pattern of the imagery: "So einleuchtend, so stimmig in sich seine Bilder erscheinen, so schwierig ist es, ihnen ihren genauen Sinn abzufragen."[45] She finally formulates the theme as follows: "Nach dem vorgelegten Interpretationsversuch besteht der Gehalt des Gedichts in der Gegenüberstellung zweier Formen von Zeitaufhebung: der erfüllte Augenblick kontrastiert der Erinnerung, die als eintöniges Mahnen an immer Gleiches auftritt."[46] She further sees night and artesian springs as allegorical figures of the abstract contrast in the two experiences of time. This excellent reading of the poem is quite consistent with our present comparison of the two poems and especially with the thematic dualities already mentioned.

Indeed, a sense of time, both in respect to passage as well as stoppage pervades both poems. "Venus and Adonis" opens in the morning and concludes around ("um"!) midnight. In a sense, the end of time has been reached with the death of Adonis. Thus, as to sense of time "Um Mitternacht" is only similar to the last ¼ of "Venus and Adonis." Somehow Mörike sensed that time as such may be felt more clearly at night as he represents it in suspension. Thus, midnight corresponds to Adonis' death. The poem's refrain, in turn, leads to a paradox which adds to its richness: midnight is both a form of present as well as past. It is the only time of a day when it would make sense to speak of a day that "has been" today: "heute gewesen." With these two words Mörike combines past and present into a haunting moment which lingers around midnight: "um Mitternacht."

In another way von Heydebrand's reading is consistent with our comparison. Aside from the obvious personification of night in "Um Mitternacht," Mörike's night has attributes of a Venus figure or at least a thoroughly feminine being with references such as "Mutter" and her ascent onto land similar to the mythological Venus'

71

rise from the ocean foam. Venus-Night is a sentient being who hears, who dreams and who is tired. This Venus figure is the origin of Mörike's personification.

In the letter part of "Venus and Adonis" night has settled on the scene. Venus mourns for her beloved youth, the dead Adonis, who has been killed during the boar hunt. The poem concludes with an atmosphere of consummate stillness after the busyness of the day with its hectic courting scene and subsequent boar hunt. Finally the mourning Venus hides herself on Cyprus from the world:

> Thus weary of the world, away she hies
> And yokes her silver doves, by whose swift aid
> Their mistress mounted through the empty skies
> In her light chariot quickly is convey'd
>   Holding their course to Paphos, where their queen
>   Means to immure herself and not be seen.   (1189–1194)

This very weariness, which lingers on after the conclusion of the poem is echoed in "Um Mitternacht:" night cloaked in her own shadow is tired of hearing the waters repeat to her the happenings of the hectic and busy day: "Vom Tage, / Vom heute gewesenen Tage." Even the word "yoke" — though put to a different use in Mörike's poem — is repeated. In Mörike's poem "Joch" seems to recall the "Wage" of time in the first stanza: time is back in balance.

Similarly, at the conclusion of "Venus and Adonis," with the death of Adonis, a quiet equilibrium has been reestablished; things are at peace; Venus is no longer plagued by the passion for the beautiful youth. Clearly, though, the peace in "Venus and Adonis," because we know what has preceded it, is much more significant than the peace of a mood in "Um Mitternacht." With the arrival of the night figure an equilibrium has been established at midnight with the lingering remembrance of the previous day. As the comparison of the poems reveals, the equilibrium that the night figure and Venus achieve is analogous.

Furthermore, the story which the artesian springs seem to whisper endlessly into the ear of night in Mörike's poem, corresponds to

nature reflecting sympathetically Adonis' death and Venus' acknowledgment of nature's mourning. In fact, before she finds Adonis'
body, all signs in nature "tell" her of his death. Even Adonis' hunting
dogs "tell" her of his death.

> And here she meets another sadly scowling,
> To whom she speaks, and he replies with howling (917—918)

On a more general level both poems are masterful representations
of nature and are based upon very accurate observation of natural phenomena. Shakespeare lingers lovingly on descriptions of
flora and fauna. The bucolic qualities of "Venus and Adonis" have
prompted much of the critical scholarship surrounding the poem to
associate it closely with *A Mitsummer Night's Dream,* in which
country scenes and sights also attest to Shakespeare's intimate
knowledge of nature. Though much more confined in scope, Mörike
also deals intensely in kinesthetic, tactile and auditory imagery in
his representation of nature. Perhaps his most striking image is night
as she "hängt" (he later emended this to "lehnt") on the side of the
mountain. A key element of natural imagery that links the two
poems is the pervasive reference to water. The artesian springs in
"Um Mitternacht" may owe their origin to this water imagery in
"Venus and Adonis." Adonis, especially, is closely associated with
cooling water in contrast to the warm and eager Venus. Thus there
is a close analogue to the artesian springs when Adonis says: "Love's
gentle spring doth always fresh remain." (801) And as Adonis is
parting for the hunt the poet adds the following simile:

> . . . after him she darts, as one on shore
> Gazing upon a late-embarked friend
> Till the wild waves will have him seen no more,
> Whose ridges with the meeting clouds contend; (817—820)

Here the water imagery specifically foreshadows Adonis' death. But
in the overall pattern water imagery as applied to Adonis has mostly
positive connotations. And, more importantly for the purpose of
our comparison, the water imagery in "Venus and Adonis" seems to
have found an echo in the artesian springs of "Um Mitternacht."

73

There is at least one additional, external reason which suggests itself why Mörike was attracted to "Venus and Adonis." We have already noted Mörike's preoccupation with love and friendship. Shakespeare's poems, especially the sonnets and "Venus and Adonis," were also inspired by a deep friendship. "Venus and Adonis" is warmly dedicated to the Earl of Southampton. Even more relevant is the fact that Shakespeare's nondramatic poetry is mostly *about* love and friendship. Mörike must have found this very appealing. Being heir to the romantics in this respect, he always seemed to cherish a literary work so much more when it had a close connection to the author's life. What A.W. Schlegel says of Shakespeare's nondramatic poems may be taken to be representative of this view: "Sie haben schon deswegen einen Wert, weil sie von einer nicht erdichteten Freundschaft und Liebe eingegeben scheinen, da wir so gar wenig von den Lebensumständen des Dichters wissen."[47]

To see a heightened value in literature to which the author attests with letters, diaries and dedications was characteristic of Mörike and the writers influenced by Romanticism. Again and again we see in the manner of Mörike's reading the attempt to "humanize" great writers, to imagine them in their day to day activities and cares. For example, during the years of his more active reading of Shakespeare he wrote to Hartlaub in March 1826.

> Mein größtes Fest wäre, zuzusehen wie L[uise] dem
> Shakespeare, etwa eh er zur Königin Elisabeth gienge
> schwesterlich die Halskrause u. d. goldene Kette
> umthäte, u. sagte dann: "so, sey fein nicht muth-
> willig gegen seine Hoheit den Grafen von —". Dann
> käme er zum sparsamen Mittagmahl wieder heim und
> hätte ihr eine blühende Granate aus den Schloß-
> gärten mitgebracht, die ihm seine Königin selber gepflückt.
> Denn die Granate, sag ich Dir, ist eine Blume für Ihn.[48]

It should be noted that the "Granate" (pomegranate) Mörike refers to, was regarded as the flower of love by the ancient Greeks. Mörike here clearly thinks of Shakespeare as a great love poet. Also, with the invention of such lovely little fictions Mörike made the towering Shakespeare more accessible to him. Perhaps his novella *Mozart auf der Reise nach Prag* (1855) represents the supreme culmination of such little fictions, with its many little anecdotes of the equally towering figure of Mozart.

In concluding our discussion of Mörike's reading of Shakespeare's poem "Venus and Adonis" we should note that Mörike's awareness that Shakespeare's poem celebrated love, both by its intent and by its content, makes such a poem more appealing. And Mörike was also prompted by it to surround his own poem with one more puzzling little fiction of a translation which is and is not a translation, as he sent it off in a dedicatory fashion to his close friend Mährlen.

Another poem in which a Shakespearean, nocturnal, dreamlike atmosphere with a setting in nature pervades, and which also grew out of the time of Mörike's active perusal of Shakespeare in the years 1825–1830, is "Gesang zu zweien in der Nacht." Specifically, "Gesang" seems to have been inspired by passages in Shakespeare's play *The Merchant of Venice*. Storz in his recent work on Mörike's poetry also sees a similarity; but in a cursory footnote he recognizes an analogue of only one line of the play in Mörike's poem.[49] Although there is no concrete evidence in the letters or *Abschriften* of Mörike's active use of this particular play, later in his life, in 1852, in a letter to his sister Clara, he reports about a conversation he had with August Gerstel, whose portrayal of "Lanzelot", the clown-servant of Shylock in *The Merchant of Venice*, he had liked very much.[50] The play's overriding theme of loyalty and that special atmosphere of the hours before dawn in the fifth act must have also attracted Mörike to the play.

"Gesang" in its lyric form and as an independent poem was not included in Mörike's collection until the second edition of 1848. In its first version of 1825 this poem was a shorter lyric monologue and part of the unpublished dramatic fragment "Spillner." Its function in this fragment was to underscore the special atmosphere of the hours before daybreak. In a more superfical link to Shakespeare we note that Mörike had originally planned these lines for inclusion into a dramatic medium with which he was experimenting in various ways. Mörike used this poem in the playlet "der letzte König von Orplid," where it was restructured as strophe and antistrophe in the dialogue of Ulmon and Thereile. Mörike may have also intended "Gesang" for an opera libretto, but there is no actual evidence for this.

Because of its musicality, linking it further with the musical passage in *The Merchant of Venice*, and its dialogue form, which is actually an alternating lyric monologue of a male and a female voice, it should perhaps be called a duet or a recitative. As an independent poem and as the recitative in "Der letzte König von Orplid" it is identical:

Sie:

Wie süß der Nachwind nun die Wiese streift,
Und klingend jetzt den jungen Hain durchläuft!
Da noch der freche Tag verstummt,
Hört man der Erdenkräfte flüsterndes Gedränge,
Das aufwärts in die zärtlichen Gesänge
Der reingestimmten Lüfte summt.

Er:

Vernehm ich doch die wunderbarsten Stimmen,
Vom lauten Wind wollüstig hingeschleift,
Indes, mit ungewissem Licht gestreift,
Der Himmel selber scheinet hinzuschwimmen.

Sie:

Wie ein Gewebe zuckt die Luft manchmal,
Durchsichtiger und heller aufzuwehen;
Dazwischen hört man weiche Töne gehen
Von sel'gen Feen, die im blauen Saal
Zum Sphärenklang,
Und fleißig mit Gesang
Silberne Spindeln hin und wider drehen.

Er:

O holde Nacht, du gehst mit leisem Tritt
Auf schwarzem Samt, der nur am Tage grünet,
Und luftig schwirrender Musik bedienet
Sich nun dein Fuß zum leichten Schritt,
Womit du Stund um Stunde missest,

Dich lieblich in dir selbst vergissest —
Du schwärmst, es schwärmt der Schöpfung Seele mit!   (I, 697—698)

Before comparing in detail "Gesang" with passages from Shake-speare's play we note the closeness of the poem to "Um Mitter-nacht." The summernight aura is frequently invoked in Mörike's poetry and is a characterisric element of the years at Tübingen and shortly after. Again the poet objectifies an inner emotion in creating the atmosphere of a summernight. There is also the magical paradox of passage ("mit leisem Tritt") and suspension of time ("der freche Tag verstummt") in the figure of midnight. In contrast to "Um Mit-ternacht" night is not personified, but is nevertheless vibrantly alive. Also, the musical elements captured in special rhyme pairs: "Ge-dränge — Gesänge," "Stimmen — Schwimmen," "Klang — Gesang," predominate more here than in "Um Mitternacht."

The similarities of "Gesang" with the recitative-like passage with which the first scene of the fifth act of Schlegel's translation of *The Merchant of Venice* opens are even more striking. The lovers Jessica and Lorenzo are alone at night, two hours before daybreak. In a kind of *Wettgesang*, competing statement and reply, reply and statement, they outdo each other in enumerating famous lovers of classical antiquity and in praising their love night. The phrase "In such a night as this" is repeated seven times. Lorenzo begins:

Der Mond scheint hell. In solcher Nacht wie diese,
Da linde Luft die Bäume schmeichelnd küßte
Und sie nicht rauschen ließ . . .   (Vol. 3, p. 87)

After this singing-match and after a short interruption by Stephano and Launcelot, Lorenzo continues the praises of their night addres-sing Jessica, as both sit down to listen to the music of the night. Here, the parallel to Mörike's "Gesang" becomes most striking:

Wie süß das Mondlicht auf dem Hügel schläft!
Hier sitzen wir und lassen die Musik
Zum Ohre schlüpfen; sanfte Still' und Nacht
Sie werden Tasten süßer Harmonie.
Komm, Jessica! Sieh, wie die Himmelsflur

Ist eingelegt mit Scheiben lichten Goldes!
Auch nicht der kleinste Kreis, den du da siehst,
Der nicht im Schwunge wie ein Engel singt
Zum Chor der hellgeaugten Cherubim.
So voller Harmonie sind ew'ge Geister:
Nur wir, weil dies hinfäll'ge Kleid von Staub
Ihn grob umhüllt, wir können sie nicht hören. (Musikanten kommen)
He! kommt, und weckt Dianen auf mit Hymnen,
Rührt Eurer Herrin Ohr mit zartem Spiel, (Musik)
Zieht mit Musik sie heim.   (Vol. 3, p. 89)

The "Harmonie" of which Lorenzo speaks requires exploration because of its complexity and its relevance to Mörike's poem. In the
original the lines are no less obscure: "soft stillness and the night /
Become the touches of sweet harmony." In modern idiom this
translates approximately: The soft, resonant stillness surrounding
us in the night, and the night itself, are fitting notes to the harmony
in the sky. Though the music suggested is not entirely accessible to
discursive analysis, there are at least three different harmonies
suggested by what Lorenzo says: There is harmony between the
spell-bound lovers. This multilevelled harmony is echoed in the
first seventeen lines of Mörike's "Gesang." Schlegel's music of the
spheres, represented by "Scheiben lichten Goldes," which are "voller
Harmonie" seem to have their correspondence in Mörike's "Sphärenklang" and "im blauen Saal," where the stars are "silberne Spindeln."
    The significance of the parallel text of Schlegel's translation of
The Merchant of Venice lies not so much in its discovery, but in the
fuller understanding it provides for some of the more obscure passages
in Mörike's poem. Mörike's mysterious phrase "der Erdenkräfte
flüsterndes Gedränge" apparently had its origin in the "sanfte Still'"
that also emanates from the earth surrounding the lovers Lorenzo
and Jessica. And Schlegel's "Engel," "hellgeaugte Cherubim" and
"ew'ge Geister" become "wunderbarsten Stimmen" and "sel'ge
Feen" in Mörike's poem. The very diction, images, the gentle rhythm
of the lines as well as the thematic levels of harmony find their
echoes in Mörike's lines. Especially striking is Mörike's use of the
declamatory "wie süß" with which Lorenzo's praises of the night

begin. It is also interesting that the extreme purity of the nocturnal perceptions by the lovers, without erotic overtones whatsoever, is identical in both works.

With the conclusion of Lorenzo's speech and the conclusion of "Gesang" the reaction of the lovers to the beauties of the night in both works begins to diverge. Beginning with "Nur wir, weil dies hinfäll'ge Kleid von Staub . . ." Lorenzo notes disappointedly, that he and Jessica, being mortal, cannot actually hear the music of the spheres. But at that very moment (according to the stage directions) real musicians appear and begin to substitute the unheard celestial with heard mortal music. This compensates nicely for the disappointment. But the spell has been broken and the subsequent dialogue indicates it. In the last passage by "Er" night is personified, measuring time step by step as it walks toward day on black velvet. In combining night with music and passage of time in this way Mörike creates one additional harmony, which is required for the successful conclusion of this lyric poem. Incorporating the dissonance of the Shakespearean passage into his poem would have meant a *Stimmungsbruch*, which would be characteristic of Heinrich Heine but not of Mörike.

Mörike avoids the slight tension or dissonance in the dialogue of Lorenzo and Jessica which seems to be required for the progression of the play. This keen quest for harmony on Mörike's part, which we see in his work and life again and again, which in this particular case may be dictated more by the genre of the lyric, but which also captured his imagination in reading *The Merchant of Venice* in the first place, may have ultimately prevented him from writing a full-blown play, where conflict and tension are essential.

"Gesang" never received the kind of critical attention that was given to the related "Um Mitternacht" and to "An einem Wintermorgen, vor Sonnenaufgang." This is perhaps because these poems have been viewed as more representative of Mörike's view of nature and his special way of sounding the mystic-mythical aura of nature. Furthermore, critical acknowledgment of Mörike's debt to Skakespeare has not usually gone beyond a footnote reference and a cursory note on the Shakespeare tradition in Germany. Von Heydebrand's comment in this connection is perhaps representative: "Für den 'Gesang zu zweien in der Nacht' mit seiner Atmosphäre von gedämpfter Sinnlichkeit, synästhetischen Erlebnissen und Feerie ist vielleicht an Shakespeare zu denken und an alles, was die Romantik – Shakespeare und die ganze Empfindsamkeit amalgamierend – an Nachtstimmungen in die Tradition eingebracht hat."[51]

The special atmospheres of Shakespeare's plays for which Mörike had a keen affinity are also found in Mörike's prose at this time. The only prose Mörike was writing prior to his work on *Maler Nolten*, which commenced in 1828, was in letters. It appears that Mörike used his correspondence in the years 1825–1828 as a forum to polish his prose by means of recreating atmospheres of certain Shakespearean plays. In a letter to Hartlaub dated April 16, 1827, for example, Mörike writes:

> Ach dürftest Du manchmal zu mir kommen. . . besonders in den Stunden nach dem AbendEssen, d.h. nach 7 Uhr mit mir in Garten gehen hinter'm Haus! Dieser ist groß und modern angelegt. Im Hintergrund steht eine halbrunde weißgegitterte Hütte mit e. Strohdach auf einem schönberaas'ten Hügel, dort blickt man unmittelbar auf eine stille Wiese, wo (außerhalb des Dorfes) ein neuer Kirchhof zu bauen angefangen wurde. Dort kann man nur Dinge wie den SommerNachtsTraum lesen.[52]

In addition to the direct reference to *A Midsummer Night's Dream* there are allusions to the leisure and to the bucolic setting of the play. Even the allusion to merriment between supper and bed-time from the play is present. Theseus in Schlegel's translation says at one time:

> Nun kommt! Was haben wir für Spiel' und Tänze?
> Wie bringen wir nach Tisch bis Schlafengehn
> Den langen Zeitraum von drei Stunden hin?
> Wo ist der Meister unsrer Lustbarkeiten?
> Was giebt's für Kurzweil? (Vol. 3, p. 68)

Though Mörike wanted primarily to please his friend with literary allusions, because earlier in school they had read the play together, he is also polishing his prose in the process. Indeed, his fondness for the word *Kurzweil* may have been stimulated by this passage.

To his friend Kauffmann Mörike also invoked the atmosphere of a Shakespearean play. Again, the purpose is as much to load his prose with precious and appropriate Shakespearean images, as it is to communicate with a friend:

Tübingen ist in der VACANZ wie ein umgestürzter Handschuh: es liegt wie in einem recht leeren und stillen Katzenjammer da, und die gegenwärtige Jahrszeit, die trübe Witterung stimmt vollkommen dazu. Der Wind tummelt sich auf dem Wörth herum, und ruht nicht, bis er die ganze Reihe von Pappeln aufs lezte [sic] Blatt wie zu Besen verkehrt hat . . . Die Wetterfahnen rufen einander in langgezogenen Tönen zu . . . wie die Klage der Äolusharfe . . . dort auf der Hinterseite der Küferei, mit der Aussicht auf das Ammerthal ist die verlassene Laube, wo ich an eben einem solchen Tag mit Bauer zum erstenmal eine getreue Übersetzung des herbstlichen Macbeth las.[53]

Did Tübingen in autumn inspire Mörike to allude to *Macbeth*, or the reverse? He gets so carried away with creating an atmosphere in his description, that he ignores the actual fact: although Mörike's description may be based on a visit to Tübingen during the vacation, he almost certainly would not have spent his time there on a previous occasion reading Shakespeare with Bauer. For his vacations he never stayed at the university. This little inaccuracy only underscores Mörike's indifference to verisimilitude. Again we note that the aura of Sheakespeare's drama left a deep impression on Mörike's sensibility.

We can initially conclude that during his first creative period of 1822–1828 Mörike's affinity for Shakespeare is revealed in every phase of his literary work. The most concrete results of Mörike's reading of Shakespeare are found in his lyric poetry especially in "Die Schwestern," "Um Mitternacht" and "Gesang zu zweien in der Nacht". But there is also evidence for his preoccupation in his letters, in his essay "Doppelte Seelentätigkeit," and in his dramatic fragment "Spillner." Mörike was intensely interested in the psychology of characters in Shakespeare, and through the Schlegel translation as a kind of intermediary, Mörike used certain motifs, especially the twin motif, poetic imagery, thematic elements such as the concept of harmony and perhaps most pervasive, atmosphere or setting.

In the subsequent chapter we will further examine Mörike's reading of Shakespeare for psychology in *Maler Nolten* and especially the creation of the mythical-poetic land of "Orplid," which belongs so firmly in the early creative phase of Mörike. Furthermore there are important concrete pieces of evidence from Mörike's extant library and *Abschriften*, which are testimony to his preoccupation with Shakespeare.

Notes — Chapter II

1 At various times Mörike copied poems, lists of titles of poems and scenes from plays by other writers. These materials are part of the Mörike *Nachlaß* at the Mörike Archiv in the Schiller-Nationalmuseum, Marbach, and at the Goethe-Schiller Archiv, Weimar, hereafter referred to as *Abschriften* SNM or *Abschriften* GSA.

2 "Mörike und der Schwäbische Dichterkreis, Bücher, Autographen, Handzeichnungen, Silhouetten, Bildnisse aus der Sammlung Hanns Wolfgang Rath. Versteigerung Mittwoch d. 29. und Donnerstag d. 30. Juni 1932 . . . Müller und Gräff, Antiquariat, Stuttgart." This catalogue lists seven more items from Mörike's library which are lost:

a. *Auszug d. Catechistischen Unterweisung zur Seligkeit.* Stuttgart, 1849.

b. Lichtenberg, G. Christoph, *Vermischte Schriften*, nach dessen Tode ges. u. hrsg. v. L.Chr. Lichtenberg u. Fr. Kries. Tl. 3–5. Wien, 1817.

c. Matthisson, Fr., *Gedichte.* 3. verm. Aufl. Zürich, 1794.

d. Schönhuth, Ottmar F.H., *Sagen u. Geschichten aus Hohenlohe*, neuererzählt. Öhringen u. Mergentheim, 1857.

e. Vischer, Fr.Th., *Aesthetik oder Wissenschaft d. Schönen.* Bd. 2–3 (in 4) u. Register. Reutlingen u. Leipzig., Stuttgart, 1847–58.

f. Young, Ed., *Nachtgedanken.* Im Versmaß d. Urschr. übers. v. Ch.E. u. Bentzel-Sternau. Frankfurt a M., 1825.

g. Varnhagen von Ense, Karl August, 1785–1858. Eigenh. Schriftstück m. U. dat. Berlin, 1.9.1856.

It should be noted that H.W. Rath was not a trained scholar, but an avid private collector and commentator of Mörike's works, papers and memorabilia. Though Rath's commentaries and archivistic descriptions are occasionally unreliable, he made some valuable contributions with his early editions of Mörike's letters: *Briefwechsel zwischen Eduard Mörike und Moriz v. Schwind*. Stuttgart, 1914; Briefwechsel zwischen *Th. Storm und E. Mörike*, Stuttgart, [1919]; *Luise: Briefe der Liebe an seine Braut Luise Rau von Eduard Mörike*. Ludwigsburg, 1921.

3 Hermann Hesse, *Nürnberger Reise* (Berlin, 1953), p. 229 and Hermann Hesse, "Beschwörungen, Rundbrief im Februar 1954. Privatdruck," p. 27.

4 See Chapter V, *Part A*: Annotated Bibliography of Mörike's Extant Library, item No. 13, *Goethe's Sprüche in Prosa*. From the dedication we know that Mörike must have read Goethe's maxims in this work a few months before his death in June 1875.

5 The notebook, "Kleines Notizbüchlein Mörikes aus dem Jahre 1818," is mentioned as item No. 43 and 44 in *Eduard Mörike und seine Freunde: Eine Ausstellung aus der Mörike-Sammlung Dr. Fritz Kauffmann* (Stuttgart: Turmhaus, 1965). Hereafter cited as Kauffmann, *Mörike-Sammlung*. Thanks to three generations of the Kauffmann family, beginning with Mörike's friend Friedrich Kauffmann (1803–1856), we have this important collection of Mörike memorabilia, including manuscripts and notations, which is now a permanent exhibit of the Stuttgart Stadtarchiv located in the Wilhelmspalais.

6 Baumann, *Letters*, p. 872.

7 Kauffmann, *Mörike-Sammlung*, item No. 46, p. 33. "Von Eudard Mörike eigenhändig geschriebener Theaterzettel."

8 Maync, *Biography*, p. 141.

9 E.L. Stahl *Shakespeare und das deutsche Theater* (Stuttgart: W. Kohlhammer, 1947), p. 270ff.

10 This letter or note is part of the Kauffmann, *Mörike-Sammlung* in Stuttgart, but it is not included in the catalogue and it is therefore not specifically identified by number. There is, however, no question that it is in Mörike's handwriting.

11 *Mörikes Aufenthalt in Wermutshausen und Schwäbisch Hall* (Schwäbisch Hall, 1950), p. 20.

12 *Eduard Mörikes Haushaltungsbuch*, ed. Bezirksheimatmuseum Mergentheim (Bad Mergentheim: Hans Kling, 1951), p. [33].

13 Hans-Ulrich Simon, *Mörike Chronik* (Stuttgart: J.B. Metzler, 1981), p. 263.

14 *Arbeiten zur deutschen Literatur 1750–1850* (Stuttgart: J.B. Metzler, 1965), p. 173.

15 *Briefe, 1811–1828*, vol. X, p. 31–32.

16 Ludwig Tieck provides us with a key explanation for Mörike's particular affinity for Shakespeare's *A Midsummer Night's Dream* when he points to its accessibility of elements of wonder: "Wenn man so eben von der Lesung

des Macbeth oder Othello zurückkommt, so wird man versucht, den Sturm und Sommernachtstraum sehr tief unter diese großen Zeichnungen zu setzen . . . Er weiht in diesen Stücken den Zuschauer in seine Zauberwelt ein und läßt ihn mit hundert magischen Gestalten *in eine vertrauliche Bekanntschaft treten*, ohne daß ihn Schrecken und Schauder von der geheimnisvollen Werkstatt in einer grauenhaften Entfremdung halten." (Emphasis, mine.) "Shakespeares Behandlung des Wunderbaren," in *Kritische Schriften*. Leipzig, 1848, vol. I.

17 *Die Tagebücher: 1821–1826*, ed. Herbert Meyer (Stuttgart: Ernst Klett, 1956), p. 300.

18 Harry Maync, "Eduard Mörike im Verkehr mit berühmten Zeitgenossen," *Westermanns Illustrierte Deutsche Monatshefte*. No. 556 (Jan. 1903), p. 494.

19 *Bismarck, Nietzsche, Scheffel, Mörike: Der Einfluß nervöser Zustände auf ihr Leben und Schaffen, vier Krankheitsgeschichten* (Bonn: A. Marcus & E. Wener, 1921), p. 87f. This cold and strictly clinical discussion leads Dr. Müller to point out Mörike's pervasive "Leistungsunfähigkeit" and "Willensschwäche." There is some question of how reliable this study is. The sentense referring to Mörike's reaction to *King Lear* is taken *verbatim* from Maync, *Biographie*, p. 477 without crediting the source.

20 *Briefe, 1811–1828*, vol. X, p. 103.

21 *Eduard Mörike: Sämtliche Werke*, ed. Jost Perfahl and Helga Unger. 2 vols. (München: Winkler, 1968), II, 585–586. Hereafter cited in the text by volume and page number. In additional references this edition is referred to as *Sämtliche Werke*.

22 *Sämtliche Werke*, II, p. 585–586. The reference to Goethe is to the section "Naturwissenschaft im Allgemeinen," in the essay "Analyse und Synthese," in Vol. 40 (Cotta edition, 1840), p. 485.

23 *Die Seherin von Prevorst: Eröffnungen über das innere Leben des Menschen und über das Hineintragen einer Geisterwelt in die unsere.* (Stuttgart & Tübingen: Cotta, 1829.)

24 August Emmersleben, "Das Schicksal in Mörikes Leben und Dichten," Diss. (Kulmbach: Universität Würzburg, 1931), p. 66. "So ist der Glaube an ein unwiderstehliches, dem Menschen vorgezeichnetes Schicksal für Mörikes Weltanschauung kennzeichnend."

25 Leipzig, 1861.

26 *Sämtliche Werke*, II, 583–584. It should be noted, that H. Unger in her work, *Mörike-Kommentar zu sämtlichen Werken* (München: Winkler, 1970), p. 150, mistakenly identifies the two-part essay "Aus dem Gebiet der Seelenkunde" and a second copy of this essay entitled "Als Beitrag zu den Studien des Herrn Prof. Max Perty" as two different essays by Mörike. These two essays are, in fact, one and the same work. There exists merely a second copy of this essay with that second title in the Kauffmann, *Mörike-Sammlung*, item No. 140.

27 *Briefe, 1811—1828*, vol. X, p. 106.
28 William Shakespeare, *Shakespeares Werke*, 4 vols., vol. III, transl. A.W. Schlegel and L. Tieck (Berlin: Paul Franke Verlag [no date], dritter Aufzug, zweite Szene, p. 46. Hereafter cited by volume and page number in the text.
29 *Biedermeierzeit*, I, p. 126.
30 Baumann, *Letters*, p. 418.
31 Vischer, *Letters*, p. 143.
32 Stahl reports in his *Shakespeare und das deutsche Theater*, p. 224, that in 1820 an inferior translation of *Twelfth Night* by A. von Zieten was performed which bore the title *Die Zwillingsgeschwister*. Wieland, Eschenburg and Schlegel never used any other title but *Der Dreikönigsabend oder Was Ihr Wollt*.
33 H. Maync in his notes in *Mörikes Werke*, I, p. 418, on "Die Schwestern," points to the egg image of *Was Ihr Wollt*. But he does not acknowledge Mörike's extensive use of the play, nor does he acknowledge anywhere the existence of Mörike's *Abschriften* of Shakespeare.
34 William Shakespeare, *William Shakespeare's Schauspiele*, transl. J.J. Eschenburg, 2nd ed., 11 vols. (Zürich: Orell & Füssli, 1798—1804).
35 Cf., vol. II, pp. 50—51.
36 Renate von Heydebrand, *Eduard Mörikes Gedichtwerk* (Stuttgart: J.B. Metzler, 1972), p. 236ff. The German word *Ton* and the English word tone are not equivalent when applied in literary analysis. Heydebrand uses *Ton* to mean a particular style.
37 Kurz, *Letters*, pp. 50—51.
38 *Eduard Mörike in Selbstzeugnissen und Bilddokumenten* (Hamburg: Rowohlt, 1971), p. 40.
39 *German Lyric Poetry* (London: Routledge & Paul, 1952), p. 169f.
40 To George and Tom Keats, Dec. 1817. *The Letters of John Keats, 1814—1821*, vol. I, 1814—1818, ed. Hyder Edward Rollins (Cambridge: Harvard University Press, 1958), p. 193.
41 *German Lyric Poetry*, p. 196.
42 *Briefe, 1811—1828*, vol. X, p. 185—186. Admittedly, Mörike's statement that his poem is a mere faithful translation from "Venus and Adonis" is an exaggeration. On the other hand, I do not believe, as the editors do in the "Erläuterungen" (p. 486), that the reference is merely "fingiert."
43 *Eduard Mörikes Gedichtwerk*, p. 28.
44 *The Works of Shakespeare. The Poems*, ed. J.C. Maxwell (Cambridge: Cambridge University Press, 1966), 11. 901—902. Hereafter cited in the text by line number.
45 *Eduard Mörikes Gedichtwerke*, p. 29.
46 *loc. cit.*
47 August Wilhelm Schlegel, *Kritische Schriften*, ed. Emil Staiger (Zürich: Artemis, 1962), p. 67.
48 *Briefe, 1811—1828*, vol. X, p. 117.

49 Gerhard Storz, *Eduard Mörike* (Stuttgart: Ernst Klett, 1967), p. 82.
50 Seebaß, *Unpubl. Letters*, p. 258f.
51 *Eduard Mörikes Gedichtwerk*, p. 31.
52 *Briefe, 1811–1828*, vol. X, p. 150–151.
53 *Briefe, 1811–1828*, vol. X, p. 247–248.

Chapter III

Love and Psychopathology: Mörike's Reading of Shakespeare
with Emphasis on the Years 1828 to 1833

Mörike's genuine affinity for Shakespeare's dramatic and lyric poetry, as seen in several poems from the years 1824 to 1828, and the
allusions in his letters to Shakespearean plays as well as to Shakespeare the human being during those years and before were discussed in the previous chapter. To trace specifically the extent of
Mörike's subsequent use of Shakespeare's *A Midsummer Night's
Dream* in the paylet "Der letzte König von Orplid" and to explore
further Shakespearean influence in *Maler Nolten* are the main en-
deavors in this chapter.

Mörike writes in his autobiographical poem "Besuch in Urach:"
"Du meiner tiefsten Kräfte stiller Herd." This he could have said
with even more justification about Tübingen, in view of his extra-
curricular reading in general and his preoccupation with Shakespeare
in particular. On his visit to Urach it was the spirit of nature that
spoke to him most strongly. On his visits to Tübingen – in actuality
and in flight of imagination – the recollections of experience and
literary inspiration which left their mark on his work are more
complex. Two words coined by Mörike immediately suggest themselves in connection with his best work of that time: Peregrina and
Orplid. To these words, in view of Mörike's actual literary output,
we should perhaps add Shakespeare as another key source of inspiration.

Peregrina and Orplid are well-known concepts in Mörike scholarship. Most critical attention – both biographical and intrinsic literary analysis – has been devoted to Mörike's famous five poem
Peregrina cycle. The notable representative of the biographical
approach is still Harry Maync with his careful discussion of the
unhappy love affair with Maria Meyer as the source of Peregrina.[1]
The most comprehensive recent representative of the intrinsic
approach, with particular attention to Mörike's use of the poetic

87

voice, the speaking situation and "Ton," is von Heydebrand.[2] Critical attention to Orplid has been less satisfactory, because scholars have generally failed to probe beyond its obvious connection to Mörike's collaboration with his fellow student and fellow traveler to Orplid, Ludwig Bauer. G. Storz' chapters, "Maler Nolten" and "Orplidische Nachklänge,"[3] as well as S.S. Prawer's penetrating comments[4] are notable exceptions, and we will have occasion to return to these studies. But first the meaning of Orplid, its relationship to the playlet "Der letzte König von Orplid," and the place in *Maler Nolten* should be recalled.

Orplid is an entirely imaginary, mythical, magical Utopia, a lost paradise which Mörike together with his friend Bauer created during long talks and shared reading in the summer of 1825. Orplid partakes of Robinson Crusoe and a lost golden age. It is an island and a city imaginatively placed in the Pacific Ocean between New Zealand and South America, guarded by the tutelary goddess Weyla. As a symbol of the creative imagination and as a fascinating and independent parallel to Coleridge's "Kubla Khan," no other aspect of Mörike's creative work is more squarely part of European Romanticism than Orplid. It has its own topography, mythology and history, with special names for rivers and lakes. Most importantly, it is inhabited by a diverse mythical race. Many letters and poems by Mörike attest to its creation. At first, neither Mörike nor Bauer thought of publication as Maync points out.[5] Then, in 1826 Bauer wrote two small plays "Der heimliche Maluff" and "Orplids letzte Tage" and Mörike wrote "Der letzte König von Orplid." Mörike's original version is apparently lost. As Storz has pointed out, the original version differed considerably from the version that was finally included as a kind of theatrical interlude or divertimento in *Maler Nolten*.[6] The best background of Orplid is perhaps given by the character Larkens in *Maler Nolten* as he introduces it. As has been pointed out by many Mörike scholars, nowhere is the relationship between one of his literary characters and Mörike closer than in what Larkens says about the origin of the playlet and the Mörike-Bauer collaboration. In the novel Larkens is the author of the play:

Ich hatte in der Zeit, da ich noch auf der Schule studirte, einen Freund, dessen Denkart und ästhetisches Bestreben mit dem meinigen Hand in Hand ging . . . Wir bildeten uns bald eine eigene Sphäre von Poesie . . . Wir erfanden für unsere Dichtung einen außerhalb der bekannten Welt gelegenen Boden, eine abgeschlossene Insel, worauf ein kräftiges Heldenvolk, doch in verschiedene Stämme, Grenzen und Character-Abstufungen getheilt, aber mit so ziemlich gleichförmiger Religion, gewohnt haben soll. Die Insel hieß *Orplid*, und ihre Lage dachte man sich in dem Stillen Ozean zwischen Neu-Seeland und Süd-America. Orplid hieß vorzugsweise die Stadt des bedeutendsten Königsreichs: sie soll von göttlicher Gründung gewesen seyn und die Göttin *Weyla*, von welcher auch der Hauptfluß des Eilands den Namen hatte, war ihre besondere Beschützerin. Stückweise und nach den wichtigsten Zeiträumen erzählten wir uns die Geschichte dieser Völker . . . Unsere Götterlehre streifte hie und da an die griechische, behielt aber im Ganzen ihr Eigenthümliches; auch die untergeordnete Welt von Elfen, Feen und Kobolden war nicht ausgeschlossen . . . Orplid, einst der Augapfel der Himmlischen, mußte endlich ihrem Zorne erliegen, als die alte Einfalt nach und nach einer verderblichen Verfeinerung der Denkweise und der Sitten zu weichen begann.[7]

Larkens continues the introduction of the playlet by giving its background and sketching some of its characters, including detail that is actually not included in its extant form. Some of his word choices are peculiar and seem to represent afterthoughts by Mörike, who was naturally concerned with creating a meaningful context for the playlet in *Maler Nolten*. Thus, for example, Larkens refers to the "Pathologische der Sache." He presumably refers to König Ulmon, the last king of Orplid, who for the last 1000 years has been bound by a loathsome love to the fairy-queen Thereile. As an allusion to Nolten and his loves of Konstanze and Agnes this coice of words would represent a curious violation of a consistent point of view by Mörike. In other words, a character in a novel should not possess an inordinate amount of foreknowledge.

As a foil to the charge of multiple external influence Larkens in the novel and Mörike in his letters suggest again and again the "Eingenthümlichkeit" of the playlet. There is indeed no *one* source of inspiration. But only an acquaintance with certain literary works and traditions, ideas in the air and specific reading in Homer and Shakespeare could account for the extreme diversity of characters and ideas in the playlet. Gerhart von Graevenitz, in his explanation of the possible source of Orplid, points to Friedrich Leopold Graf zu Stolberg's novel *Die Insel* (1788) with the difference that "Für Stolberg ist die erträumte Gelehrtenrepublik Mittelpunk," whereas "Für Mörike die Erlösung Ulmons von seiner 'verhaßten Liebe' und seiner tausendjährigen Unsterblichkeit."[8] Von Graevenitz goes on to concede that in the Mörike text there is no comparable patriotic mission to bring about reform based on ideas in Leibniz and Zinzendorf.

Before dealing specifically with the Shakespearean source, let us review several other tangential sources which left their mark on the world of Orplid. This review is all the more relevant since it seems that with the inclusion of poems, letters, legends, a dramatic interlude, and a musical score Mörike wanted to impress the reading public with a diverse richness in his debut *Maler Nolten*. Furthermore, it cannot be overemphasized that Mörike possessed enormous assimilative skills.

In letters to Mörike Bauer frequently referred to their common debt to Homer and Shakespeare. In a letter dated as early as Sept. 6, 1824, he writes Mörike: "Wenn ich an Dich gedenke, ist mirs, wie wenn ich im Shakespeare gelesen hätte."[9] In a letter dated Juni 27, 1826 he recalls having read Homer and Shakespeare, while trying to recollect the exact origin of Orplid a year after its invention. "Nach Jakobi, also nach dem 25. Julius, muß es gewesen sein . . . ehe ich fortging, lasen wir noch einmal im Homer, und solange wir im Homer lasen, war Orplid noch im Himmel bei den seligen Göttern."[10]

Homer's *Odyssey* served as a source for the "sichere Mann" in "Der letzte König von Orplid." He is only indirectly mentioned in the playlet, when the fairy-child Silpelit disappears and plays with him. This giant seems partly based on Polyphemus in the *Odyssey*. In this connection I would like so suggest a revision of the date of Mörike's lenghty narrative poem "Märchen vom sichern Mann" from 1837 to 1825 on the basis of a heretofore unknown and unpublished letter fragment, probably addressed to Friedrich Kauffmann, dated "Vor dem 19. Juli 1825." The letter reads in part:

[der sichere Mann hatte] gegen Ende seines Lebens die fixe Idee gefaßt, ein Prophete zu seyn und stand, in der Schattenwelt ankommend, plözlich mit einer Menge ausgehobener Stubenthüren unterm Arm da, welche an den Angeln mit Sailen nach Art eines Buches zußammengeheftet waren und die er ohne Zweifel bei nächtlicher Weile in Gasthöfen u.s.w. gestohlen hat.[11]

These details and several more in this letter match those in the poem "Märchen vom sichern Mann" first published in 1838. It is not clear from the letter whether the details are in the form of drawings or prose descriptions, since whatever Mörike sketched entered Bauer's possession, as he reports in this letter. But even more important than a revised date of origin is the quasi disappearance of the "sichere Mann" from the version of the playlet in *Maler Nolten.* It suggests a shift in Mörike's attention from Homeric, legendary influence in 1825 to Shakespearean, immediate and psychological influence in the year 1828 to 1832.

Another minor inspiration was apparently Goethe's "Helena Akt," published in 1827; its full title was, "Helena. Klassisch-romantische Phantasmagorie. Zwischenspiel zu Faust." In the version in *Maler Nolten* "Der letzte König von Orplid" bears the subtitle "Ein phantasmagorisches Zwischenspiel." But except for the daring transcendence of a realistic time frame in "Orplid" no further parallels seem to exist between these two works. For juxtaposition of real with supernatural characters Mörike had many other models in the tales of E.T.A. Hoffmann and Tieck.

Another possible source of inspiration, not yet investigated in Mörike scholarship – one which we might assign to the humanistic tradition and which is probable, given the atmosphere of theology and philosophy at Tübingen – could be seen in ideas from Plato's *Symposium.* Mörike was never more philosophical than in his discursive as well as poetic statements on love. It is Ulmon's fate on Orplid to be poised between the love of a seductive fairy and faithful memory to his wife Almissa. He is forced by the ancient gods to wait wearily for death and immortality. Several times he openly expresses his longing for death. He finally achieves this immortality by fending off his impure, trivial, present love-out-of-wedlock for Thereile, with clear recollections of his good, noble, sanctified and past love for his wife Almissa. His obedience to the instructions in the book of fate to shoot an arrow into the magic willow in which Thereile had hidden traces of their combined blood is not as important as his ability to recollect. The ancient gods' real test is to make him able to face himself, his own identity in traces of his recollections. Along very similar lines Diotima reminds Socrates in the *Symposium* that "love is of the immortal."[12] The attainment of love by man is bound up with the urge to repeat generation just as attainment of immortality is bound up with repeated recollection. The immortal gods have perfect recall and are not engaged in recollections. But man's striving to recollect arises from the urge to be immortal. Mörike in "Orplid" engages Ulmon in this process of attaining immortality. A second similarity to a key idea in the *Symposium* emerges from Larkens's reference to the Greeks in his introduction of "Orplid." This reference should not be seen, I believe, as limited to Greek mythology and Homer in the *Odyssey*. Larkens ostensibly ascribes the fall of the people of Orplid to a refinement of taste, a form of pride, which would have left no room for the ancient gods if allowed to continue unchecked. Similarly to this charge, Aristophanes in the *Symposium* suggests that because of pride and rebelliousness, androgynous man was split in half, and that love ever since should be viewed as man's desire to become re-united with his other half.[13] Mörike's multi-faceted view of love in "Orplid," in poem after poem as well as in his prose work and *Maler Nolten* makes it almost inevitable that he was also acquainted with Plato's definitions of love.[14]

And how does "Orplid" fit into the scheme of *Maler Nolten?* For the most persuasive answer to this question I am indebted to S.S. Prawer.[15] Prawer sees Ulmon as the representative of the post-Goethean generation, an epigone, whose problem is that he cannot act and think spontaneously, whose creativity is hindered by reflection and reminiscenses. As his parallel in the novel, Nolten rejects experience. Wilhelm Meister welcomed experience but Nolten's artistic sensibility cannot cope with it. Prawer's historical perspective here is particularly potent because he does not attach pejorative connotations to Mörike's art, which could arise from the somewhat problematic concept of epigone or late-comer.

The most important influence on "Orplid," however, seems to have been Shakespeare's *A Midsummer Night's Dream*. Maync was by no means the first scholar to hint at this connection.[16] But as with so many other connections suggested by Mörike's reading, this has not been further pursued.

We have noted in a previous chapter that Mörike saw in Shakespeare a great love poet. We also noted Mörike's affinity for *A Midsummer Night's Dream* imagery, atmosphere and its supernatural elements which complemented so well Mörike's own tendency to create myths and mythical characters. All of these elements are also of major importance in "Orplid." But perhaps most important, Mörike saw in *A Midsummer Night's Dream* a structurally unified model.

Shakespeare managed in *A Midsummer Night's Dream* to compose a coherent play out of a four-part plot originationg on four levels of society. This four part structure consists of Theseus and Hippolyta and their wedding plans; the love entanglement of Lysander and Hermia on the one hand and Helena and Demetrius on the other; the fairies, headed by Oberon and Titania; and the clownery of the local tradesmen under the direction of Quince and Bottom putting on a play in honor of the marriage.

This labyrinthine but successful structure Mörike tries to imitate in "Orplid." Mörike also starts with a basic set of four groups which he needed to integrate meaningfully. Corresponding to the court of Theseus, which acts as a framing device, Mörike's frame is the townspeople, including Löwener, Suntrard, Harry the Englishman and Kollmer. Kollmer, similar to Theseus is the most level-headed and realisric character, who puts things into perspective as if he were a Greek chorus commenting on the action. There is no group in "Orplid" which corresponds to the Lysander-Hermia-Demetrius-Helena love chase. Only in an oblique way can Thereile's pursuit of Ulmon be seen as a parallel to that. There is, however, the encounter of Silpelit and the "sichere Mann" which qualifies as a second group and for which there is, in turn, no corresponding group in Shakespeare's play. It has its own peculiar character, taking place off stage. Ulmon, Thereile and Silpelit form the third and the most important group, exhibiting many correspondences with the Oberon-Titania-Puck group. Like Oberon and Titania, Ulmon and Thereile have a love dispute. But here the similarity between these two pairs seems to cease. The dispute between Titania and Oberon is over a boy attendant; hence the dispute is by no means unreconcilable. In fact it seems to give Shakespeare a forum for love's little bickerings and jealousies to be aired. Ulmon's and Thereile's dispute is over a deeper and more permanent problem. Seen from his point of view, he is inextricably enchanted by a beautiful witchlike creature, attracted and repelled all at the same time. There are at least three times when his relationship to her is expressed by means of oxymoron. Describing her he says of her smile: "Ein Lächeln, wie drei Tropfen süßes Gift." (III; 116) His ties to her he calls "seliges Erkranken" and Kollmer characterizes it as "verhaßte Liebe." (III, 104) From her point of view, she is infatuated with this tragic mortal but comes to realize that even if he gave in to her, human beings and supernatural beings cannot be united for long. But pathos for her situation cannot arise because the reason for her love to Ulmon is inknown, hence motivation is missing and she remains two-dimensional.

The fourth group, including the comic Wispel and Buchdrucker, corresponds to the clownish tradesmen group in *A Midsummer Night's Dream*. Wispel and Buchdrucker are genuinely funny characters, but they are tied awkardly to the central figure Ulmon by having in their clumsy hands, of all things, the book of fate, by means of which Ulmon ultimately extricates himself from Thereile's control. This completes the overall structural parallels of the two works, limited as to group constellation and relationship.

Confining myself for the moment to structural considerations, it must be conceded that Mörike's structural imitation failed. It failed in the sense that we never feel as spectators, that there is an underlying coherent theme or symbolic or allegorical level to which the four disparate groups and individuals are subordinated. The comic banter of Wispel and Buchdrucker clashes sharply with the dreary death-longing of Ulmon. The problem with Ulmon's role is that as a towering figure of a king, who is the lone survivor of his race, longing for re-unification with the purity of his wedded wife Almissa through death, praying for death every minute of his existence in the playlet, he does not fit in with any other group or poetic unity. Or putting it another way, the fairies, the comic figures, the townspeople are forced onto the same stage with this figure, who surely represents an all too autonomous "germ" of the original set of mythic beings with which Mörike had peopled Orplid in 1825.

Perhaps because he was aware of the problematic structure, Mörike added through Larkens a disclaimer by calling "Orplid" "eine undramatische Kleinigkeit." (III; 96) And, indeed, Mörike's "Orplid" resembles much more a courtly masque or a sub-species of such a masque like Milton's *Comus* and Goethe's Mummenschanz-scene in *Faust II*. To represent characters primarily in their essence, permeating the atmosphere with allegorical figures becomes central. But masques must also succeed with their poetry and create a unified emotion. The luscious beauty of the lines from "Gesang zu zweien in der Nacht," for example, seems wasted and misplaced in "Orplid." It, too, is an entirely autonomous unit from Mörike's earlier creative period. While Shakespeare's *A Midsummer Night's Dream* seems to have served as a structural model, Mörike did not succeed in unifying his diverse imaginative creations of 1825 into the interlude in the novel of 1832.

On the other hand, Shakespeare's influence on *individual traits of characters and motifs* in "Orplid" has been assimilated more successfully by Mörike. Characters themselves are multifaceted but consistent within themselves. The parallel between the fairy child Silpelit as an amalgamation of Puck and Titania's dark boy attendant is particularly fascinating. Silpelit is of superior rank among the fairies because she shares Ulmon's fate of being enchanted by Thereile. She is much more independent than the other fairies such as Malwy and Talpe. She wanders off independently and plays with the giant "sichere Mann." In this independence "she" resembles Puck. In fact, from her inception or conception "she" was a he: Mörike had promised his sister Klara while on vacation in 1825 to bring Silpelit along. This is how he reports her reactions to Hartlaub: "In jenes kleine Gemach trat ich zuweilen mit der Einbildung, es sei eigentlich ein Feenstübchen. Letzthin kommt Klein-Klara zu mir herüber mit der Magd, die mein Tübinger Felleisen trägt, ich soll es aufmachen. 'Ist er drin?' Wer denn? 'Der Silpelit,' sagte sie leise."[17] In the much later poem "Märchen vom sichern Mann," where Silpelit becomes Lolegrin, "she" is a male figure. Silpelit is also half-human in "Orplid," being the daughter of Kollmer and a fairy.

But Silpelit also resembles the mysterious Indian boy attendant in *A Midsummer Night's Dream*: In fact, in an echo to how Titania obtained the boy, Ulmon comments on Thereile's possession of Silpelit: "Vielleicht die Fürstin hat / Es grausam aus der Wiege einst entführt." (III, 118) Another parallel between Silpelit and Titania's Indian boy is Thereile's fierce request for the whereabouts of Silpelit. This request is totally unmotivated in "Orplid." If we now remember, however, the equal ferocity of Titania's battle with Oberon for continued possession of her Indian boy, Thereile's request emerges as more meaningful.

In *A Midsummer Night's Dream* Titania tells the following little story about her Indian boy and his mother — one of the most remarkable excursions of Shakespeare's imagination, all the more so because the child's background is of no importance to the play as a whole:

> The fairy land buys not the child of me.
> His mother was a vot'ress of my order:
> And, in the spiced Indian air, by night,
> Full often hath she gossiped by my side;
> And sat with me on Neptune's yellow sands,
> Marking th' embarked traders on the flood;
> When we have laughed to see the sails conceive
> And grow big-bellied with the wanton wind;
> Which she, with pretty and with swimming gait
> Following (her womb then rich with my young squire),
> Would imitate, and sail upon the land,
> To fetch me trifles, and return again,
> As from a voyage, rich with merchandise.
> But she, being mortal, of that boy did die;
> And for her sake do I rear up her boy;
> And for her sake I will not part with him.[18]

This poetic flight apparently affected Mörike deeply. It is characteristic of him to assimilate Shakespeare at his most fanciful. Mörike was all the more struck with the wind and water images in the poem, because he associated Shakespeare with the elemental forces of wind, water and fire in many of his poems in which an affinity for Shakespeare reverberates under the surface. In a kind of spin-off from the

Indian boy and his mother as well as from Silpelit in "Orplid," Mörike seems to have created the following double portrait in his poem "Jung Volkers Lied," spoken by Jung Volker himself:

> Und die mich trug in Mutterleib,
> Und die mich schwang im Kissen,
> Die war ein schön frech braunes Weib,
> Wollte nichts vom Mannsvolk wissen.
>
> Sie scherzte nur und lachte laut
> Und ließ die Freier stehen:
> "Möcht' lieber sein des Windes Braut,
> Denn in die Ehe gehen!"
>
> Da kam der Wind, da nahm der Wind
> Als Buhle sie gefangen:
> Von dem hat sie ein lustig Kind
> In ihren Schoß empfangen.   (I, p. 700)

It seems to me that the parallels of Titania's story and Jung Volker's account emerge beautifully as an example of poetic cross-fertilization: "Schön frech braunes Weib" corresponds to the dark exotic "Indian vot'ress." Their merry laughing at mortal lovers (for Titania's woman these are represented by the departing traders, and for Volker's mother represented by the dumbfounded "Freier") indicate a marvelous feminine self-sufficiency and a spurning of mortal conception for the spiritual conception of the wind. In both accounts the supernatural or spiritual impregnation by the wind (in Greek the word for wind meant spirit) produces an extraordinary fairy child. In Shakespeare's passage the added meaning of "mortal" comes about *because* the mother was mortal, she did not survive the union with the wind. Titania's woman imitates the wind's effects with comic gestures. The suggestion is that she was impregnated physically by the departing "trader" but spiritually by the wind. In contrast, in Mörike's poem, the physical union is excluded from the description. But, of course, the extra-marital or extra-human union adds to the exotic quality of Jung Volker-Silpelit.

As Storz has pointed out in his discussion of "Orplidische Nachklänge:" "Das uralte Motiv der Gesellung von Naturgeistern und

Menschen hat unseren Dichter unablässig, von den frühen Jahren bis zur Reifezeit, beschäftigt: Das dokumentiert sich sichtbar in der Reihe von Silpelit, Justine, Lau."[19] To this series of mythic beings from Mörike's work we should add, in my view, the male figure Jung Volker.

Mörike did not include this poem in "Orplid." But Mörike's poems include several others which, though independent of the playlet itself, nevertheless grew out of it. Still another is "Gesang Weylas." Other poems partaking of Orplid and included in one form or another in the playlet are: "Gesang zu zweien in der Nacht," "Märchen vom sichern Mann," "Elfenlied," and "Die Geister am Mummelsee."

Storz explores the later versions of these poems with their variations in "Orplid," but he does not link shifts in perspective by Mörike with Mörike's reading and stimulation by friends and by Mörike's realtionship to society in general. Although limiting himself to purely literary considerations Storz argues persuasively that Mörike tries to free himself from his "subjective" world of the year 1825 by turning to more objective media of expression; but the facts that he rewrote "Orplid" in the fall of 1830 for inclusion in *Maler Nolten* and probably composed "Die Geister am Mummelsee" and "Elfenlied" in 1828 for inclusion in his private collection "Das grüne Heft" mean that the lure of Orplid remained strong.[20] If the implication of Storz's argument is that the importance of Orplid on Mörike's later work in general has been underestimated, it follows that Shakespearean influence has been underestimated as well.

Continuing our discussion of individual traits and motifs of *A Midsummer Night's Dream* and "Orplid," two major elements in them are the broad comedy and farce by Bottom and his group in Shakespeare and Wispel and Buchdrucker in Mörike; secondly, there is the motif of the magic arrow, a kind of *deus ex machina* device in both works.

Much of the comedy by Bottom and his friends arises from play with language, rhetoric, puns and semantic confusion. Bottom prides himself on his fine voice; wanting to play Thisby in the tradesmen's portrayal of the love story of "Pyramus and Thisby," he mispronounces it "Thisne" (an echo of this name surely resides in Mörike's invention of the name "Wispel"): "Ninus tomb" is mispronounced "Ninny's tomb" by another player. When Bottom means ballad it comes out, "ballet;" and when he means disposition he says, "exposition." Meaning to be polite and formal the transformed Bottom, unaware of having the head of an ass, addresses the little insignificant creatures Cobweb and Mustardseed as "monsieur" and "signior." This also exhausts his knowledge of French and Italian.

Similarly, Wispel in scene eight (the only comic scene in "Orplid") prides himself in his speaking voice: "eine weiche Aussprache eine Diktion, die mich besonders bei den Damen sehr empfehlen muß." (III, 125) Like Bottom he pretends to be learned only to confuse konversieren with "konservieren" and Phenomenon with "Phantom." Like Bottom he tackles French which is limited to oaths such as "Ciel" and "Grand Dieu." His Italian is confined to what he imagines to be Italian intonation: "süßem italienischem Charakter:" His companion Buchdrucker is even more clumsy than Wispel and a good measure coarser. Mörike had apparently Bottom's crudities in mind, such as, "every man look o'er his part," when he has Buchdrucker utter such epithets as "du hundsföttischer neidischer Blitz." Wispel finally even alludes to a hole in the wall through which he is planning to overhear Buchdrucker's dealings next door: "Soll ich durch den Spalt wispern und sagen er soll in einer halben Stunde wiederkommen?" (III, 130) Here Mörike's borrowing from Shakespeare's low-comedy use of the hole in the wall through which the lovers Pyramus and Thisby communicate originates, in turn, with Shakespeare's use of Ovid. In perhaps the last use Mörike makes of Shakespeare's dreaming, sleeping characters in the Wispel-Buchdrucker episode, he adds in the stage directions: "Endlich schläft Wispel ein." (III, 132) Only if we remember Mörike's indebtedness to *A Midsummer Night's Dream* does such a stage direction become meaningful.

The view held widely in Mörike scholarship that Mörike's comic figures are totally of Mörike's invention is quite untenable. Storz, for example, maintains: "Die Clownerien selbst und die Spaßmacher sind indessen ganz und gar von eigener Erfindung und Prägung: Mörike hat die Figuren des Wispel und seines Widerparts, des Buchdruckers, in mimischen Improvisationen vor den Stiftsfreunden ent-

worfen und sie in jahrelanger, gelegentlicher Wiederholung des ko-
mödiantischen Spaßes immer bestimmter konturiert und verfe-
stigt."[21] I would suggest a modification of the assumed values of
Eigenständigkeit and *Eigentümlichkeit*, which are again and again
upheld in Mörike scholarship. Precisely *because* of the influences
assimilated in the figures of Wispel and Buchdrucker, Mörike's comic
figures are rescued from the sometimes all too conciliatory and
idiosyncratic sphere of humor for which his most characteristic word
is *treuherzig*.

There is also a kind of *deus ex machina* motif from *A Midsummer
Night's Dream*, that finds its way in a transformed fashion into "Orplid." In need of a magic love potion Oberon instructs Puck to get
petals of the flower "love-in-idleness" or pansy. By having them
applied to Titania's eyelids Oberon achieves his revenge on her: she
falls in love with "the next live creature" that she sees upon awaken-
ing. The saying goes, Oberon explains to Puck, that one of Cupid's
arrows went astray, falling on the pansy and imbuing it with love-
inducing magic.

Ulmon, in turn, after consulting a mysterious "Buch des Schicksals," (possibly a parallel to Prospero doing so in *The Tempest*)
follows divine instructions by shooting a golden arrow into a willow,
which contained traces of Thereile's and Ulmon's blood (another
possible parallel to Ariel being imprisoned in a tree in *The Tempest*).
This releases Ulmon from the love bound. As Puck is the go-between
in Shakespeare's play, so is Silpelit Ulmons secret accomplice. In
addition to straightforward love-potion magic applied directly to
the eyelids of Puck, in "Orplid" the love release also works from a
distance. Here is Mörike's belief in "Sympathie," a physical effect
achieved at a distance in bodies which share a common core. Describing the process which also affects Silpelit Ulmon states:

> Bald aber rinnet von dem goldnen Pfeil
> Der Liebe Purpur aus des Baumes Adern,
> Und alsbald aus der Ferne spürt dein Herz
> Die Qual der schrecklichen Veränderung,
> Doch nach vertobtem Wahnsinn wird im Schlummer
> Sich Ruhe senken auf dein Augenlid.   (III, 140)

Indeed, in the reference to eyelids Mörike evokes the love magic of *A Midsummer Night's Dream* once more.

As always, Mörike was keenly attuned to Shakespeare's poetry, especially his conceits and images. One of those images in *A Midsummer Night's Dream* is Titania's comparison of herself and Bottom while she is under the spell of love:

> So doth the woodbine the sweet honeysuckle
> Gently entwist; the female ivy so
> Enrings the barky fingers of the elm.
>
> (IV, i, 41–43)

Mörike could not resist this image. In a disclaimer after the performance of the playlet of any major parallels between the recently deceased king and Ulmon, the narrator in *Maler Nolten* explains that the late-lamented king, like Ulmon, also had not had enough strength and will power left to fend off "einen jugendlichen Epheu, der sich liebevoll an ihm hinanschlinge." (III, 153)

Schlegel's translation of Titania's adoration of Zettel, der Weber, was by no means a lessening intermediary, but instead a poetically translucent medium:

> So lind umflicht mit süßen Blütenranken
> Das Geißblatt; so umringelt, weiblich zart,
> Das Epheu seines Ulmbaums rauhe Finger:[22]

In concluding our exploration of the influence of *A Midsummer Night's Dream* on "Orplid" we also become aware of a broad thematic parallel. That is to say, one of Shakespeare's achievements in his play is a delightful kaleidoscopic multiplicity of attributes of love emerging from the many love entanglement: love is foolish, love is unpredictable, love is jealous, love is forgiving, love is idle, love is blind, etc. On the other hand, Mörike's definition of love is more limited at this point; it is overshadowed by a mysterious and morbid darkness. But in a sense, if we continue the series of Shakespeare's attributes of love, we would surely reach a paradox. And Mörike abbreviates his series of definitions of love by injecting a somewhat premature paradox in "Orplid" into the nevertheless universal truth that love is a form of painful pleasure. Secondly, Mörike's adoption of the structure of *A Midsummer Night's Dream* fails, because his diverse groups seem to cling too tenaciously to earlier independent and non-dramatic existences, leaving them in an incompatible stasis in the playlet. Finally, in his use of individual traits and motifs Mörike reveals an extraordinary and enriching power of transformation, especially in Silpelit, Jung Volker and Wispel.

Before exploring further Shakespeare's influence in *Maler Nolten*, especially Agnes' insanity, we must consider Shakespeare's broader influence on Mörike and a shift from allusions to gentle, harmonious dreamy atmosphere to those of darkness, tragedy, insanity and death. In the earliest conceptions of Orplid and in Mörike's early reading of Shakespeare through 1825, as we see in the letters and poems, there are no thoughts of doom, death and destruction. Orplid, originally, was not overcast with the pallor of a tragic fall and an inextricable love-hate complex. Initially we suggested that the best introduction to "Orplid" is Larkens' comments in *Maler Nolten*; but this view, though generally held in Mörike scholarship, may need to be modified. Mörike's reading of Shakespeare in the years 1828–1832, as seen in letters and poems, reveals a significant shift of perspective and emphasis from the merry, dreamy atmosphere and love-play of *A Midsummer Night's Dream* and possibly *The Tempest* to an attention to tragic and death-related elements in Shakespeare. Instead of *A Midsummer Night's Dream, Twelfth Night, The Merchant of Venice*, and *The Tempest*, (all supreme statement on the ultimate power of harmony that resides in love) Mörike turns to *Macbeth, Hamlet, King Lear*, the dark death-reflections of *Measure for Measure* (especially Act III, Scene i), and *Romeo and Juliet*. The notable exception is Mörike's conciliatory letter to Mährlen, dated May 21, 1830, in which he alludes to *Henry IV* and acknowledges his deep affection for Mährlen by quoting Schlegel's translation in a somewhat altered form:

Es geht mir mit Dir wie dem Falstaff . . . der seine unverwüstliche Liebe zu einem alten unwürdigen Compagnon mit den Worten entschuldigt: Stündlich hab ich des Menschen seine Gemeinschaft verschworen! Aber es geht nicht. Der Mensch muß mir einen Trank beigebracht haben, oder ich will ein Bündel Radieser sein.[23]

But the exception (that is to say, quoting the supremely comical character of Falstaff while something tragic and darkly threatening made its way into Mörike's view of life) proves the rule. Earlier, in the context of his attempted escape from the *Vikariatsknechtschaft*, Mörike concedes his inability to strike out with decisive action by quoting from Hamlet's to-be-or-not-to-be soliloquy in a letter to Mährlen, dated April 15, 1828:

> Unternehmungen voll Kraft und Mark
> Wird des Gedankens Blässe angekränkelt.[24]

This is Mörike's own, somewhat difficult variation and condensation. The Schlegel translation reads:

> Der angebornen Farbe der Entschließung
> Wird des Gedankens Blässe angekränkelt,
> Und Unternehmungen voll Mark und Nachdruck
> Durch diese Rücksicht aus der Bahn gelenkt,
> Verlieren so der Handlung Namen . . . (III, 50)

We recall that an inability to act by Nolten (as opposed to Wilhelm Meister's ability to do so) is seen by S.S. Prawer as the source of ultimate catastrophe in *Maler Nolten*.[25] In this light Nolten can hardly be seen exclusively as a projection of the post-Goethean Mörike.

In the letter to Kauffmann October 30, 1828, Mörike describes Tübingen as if it were a windswept desolate heath in the fens of Macbeth's Scotland.[26] He broods over Tübingen's sunny past, now devoid of people. We might hasten to add, however, Mörike delights here also in his own power of evocation, so that the melancholy arising from the loses of human fellowship is mitigated and artistically sublimated by being cast into a remarkable epistle on autumnal nature.

Despite his exhilarating and sunny love for Luise Rau, commencing in May, 1829, Mörike writes to her about tragic aspects of

Hamlet and *Romeo and Juliet*. In a letter to her dated May 19/20, 1830, he includes his own sketch of the insane Ophelia and describes it in an accompanying passage as if to test his skills before including similar scenes of the insane Agnes in *Maler Nolten*:

> Hier, mein Schätzchen, erhälst Du eine Tuschzeichnung von meiner Hand, an der freilich noch dies und jenes zu tun übrig bliebe. Indessen mags so hingehen. Es stellt die Szene aus "Hamlet" vor, wo die unglückliche Ophelia im Wahnsinn, phantastisch aufgeputzt mit Blumen, Stroh usw., ins Zimmer tritt und dergleichen Gaben verteilt. Ihr Bruder Laertes und die Königin sind zugegen. Komposition und Ausdruck ist ziemlich geraten.[27]

Perhaps fearing he would miss a crucial aspect of her surroundings, for possible use in *Maler Nolten,* Mörike captures Ophelia and the dramatic context in a drawing. His slight alteration of the blocking of characters from the original (there is no scene with this precise Ophelia, Queen and Laertes combination) does not seem to be purposeful and is probably accidental.

Mörike makes one of the most cogent critical observations (which is also part of the shift toward the tragic vision) in comparing what he gleaned from the views of death in *Hamlet* and from *Measure for Measure* in a letter to Vischer, dated May 23, 1832:

> Ich las kürzlich — zum erstenmal! — "Maß für Maß!" Tieck nennt es ein "tiefsinniges Stück" und erklärt's für eins der spätesten des Shakespeare. Eine der merkwürdigsten Stellen ist: wo Isabella ihrem Bruder, der durch ein Vergehen in der Liebe (oder weil er, wie es an einem anderen Ort heißt, den Trichter in eine Flasche gesteckt) nach den Gesetzen das Leben verwirkte, im Gefängnis die Möglichkeit seiner Lossprechung entdeckt, auf den Fall, daß sie, seine Schwester, dem Regenten ihre Unschuld opfern wollte.[28]

Then Mörike quotes extensively from the dialogue between Isabella and her brother Claudio in Act III, Scene i. Deeply struck by the situation of Claudio begging his sister to yield to the lust of Angelo in order to spare her brother's life, Mörike refers specifically to the following contemplation of death by Claudio. Isabella, equally distraught had cried: "Und Leben ohne Ehre ist hassenswert." To this Claudio replies:

> Ja. Aber sterben? − Gehn, wer weiß, wohin, da liegen, kalt, ein eingesperrt, und faulen; dies lebenswarme, fühlende Bewegen verschrumpft zum Kloß! und der entzückte Geist getaucht in Feuerfluten, oder schaudernd umstarrt von Wüsten ew'ger Eisesmassen; gekerkert sein in unsichtbare Stürme und mit rastloser Wut gejagt rings um die schwebende Erde: oder Schlimmres werden als nur das Schlimmste, was Phantasie uns schwärmend, zügellos heulend erfindet: das ist zu entsetzlich; − das müdste, jammervollste irdische Leben, das Alter, Meineid, Scherz, Gefangenschaft dem Menschen auflegt, − ist ein Paradies gegen das, was wir vom Tode fürchten![29]
> [Schlegel: *schwerste* instead *müdste*]

Mörike continues his citations and concludes his commentary by adding: "Ich gestehe Dir gerne, daß das was Claudio *zumal in dieser Verbindung* vom Tode sagt, mir merkwürdiger dünkt, als das viel gepriesene: 'Sein oder nicht Sein.'"[30] This is indeed a valid insight by Mörike. It surely is of special significance to our understanding of Mörike's art at the time and our knowledge of the intensity of his reading, that this quote is perhaps the lengthiest from his readings in all of his letters to learned critics, fellow writers and friends.

These comments and preoccupations are all the more significant in regard to Mörike's writings of *Maler Nolten* at the time. Mörike, in fact, discusses his novel in this very letter to Vischer and tells him about his intentions for his conclusion: "Indessen ist − teils eine Unvorsichtigkeit des Maler, teils die unerwartete Erscheinung der Elisabeth Veranlassung, daß Agnes in ihrem Wahnsinn rückfällig wird: Sie geht in diesem Zustande unter . . . Noltens Tod ist Folge teils eines gewissen wunderbaren oder wunderähnlichen Umstands, den ich jetzt nicht nennen will."[31] In the process of bringing his novel to a tragic conclusion Mörike read Shakespeare with a keen eye for how the horror and imminence of death can be brought about for Agnes and Nolten, who are under the spell of doom. Thus Mörike's reading of Shakespeare during the years 1828−1832 served directly to clarify and enrich his art in *Maler Nolten*.

Before exploring the Ophelia-Agnes parallels in *Maler Nolten*, another remarkable instance of Mörike's reading needs to be accounted for. In June 1831 Mörike made an interesting discovery. He found a fragmentary and tattered copy of the first edition of Hans Sachs' voluminous *Das ander Buch* of 1560 (see Chapter V, Item No. 41 in *Part A*: Annotated Bibliography of Mörike's Extant Library). In this volume Mörike found a narrative poem by Hans Sachs, dated 1558, which is in essence the story of Hamlet. Although it has long been recognized that the historical source of Shakespeare's *Hamlet* is Saxo Grammaticus' *Historia Danica* (1180—1208), and that there are many intermediate, historical versions such as Belleforest's *Histoires Tragiques* (c. 1570) as well as Eppendopff's German translation (1659) of Albert Krantz' *Chronica* (1558), this Hans Sachs version has been ignored and neglected to this very day![32] The poem surely is a significant literary as well as historical document in German literature. From Mörike's point of view, seeing Shakespeare as the great master of psychological portrayal, the scene in the Sachs poem in which Amplet chastises his mother (Fürstin) and kills the spying listener (Heuchler) in a fit of pretended madness, must have been particularly memorable. The following excerpt represents lines 69 to 86 of the 112 line chronicle poem; it roughly corresponds to Act III, Scene iv of Shakespeare's *Hamlet*:

Nach dem die Fürstin hinein kam
Auch jr sun Ampletus mit Nam
Der strafft sie hart das sie dem Mann
Wer gehorsam vnd vnterthan
Der sein Vatter ermördtet hett
Die Mutter aber straffen thet
Den son von wegen seiner thorheit
Der son breit auß sein arm weit
Als ob er fliegen wolt daruon
Springt auff das Bet kret wie ein Hon
Als er nun auff den Heuchler tratt
Sein untrew er gemercket hat
Vnd jn mit seinem schwerdt erstach
Zerhawt jn zu stücken hernach
Vnd sud die stück zu abentewer
In einem Hafen bey dem Feuer
Darnach schüt er es für die Sew
Die fraßen jn on alle schew[33]

From the tough and sincere voice of the narrator Amplet's pretended madness emerges powerfully as the dominant trait in the characterization. This description is not without subtleties. Ostensibly, Amplet's reason for jumping on the bed and crowing like a rooster is to demonstrate his continued madness. But since his mother is all along aware of his "thorheit," the narrator seems to suggest that Amplet enjoys his pretended madness. Amplet's subsequent macabre multilation of the Heuchler further complicates matters, since it raises some doubts in regard to the "pretended" madness.

The psychopathology of all of this could not have escaped Mörike. In this light Mörike's view of Hamlet and his Germanic *Doppelgänger* Amplet belongs to the tradition of psychological interpretations, commencing early in the nineteenth century with Coleridge's and having its perhaps best known exponent in Ernest Jones' Freudian interpretation in 1910.[34]

Mörike subsequently sent his Sachs volume with the dedicatory poem (see Chapter V, Item No. 41) to the psychiatrist Albert Zeller. Albert Zeller at the time in 1831 was about to be appointed director of the clinic for the mentally ill in Winnental, where Lenau spent most of his waning years. Although there are unfortunately no letters extant from the exchange of ideas between Zeller and Mörike, our poet had in fact consulted Zeller in Stuttgart about the psychopathological aspects of his characters in *Maler Nolten*. Referring to his novel Mörike reports to his brother in a letter dated Dec. 6, 1831: "Daß die Braut später aufs neue wahnsinnig wird und dabei umkommt, konnte nicht anders sein. Ich habe es hinlänglich vorbereitet. Ein gewisser Dr. Zeller, der sich viel mit Psychiatrie abgibt und demnächst als Arzt an ein solches Institut kommen wird, hat die Novelle gelesen und den psychologischen Gang, den ich von p. 66 sqq. mit Agnesen verfolge, zugleich richtig und schön gefunden."[35] Thus it is clear that Mörike sent Zeller the Sachs volume to express his gratitude for whatever advice he had received.

Again, because Mörike thought the psychiatrist would enjoy such a "case" as the Amplet-Hamlet, Mörike sent his newly discovered Hamlet to him. Here, then, is another indication of the perspective from which Mörike read Shakespeare, specifically *Hamlet*. In the dedicatory poem Mörike says: *Mit wundern las ich was dort steht /*

Von einem Dänen-Prinz Amlet. Mörike was acutely conscious of Shakespearean psychological realism and psychopathological characterization. And Hans Sachs' version can indeed corroborate such a reading of *Hamlet.*

Perhaps no other character in Mörike's work exhibits as many psychopathological elements in her behavior as Agnes in *Maler Nolten.* As Storz puts it, Agnes presents a "Krankheitsbild tiefenpsychologischer Art . . . Nichts fehlt an ihm als die moderne Terminologie von 'Trauma', 'Verdrängung' und 'Neurose'."[36] I disagree with Storz, however, when he maintains that the characterization of Agnes does not receive full attention by Mörike.[37] Although she is separated from Nolten during much of the central part of the plot, she completely dominates the final one-fourth of the second part of *Maler Nolten.* This is also true for the revised version of *Maler Nolten,* in which the first part was changed extensively, but the final part in which Agnes' psychological disintegration occurs remained untouched by Mörike. In other words, after its publication in 1832, during more than twenty years of critical echoes, and during the years 1855−1874 when Mörike tortuously revised his novel, he did not see fit to alter Agnes' characterization substantially. The basis for our discussion, as it was for "Orplid" also, is the original version.

Whatever peculiar psychological complexes Mörike had in mind for Agnes, complexes which are lumped together by the word "Wahnsinn" which is applied to her condition serveral times, we might initially define the process she goes through during the final stages of her existence as a regression-disintegration. Her character is indeed shown in a descending development. But most important for our purposes, the aspects of her change only become fully clear, and only fully emerge as a pattern, when compared with the similar process through which Ophelia goes in Shakespeare's *Hamlet.*

In their final decline Ophelia and Agnes share the overall similarity not so much of pictures of "deep tragedy" and falls from height combined with inevitability, but rather of "pathetic beauty," as A.C. Bradley observed in his discussion of the role of Ophelia in *Hamlet.*[38] But on a deeper level, is seems to me that this pathetic beauty can only be maintained in both characters, despite the movement toward death, by associating both Ophelia and Agnes increasingly with the natural beauties of the elemental forces of fire, wind and water. In other words, what Mörike learned from Shakespeare's portrayal of Ophelia is how the internal psychological disintegration of a mind can be illustrated and reinforced by the identification of the character with external, random and at times chaotic interplay of the natural elements. Perhaps the most famous Shakespearean objective correlative of which Mörike also knew is the storm scene in *King Lear*. In tracing psychological parallels of Ophelia and Agnes I will proceed chronologically in both *Hamlet* and *Maler Nolten*.

The beginning of the end for Ophelia is her first appearance after the death of her father in Act IV, Scene v. The stage directions describe her as "distracted." She is a picture of utter desolation. The trauma to her personality as seen by the king was the death of her father. But, of course, to this we must add her rejection of Hamlet and vice versa, the fact that the exiled Hamlet may be lost to her forever, and that her brother is absent in France. She has no mother to stand by her side.

There is a peculiar mixture of sanity and insanity in what she sings at her entrance in IV, v. The loss of a grasp of reality is mainly demonstrated by her confusion of lover with father: in the first stanza of her song she asks "How should I your true-love know / From another one?" and in the second stanza she sings: "He is dead and gone, lady." This confusion of lover and father suggests also a breakdown of self-awareness. The King expresses her indentity crisis with: "Divided from herself and her fair judgment." (IV, v, 1. 85) The fact that she sings when normal discourse is called for adds an involuntary and compulsive aspect to her loss of a grasp of reality. The complexity of "logical" extemporaneous speech, in a sense, gives way to the "illogical" simplicity of a folksong-like reply. Answering the Queen by singing a song not of her own making also shows a loss of reasoning power. Singing also suggests a more elemental or at least more "natural" bearing. Furthermore, her reference to flowers, "Larded all with sweet flowers" (VI, v, 38) adds another elemental or natural quality to her.

In her second song, beginning with "To-morrow is Saint Valentine's day," another important aspect of her psychological disintegration is overtly sexual references:

> Young men will do't if they come to't.
> By Cock, they are to blame.   (VI, v, l. 60—61)

This bit of harmless crudity seems to represent a hint by Shakespeare that a loss of sanity or a disintegration of the check of the discerning mind will release the darker, subconscious and libidinal urges of even the purest maiden. These lines could be quite realistic coming from the mouth of a different woman. They also represent a momentary lucidity on the ways of the world and in an ironic sense make Ophelia appear to be truly sane for the first time. By singing about the lust of young men, rather than about innocuous courting, she shows, ironically, a better grasp of reality than before going mad.

In fact, Ophelia exits with quite sane and lucid comments in prose, making her occasional lapses into insanity with oblique replies by means of songs even more disconcerting to her listeners.

In her next entrance, later in the same scene, the undercurrent of a return to nature and to the elements in the imagery and diction becomes more intense. In Laertes' pained reaction upon seeing his mad sister there are allusions to fire and heat. Even if this is more of a projection of his own feelings rather than a representation of the heat of raving insanity, elemental forces are still evoked:

> O heat, dry up my braing; tears seven times salt
> Burn out the sense and virtue of mine eye!
> (11. 154—155)

Leartes' sensing of heat is balanced by Ophelia's gentle references to water and flowers: "And in his grave rained many a tear" (l. 166) and "I would give you some violets but they withered all when my father died." (1. 183) Since she is all along associated with flowers, the implication of this line is that the heat of madness is withering the flower Ophelia. She then makes her final exit with another song. Significantly, the song concludes with a deeply religious note, suggestive of an apotheosis: "And of all Christian souls, I pray God. God by you." (1. 198)

In IV, vii the Queen reports Ophelia's drowning. The Queen compares her to a mermaid. Her return to the elements through death by water is complete:

> And mermaid-like awhile they bore her up,
> Which time she changed snatches of old lauds,
> As one incapable of her own distress
> Or like a creature native and indued
> Unto that element . . .   (11. 175—179)[39]

Continuing the association with natural elements, Shakespeare maintains the fire imagery with Laertes in contrast to Ophelia: "I have a speech o' fire." This comment of a forward-looking revenge foreshadows Laertes' own end as another return to the elements, but in a fit of rage.

Agnes' psychological disintegration and regression toward the elemental level seems to be based largely on the same process which Ophelia goes through in *Hamlet*. Although Agnes' trauma does not include the death of a father, she labors under the added threats of a history of emotional instability and of demonic possession by the gypsy Elisabeth. Elisabeth represents also the force of "tragic fate" in the course of the characters' lives, according to the very plausible interpretation of R. Immerwahr.[40] But the primary trauma to Agnes' psychological balance is Nolten's confession to her of having been unfaithful during his long absence. Furthermore, Larkens, in Nolten's place, had carried on the correspondence with her.

Agnes at this point is as forlorn as Ophelia. She is without family, away from home; there is no one to hold on to any more. She reacts to Nolten's confession with an immediate psychological withdrawal. Like Ophelia she seems to express herself reflexively and compulsively through songs. But much less apparent is the parallel to Ophelia of the influence of natural elements in the dramatization of her decline. Just before Nolten pours out his confession, a thunderstorm surrounds the pair. In a symphonic foreshadowing of a return to the elements the fire and storm imagery of "des feurig aufgeregten Ele-

111

ments" is replaced after a while by the water image of "Der Himmel hatte sich erschöpft, der Regen hörte auf." (III, 336)

The next time the people at the castle meet Agnes, she has been lured outside by the demonic Elisabeth. Elisabeth's eerie singing represents the second major trauma on Agnes' psyche. Taking advantage of his broader medium of prose rather than dramatic dialogue, Mörike, who was deeply conscious of the demonic power of music (especially in his favorite opera "Don Giovanni") describes in detail how music can exert its demonic and elemental power over the human will, by having Elisabeth lure Agnes outside in her nightgown. This demonic power of the singing voice and of music, which Mörike associates with wind in much of his poetry, has no parallel in *Hamlet*.

In another similarity to Ophelia Agnes has moments of lucidity. Once she even exhibits "eine erfreuliche Heiterkeit," which portends a false recovery. Agnes also goes through a loss of identity, revealed in her first incoherent talk with Nolten after the confession. In this talk she confuses the dead Larkens with Nolten, as Ophelia had confused lover and father. For emphasis the narrator summarizes: "So schien die sonderbarste Personenverwechslung zwischen Nolten und Larkens in ihr vorgegangen zu sein; vielmehr es waren diese beiden in ihrer Idee auf gewisse Weise zu einer Person geworden." (III, 382) Here we also encounter Shakespeare's egg metaphor in *A Midsummer Night's Dream* again. In her confusion Agnes says to Nolten: "Ein Ei gleicht dem andern nicht so, aber eines von beiden ist hohl." (III, 382) However, unlike in the poem "Die Schwestern," the use of the metaphor is non-idyllic now, and even sarcastic. In her hallucinations about the two men she is darkly aware that one of them is a false lover, indeed, that the false lover has aligned himself with the devil. In this connection she greets Nolten: "Guten Morgen Heideläufer! Guten Morgen Höllenbrand." (III, 382)

In these greetings we can also see a loss of innocence experienced by Agnes. Like Ophelia she suddenly uses rude expressions. In addition to that Agnes also speaks in a sarcastic tone: "Nun, stell Er sich nicht so einfältig! Schon gut, schon gut! ich bin unbeschreiblich gerührt. Er bekommt ein Trinkgeld fürs Hokuspokus. – Bleib Er nur – bitte gehorsamst, ich seh's recht gut, nur immer zwölf Schritt vom Leibe. Was macht denn seine Liebe braune Otter? – haha, nicht wahr? Mein kleiner Finger sagt mir zuweilen auch etwas." (III, 382) In two further instances this loss of innocence in the sense of unrestrained behavior is shown. First, Agnes plots an escape from the castle — a daring change from her placid passive loveliness before the traumas. Secondly, in her talks with the other women present she exhibits a bit of vulgarity in asking indiscreetly about her presumed false lover: "Wie küßt's sich denn mit ihm?" (III, 388) Continuing her tirade she turns to one of the ladies and says: "Und, Fräulein, wenn du wieder mit ihm buhlst, mir kann es ja eins seyn, aber gewarnt hab' ich dich." (III, 387—388)

Mörike's retention of sexual allusions and crudeness in the unexpected outbursts by Agnes, as parallels to Ophelia, may well be based on his familiarity with a discussion of this problem in Goethe's *Wilhelm Meisters Lehrjahre*. In his explanation to Aurelia's objections to Ophelia's "Zweideutigkeiten und lüsterne Albernheiten" in the fourteenth and sixteenth chapters of Book IV, Wilhelm Meister defends these elements as important indications of Ophelia's subtle sensuality as an integral part of her character throughout the play. This sensuality, so Wilhelm reasons, is ultimately revealed by Ophelia's songs "in der Unschuld des Wahnsinns,"[41] It is highly likely that Mörike wanted to retain the outbursts of crudeness and rudeness in regard to the characterization of Agnes, as Wilhelm wanted them retained in his characterization of Ophelia. In other words, Mörike seems to suggest that Agnes is more than the embodiment of virginal purity and innocence as seen by Nolten. In this light a view of Agnes as the idealization of the idea of "Reinheit" as defined by H.P. O'Swald needs to be somewhat modified.[42]

When Agnes talks to the other ladies present, she asks one of them what the Latin word for spark is. After she receives the answer she says: "Scintilla . . . so, so, das ist ein musterhaftes Wort, es gibt ordentlich Funken." (III, 387) Again, on the one hand the reference to sparks is Agnes' unwitting sexual allusion to Nolten as the devilish (hell-fire) lover. But in addition to that, Mörike's purpose here is also to associate Agnes with the elemental forces of fire and water and especially wind. In this association with the elements Mörike's debt to Shakespeare's portrayal of Ophelia is most pronounced.

As a kind of subconscious incantation, perhaps part of her final urge to keep the wind from brushing her away, she says: "Der Wind weht dort! Ich muß das Windlied singen; es ist ratsam heute." She then sings:

Sausewind! Brausewind
Dort und hier,
Deine Heimath sage mir!
. . .

Lieb' ist wie Wind
Rasch und lebendig,
Ruhet nie
Ewig ist sie
Aber nicht immer beständig. (III, 396—397)

Not long before reciting this extremely simple song she was reading complex poems supposedly written by Lakens. The present simplicity, plus several more stanzas like it, seems to symbolize the greater rapidity of her mental disintegration. Despite the simplicity of the song, the problem of love, like the wind, being both restless and eternal further undercores Agnes' pathetic situation. Agnes seems to be darkly aware that she is becoming more and more subject to the wind and to the supernatural force residing in it. As Job heard the voice of God in the wind, for Agnes the wind contained a similar force of the voice of fate and the spirit of nature.

In the second encounter with Nolten, after his absence for therapeutic reasons in view of Agnes' condition, he is received by Agnes with wild and lewd embraces. Associating her state of mind with the white heat of madness, the narrator sketches images of fire: "Der Maler liegt, eh er sich's versieht, an ihrem Hals und saugt von ihren Lippen eine Glut . . . der Wahnsinn funkelt frohlockend aus ihren Augen." (III, 398)

In one final lucid moment Agnes sees herself more clearly than ever in the thralldom of the elements: "Siehst du . . . ich bin nur eben wie das Schiff, das leck an einer Sandbank hängt und dem nicht mehr zu helfen ist . . . Was kann aber das arme Schiff dafür, wenn mittlerweile noch die roten Wimpel oben ihr Schelmenspiel im Wind forttreiben . . .?" (III, 399) Mörike here apparently felt just as keenly as Shakespeare did that the decline of a character can be heightened to the most beautiful level only when the character also has some lucid awareness of her condition. This seems to be the case here. To Henni Agnes says, as if she had Ophelia's flowers in mind: "O Henni — welk, welk, welk, es geht zum Welken!" (III, 400)

Agnes' last words, like Ophelia's are uttered in a poem and again like Ophelia's her last words are a Christian evocation, culminating in a gentle apotheosis. She exclaims:

> Hüter! Hüter! ist die Nacht bald hin?
> Und was rettet mich vor Tod und Sünde? (III, 402)

During the following night she also finds death by water as Ophelia does. She drowns in a well. Perhaps the full cycle of her decline is reached with the storm that rages in the night following her death. Mörike clearly portrays Agnes' death as a return to the elements. There is also music in the storm as if it had admitted Agnes into its breath. The following lines, as Meyer points out, are an echo of the motto which Mörike had added to his poem "Die Elemente" (1824).[43] Nolten, as well as Henni, who more and more comes to resemble Agnes as a kind of double, overhears the storm: "Es deuchten ihm seufzende Geisterchöre der gebundenen Kreatur zu sein, die auch mit Ungeduld einer herrlichen Offenbarung entgegenharren." (III, 407)[44] Both Nolten and Henni are part of that life (Kreatur) which is awaiting release or revelation.

With this echo of a poem of 1824, Mörike, in a sense, comes full circle in his novel in 1832. That is to say, with the allusion to this early poem Mörike also evokes his early encounters with Shakespeare, with the poet of nature, of the wonderful, of atmosphere and of elemental forces as in "Venus and Adonis." There are no tragic or terrifying or nihilistic overtones in Agnes' disintegration; it seems to be a natural as well as a supernatural occurrence without implications of alienation in Mörike's point of view. There is even an awesome beauty about the decline and death of Agnes in the sense of Bradley's "pathetic beauty" as applied to Ophelia.

E. Staiger interprets Mörike's views of the transitoriness of love as part of the poet's awareness of being an epigone or late-comer to a more splendid and immediate tradition, exemplified in the words of Goethe, Schiller and Hölderlin.[45] Although Staiger reaches this conclusion in connection with his analysis of the poem "Das verlassene Mägdlein," he surely would apply this conclusion to Agnes, who is also an abandoned girl, conceptualized by the poet with a "resignierten Blick." Mörike, in this view, can portray love only as recollection. The portraits of young women who have lost their love are projections of Mörike's views of love in general. This interpretation is indeed persuasive. But, I believe, for the function of the elements in this context, we have to look beyond a biographical myth. Rather than seeing the elements as Staiger does: "Die Elemente sind aber die alte Macht, aus der sich Mörike im gewöhnlichen Leben des Tages verbannt weiß,"[46] it seems to me that those elements were part of a force even Mörike's shaping imagination was only darkly aware of. He tries to embody this force, however, in Agnes' reaction to the wind and in the reactions to the "Geisterchöre" which both Henni and Nolten hear in the night after Agnes' death. In addition to the deep kinship between man and the elements as revealed by Mörike in *Maler Nolten* there are also veiled suggestions, after the death of Agnes, that the pain of human life has been transcended by an eternal and mysterious union of Agnes with the spirit of wind and nature into some form of immortality. The fact that Nolten and Henni have heard the "Geisterchöre" which seemed to have admitted Agnes into their unified voice, suggests that Nolten, Agnes' lover, will also be unified with these voices and that he too will become part of the elements and the eternal. Nolten, after all, survives Agnes only a few weeks. And during that night following Agnes' death, he too is lured outside by music in the wind that only *he* could hear. And when Henni and his father find Nolten lying unconscious on the ground, it is only one additional indication of his ties to Agnes. It seems that the music and the wind further symbolize the "Sympathie" with Agnes, combined with the force of fate and spirit of nature which rush Nolten toward death to join Agnes. In this sense love and eternity are finally achieved through the medium of the elements in a kind of

116

mystical "Liebestod." With the description of the stormy night after Agnes' death Mörike adds a postscript to Agnes' portrayal which is quite in contrast to the death of Ophelia in *Hamlet*. That is to say both Ophelia and Agnes die in the same way; both become unified with the elements. But in addition to becoming part of nature after death, Agnes is surrounded with hints of immortality.

In connection with a gentle apotheosis and in view of her madness Mörike may well have had Gretchen in *Faust's* Kerker-scene in mind in his characterization of Agnes. But because of the step by step progression of mental disintegration and because of the close association with the elements, Agnes' portrayal owes more to Shakespeare's Ophelia than to Goethe's Gretchen.

Shakespeare's psychology is indeed rich enough to invite Mörike to augment his abstemious experience by adding to his knowledge of human psychology through his reading. I am agreement with R. Immerwahr when he points out that Mörike's portrayal of Agnes, Constanze and Elisabeth in *Maler Nolten* is the mythic and artistic projection of his personal experience.[47] But in addition to this, it must be remembered that Mörike led a withdrawn and modest life, relatively poor in enriching experience. He therefore was dependent to some extent on what he could glean from the intricate characterization and aspects of psychopathological behavior. Finally, Mörike also has an inborn affinity for Shakespeare's poetic rendering of love, nature and the elements. This affinity bears the richest fruit in Mörike's poetry before 1833.

Notes — Chapter III

1 Maync, *Biography*, pp. 78–110.
2 Renate von Heydebrand, *Eduard Mörikes Gedichtwerk* (Stuttgart: J.B. Metzler, 1972), pp. 73–81.
3 *Eduard Mörike* (Stuttgart: Ernst Klett, 1967), pp. 180–188 and 197–216.
4 "Mignon's Revenge: A Study of Mörike's *Maler Nolten*," *Publication of the English Goethe Society*, vol. XXV (1956), pp. 63–85.

5 Maync, *Biography*, p. 116.

6 Storz, p. 182.

7 *Eduard Mörike: Werke und Briefe, historisch-kritische Gesamtausgabe, Maler Nolten*, ed. Herbert Meyer (Stuttgart: Ernst Klett, 1967), vol. III, pp. 95–96. Hereafter cited in the text; all references to *Maler Nolten* are to this edition.

8 *Eduard Mörike: Die Kunst der Sünde Zur Geschichte des literarischen Individuums* (Tübingen: Max Niemeyer, 1978), p. 152.

9 Ludwig Amandus Bauer. *Briefe an Eduard Mörike*, ed. Bernhard Zeller und Hans-Ulrich Simon (Marbach: Ernst Klett, 1976), p. 36.

10 *Ibid.*, p. 57.

11 *Briefe, 1811–1828*, Vol. X, p. 102.

12 *The Works of Plato*, ed. Irwin Edman (New York: Random House, 1956), p. 375.

13 *Ibid.*, p. 357.

14 In recent years Mörike's complex views on love have received some attention in the lucid discussions by Benno von Wiese, *Eduard Mörike* (Tübingen und Stuttgart: R. Wunderlich, 1950, rpt. 1978), pp. 144–169; and by Raymond Immerwahr in "The Loves of Maler Nolten," *Rice University Studies*, vol. 57, No. 4 (1971), pp. 73–87.

15 "Mignon's Revenge," p. 72ff.

16 In the separate publication *Iris* (1839), which also includes Mörike's libretto "Die Regenbrüder" and the story "Lucie Gelmeroth," Mörike published "Der letzte König von Orplid" with some minor changes. Soon after its appearance a review in "Blätter für literarische Unterhaltung," mentions "Nachklänge" from *A Midsummer Night's Dream*. Mörike, always sensitive to charges of borrowings, adds excerpts from this review in the context of a sarcastic commentary in a letter to Hartlaub, dated May 29, 1840, without, however, denying the reviewer's suggestions; see Baumann, *Letters*, p. 485.

17 Renz, *Letters*, p. 27.

18 William Shakespeare. *The London Shakespeare, The Comedies*, vol. I, ed. John Munro (New York: Simon and Schuster, 1957), II, i, 1. 123–137. Referred to hereafter in the text.

19 Storz, p. 211.

20 *Ibid.*, p. 200ff.

21 *Ibid.*, p. 186.

22 *Shakespeares Werke*, transl. A.W. Schlegel and L. Tieck (Berlin: Paul Franke, no date), vol. III, p. 58. Hereafter cited in the text. Just as there are echoes of *Orpheus* and *Lied* in Orplid, there are also echoes of *Thispe* in Wispel; and here in the lines spoken by Titania, the crusty *Ulbaum* may very well have been the sound and figure which Mörike transmogrified into Ulmon!

23 Seebass, *Unpubl. Letters*, p. 51.

24 *Briefe, 1811−1828*, vol. X, p. 208.
25 "Mignon's Revenge," p. 74ff.
26 *Briefe, 1811−1828*, vol. X, p. 247f.
27 L. Rau, *Letters*, p. 92.
28 Vischer, *Letters*, p. 83.
29 *Ibid.*, p. 80−81.
30 *Ibid.*, p. 81.
31 *Ibid.*, p. 83.
32 The most recent and most complete bibliography on Hans Sachs is in the monograph: Barbara Könneker, *Hans Sachs*. Stuttgart, 1971. This study lists many works which deal with Sachs' sources and with subsequent literary connections such as Goethe and Sachs. The only work listed which is directly relevant is: Wolfgang Golther, "Hans Sachs und der Chronist Albert Krantz," in *Hans Sachs Forschungen: Festschrift*, ed. A.L. Stiefel (Nürnberg, 1894), pp. 263−277. Golther's article contains no discussion or awareness of the "Amplet" story. Golther merely lists the title "Fengo ein Fürst in Itlandt erwürget sein Bruder Horwendillum," on page 266 as part of the tabulation of chronicles which Sachs used in his Krantz source. Perhaps the most complete Hamlet source study is: J. Schick, *Corpus Hamleticum: Hamlet in Sage und Dichtung Kunst und Musik*, 2 vols. (Vol. I Berlin, 1912 & vol. II Leipzig, 1932). This study pursues the following topos back to its Byzantine origin: "Das Glückskind mit dem Todesbrief: Europäische Sagen des Mittelalters und ihr Verhältnis zum Orient." J. Schick's second volume contains a chapter on Hans Sachs pp. 198−199. Schick does not list Sachs' "Amplet" story, nor does he list Krantz or Saxo Grammaticus as one of Sachs' sources. Schick's Sachs chapter deals exclusively with Sachs' *Meistersang* "Des försters sun" and with the comedy version of this entitled "Comedi mit 12 Personen, der König Dagobertus auss Franckreich, mit des Försters Kind und hat 5 Actus." The *Meistersang* as well as the *Comedi*, Schick argues, originate in Sachs' use of *Gesta Romanorum*. This source contained apparently another Hamlet topos. But Schick makes no reference to Sachs' "Amplet." Sachs' story is included in the definitive edition of Sachs' works which was carried out by the "Bibliothek des Literarischen Vereins in Stuttgart:" *Hans Sachs*, ed. Adelbert Keller (Tübingen, 1874), Vol. VIII, 591−594. No reference is made in this edition to Sachs' sources or to a possible parallel between Sachs' story and Shakespeare's play. There is only a brief acknowledgement of the existence of this "Amplet" in Goeffrey Bullough's *Narrative and Dramatic Sources of Shakespeare*, Vol. III (New York: Columbia University Press, 1973), p. 9f. But unlike that other anonymous German Hamlet play, *Der Bestrafte Brudermord* (1781) which owes its origin to a Shakespeare version performed by traveling groups of actors in the seventeenth and eighteenth centuries on the continent, Hans Sachs' "Amplet" poem published in 1560, had its own, unique line of derivation, apparently independent from Shakespeare.

119

33 SNM 48675.

34 "The Oedipus Complex as an Explanation of Hamlet's Mystery," in *The American Journal of Psychology*, XXI (1910), pp. 1−37.

35 Baumann, *Letters*, pp. 284−285.

36 Storz, p. 164.

37 *loc. cit.*

38 *Shakespearean Tragedy* (1904; rpt. New York: Fawcett, 1967), p. 135.

39 Schlegel's translation of "mermaid-like" in the Queen's account of Ophelia's death is "sirenengleich." Sirenengleich adds a demonic dimension to mermaid. Here we have another example of the German romantics' grafting onto Shakespeare mythic imagination aspects of the demonic. Sirenengleich serves Mörike's purpose much better than the more faithful translation of "meerjungfergleich." Schlegel's term contains the added dimension of the demonic power of song and music which pervades *Maler Nolten*.

40 "The Loves of Maler Nolten," *Rice University Studies*, 57, No. 4 (1971), p. 74.

41 Johann Wolfgang Goethe, *Goethes Werke*, ed. Erich Trunz (Hamburg: Christian Wegner, 1969), VII, p. 246ff.

42 "Die Idee der Reinheit im Werk Eduard Mörikes," Diss. (Seattle: University of Washington, 1969), p. 123ff.

43 Cf. Herbert Meyer's chapters, "Entstehungsgeschichte der ersten Fassung," and "Entstehungsgeschichte der Umarbeitung," in *Maler Nolten: Lesarten und Erläuterungen*, V (Stuttgart: Ernst Klett, 1967), pp. 11−18 and 19−31.

44 The exact version of the motto for the poem "Die Elemente" is: "Denn das ängstliche Harren der Kreatur wartet auf die Offenbarung der Kinder Gottes." (St. Paul to the Romans, 8, 19). In English the King James version reads: "For the earnest expectation of the creature waiteth for the manifestation of the sons of God."

45 *Die Kunst der Interpretation* (Zürich: Atlantis, 1955), p. 151ff.

46 *Ibid.*, p. 182.

47 "The Loves of Maler Nolten," p. 73ff.

Chapter IV

Critical Distances: Mörike's Reading
of the Poems of Feodor Loewe

The most important sources for an assessment of Mörike's own literary-critical views as well as of his place in literary tradition and his relationship to contemporary writers are his letters. In this connection such additional sources from Mörike's *Nachlaß* as diary-like essays and journal entries in calendars were included in the research of Renate con Heydebrand's study, *Eduard Mörikes Gedichtwerk*[1] and Hans-Ulrich Simon's *Mörike Chronik.*[2] Additionally, there are a number of handwritten, unpublished notes, suggestions for corrections and improvements and editorial notes in regard to other poets' work – especially those of Karl Mayer and Wilhelm Waiblinger – that contain important clues about Mörike as reader and critic.[3]

To be sure, the kind of critical readings that Mörike's work on Mayer, Waiblinger, Loewe and other minor contemporary poets have in common, must be distinguished from the kind of assimilative reading with which Mörike approached the work of Shakespeare and Goethe. Although he actively read the great masters throughout his life, this productive, crossfertilizing reading occurred simultaneously with the writing of his own most important work and, except for intermittent sparks of creativity (1855–56: *Mozart auf der Reise nach Prag* and 1862–63: "Erinna an Sappho", "Bilder aus Bebenhausen"), had found its fruitful conclusion in the years 1838–43. His work with minor, contemporary poets commenced at this latter point in the early 1840s and consists of corrections and advice, limited strictly to one genre: lyric poetry. In the first case, as I have attempted to delineate in the previous chapters, his preoccupation with Shakespeare led to a deepening of ideas about love, death, psychopathological motivation of fictional characters as well as to key lyric images. In contrast to this, in the critical reading of lyric poems the "harvest" is much sparser and limited to bits and pieces

121

of critical language. Nevertheless, reflected in this critical language, as we shall see below, we find Mörike's own extreme care of masterful poetic craftsmanship. And although a comprehensive overview of his critical reading of minor poets has to await progress of the critical-historical edition of his works, a hint of what is involved can be gained now in an exploration of his work on Loewe.

Of the unpublished materials that can shed additional light on Mörike's literary-critical views, his notations regarding Feodor Loewe's poems, as a discrete, self-contained manuscript, are interesting and representative.[4] The "Bemerkungen" consist mostly of a listing of titles and first lines from the second edition of Loewe's *Gedichte*, published in 1860 by Cotta in Stuttgart. To his listing Mörike added intermittent comments, questioning phrases, changes and exclusions, as if he were acting in the role of editor or publisher. These critical notations may have served as an evaluation for a possible third edition that never materialized.[5] On the basis of Mörike's predominantly reserved and negative tone, Loewe, in turn, may have decided to have his *Neue Gedichte* (1875) published by Wittwer, who is also located in Stuttgart, instead of by Cotta, who had published the first and second edition of the first volume. However, there are no letters or other written evidence to prove this one way or the other. Neither do the four extant letters by Mörike to Loewe from the years 1862 to 1874 and the sole unpublished letter by Loewe to Mörike contain any additional data as to who the recipient of the "Bemerkungen" may have been, nor exactly when they were written.[6] Furthermore, as we see in the marginalia by him in books in his possession as well as in the *Abschriften* SNM and GSA (see below, Chapter V, "Annotated Bibliography of Mörike's Extant Library"), Mörike was fond of putting together his personal lists of selected poems by various writers.

As to the four letters, the first of which was written to Loewe January 2, 1862. No doubt by that time Mörike was already in possession of the second edition under consideration here, because he thanks Loewe "für so Viel" by enclosing, in turn, a copy of his own poem "Besuch in der Kartause."[7] Mörike's reference to "Viel" may very well have included the second edition of the poems as well as free tickets to the Stuttgarter Hoftheater, where Loewe had been an actor since 1841 and, additionally, a director since 1846. In one of Mörike's very last letters, dated December 30, 1874, addressed to Loewe, there is the only mention of Loewe's literary activity, but this is limited to an expression of thanks for the pre-dated *Neue Gedichte* of 1875.[8]

Additional important indications of Mörike's relationship to Loewe, mostly based on mentioning of Loewe's name in letters Mörike sent to others during the years 1860 to 1874, are contained in Simon's *Mörike Chronik*.[9] But nothing in these indications reveals whether Loewe had ever received Mörike's "Bemerkungen" himself or whether they were solely intended for editorial consideration by third parties. Friedrich Seebaß does not follow up on his comment in connection with the letters of January 2, 1862 and November 1862 that "ein freundlicher Verkehr mit Mörike blieb nicht immer ungetrübt."[10] Seebaß's conjecture seems to be based exclusively on his reading between the lines of Mörike's letters. Indeed, one could come to the conclusion that Mörike tried to avoid personal contact with Loewe, because he repeatedly laments either his inability to visit Loewe or, conversely, Loewe's failure to visit him. Such avoidance of personal contact tends to lend a negative resonance to Mörike's "Bemerkungen." It was probably during the very active social life of the years 1862–67 in Stuttgart, during which time Mörike also tried to induce Loewe to assist him in the support of several young artists (i.e. C.R. Köstlin and Friedrich van den Berghe) who sought Mörike's help, that the "Bemerkungen" were written.

Mörike's work as literary advisor during the 1860s may have come about in part in consequence of having to repay a financial loan he had with Cotta since 1859.[11] On the other hand, much to his increasing chagrin, he was frequently consulted by young, budding poets – his reputation having reached a high point in the early 1860s.[12] There is a basic similarity in his assessments of manuscripts by young poets as we see, for example, in his comments to Grüneisen,[13] in regard to the poetry of Karl Siebel (November 17, 1860) and in his letter addressed "An einen unbekannten Dichter," dated August 26, 1860.[14] Four aspects predominate in his comments: First, the young poet should publish initially only "stückweise," a few separate poems in journals. Secondly, the poems should be left to cure "drei oder vier Jahre." Third, the great models should be consulted. In this connection Mörike also likes to quote Latin sententious maxims such as those by Plinius.[15] His keenest criticism Mörike reserves for attempts to gain artistic success by forcing one's creative powers to yield productivity. Mörike had condemned this as early as the 1840s while doing editional work on Waiblinger's poems and several more times after that. Thus, for example, in the letter to Grüneisen, who had asked him to evaluate the poems by Siebel, Mörike indicates his condemnation by citing a phrase from one of the poems; "'Wird auch die ganze Welt nicht sein / Ein Kranz ist ihm verheißen / Und müßt er auch den Lorbeer sich / Vom Himmel nieder reißen.'" About such violent poetic ambition Mörike comments: "So kann er [Siebel] denn noch lange auf seinem Weg fortgehn, bis ihn an seinem Kranz ein Blatt ums andre verwelkt, und er zuletzt verbittert und sich selbst verödet, nur den Verlust der schönen Zeit und edlen Kräfte zu beklagen haben wird."[16]

In the case of Loewe Mörike also detected driving ambition in connection with Loewe's career at the Stuttgarter Hoftheater. There can be little doubt that Mörike's critical judgment of Loewe's collection of poems was in part colored by his distaste for Loewe's ambition. Apparently in full agreement with the negative judgment about Loewe by the theater historian Devrient, Mörike quotes from that review in a letter to Luise Walther.[17] Additionally, Mörike may still have borne some resentment toward Loewe because as early as 1841 Mörike's Festspiel *Das Fest im Gebirge* had been rejected by the Hoftheater in favor of a text by Loewe.[18] Although we have no written record of Mörike's reaction to this rejection, his relationship to Loewe may have therefore been doomed from the very start.

The fact that Loewe's poems were not favorably reviewed can also not have escaped Mörike's attention. Although he had not yet read the review of the first edition of Loewe's poems of 1854 when he thanks Gustav Pressel in a letter dated November 2, 1854, sooner or later Mörike must have become aware of that review.[19] The negative assessment of Loewe is highlighted by the fact that in comparison with two other neophytes (Hermann Lingg and J.G. Fischer) he fares worst by being labeled an uninspired dilettante: "Er ist ein sehr gebil-

deter Geist . . . der viel genossen hat, und nun reflectirt was er gewonnen, was er erreicht habe, dem diese Reflexion aber oft die
frische Lust, den unmittelbaren Genuß verderbt, der nicht einer
tiefen Qual, aber einer lästigen Plage entgehen möchte, und den diese
Plage bis in sein Dichten hinein verfolgt: 'muß es geplagt seyn, soll
ein Lied mich plagen.'"[20] In a strikingly similar condemnation to
this anonymous review, Mörike had also once let off steam in a small
poem, written some sixteen years earlier:

> An —
> Laß doch dein Dichten! hast ja Geld;
> Tropf! brauch's, die Poesie lebendig zu betreiben!
> Was gilt's, dich freut das Schönste in der Welt
> Nur halb, vor lauter Angst, du müssest es beschreiben! (I, p. 851)

In the early 1860s, some twenty-five years after this poem, Mörike
expressed his criticism in ways that could be more readily commun-
icated to young poets or to a publisher. His selective critical comments which accompany his preferential list of Loewe are an example
of such constructive, critical work. The following is a complete transcription of his list of titles of first lines along with his sundry comments:

[Mörikes Bemerkungen zu Feodor Loewes Gedichten] [21]

S.	9.	*Die Sage spricht, wo tief* [ein Schatz.]
	11.	*Ein seltnes, räthselh* [aftes] *Buch.*
	15.	*Mein Aug geht gar zu gern* [bei deinem Aug' zu Gast.]
	18.	*O Hain, wie deine Kronen all.*
	23.	*O komm mit mir* [zur duft'gen Laube komm.]
	26.	*Ich fuhr im Kahn* [mit meinem Lieben Weh.]
	27.	*Das tück'sche Meer verschlang* [ein liebes Blatt.]
	32.	*Ich lese stumm in deinen Anges* [icht] *c die Schlußzeilen?*
	33.	*Der Schwalbe gleich,* [die froh die Kunde bringt.]
	34.	*Es ist ein tiefes Wort,* [tief wie das Meer.]
	37.	*Von meinem Lieb verwahr ich.*
	39.	*Einmal nur für alle Orte,* [liebe Seele glaube mir.]
	55.	*Gebirgsmorgen. c "gleich den fl* [ammenden] *Lavaflüssen"?*
	82.	*Am See 1. c Singen den Wellen? / 2. 3. 4. 5.*
	96.	*Reiterlied.*

100.	Die Brünnlein die da fliessen.
105.	folgg. In den Stücken aus Venedig vieles Bedeutende und Schöne.
149.	Pan schläft. c die viertletzte Zeile will mir nicht ganz einleuchten.
158.	Rache u. Sühne. 1. 2.
161.	Distichen. besonders: 3. 7. 12. 13. 15. 17. 18. 20. 21. 22. 23. 28. 29. 32. 34. 36. 37. 38. 40.
185.	Der Tod der Mutter.
190.	Bei Hardeggs Tod.
196.	Ein bleiches Haupt.
206.	Ein Tischnachbar.
219.	Das erste Bildniß.
223.	Der Bergmann.
243.	Klytämnestra.
247.	Serapis / vielleicht würden die 3 letzten Reimpaare besser wegfallen /
252.	Schwäbische Erbschaft.
253.	Walther v. Kernberg.
261.	Vor Göthes Standbild. c Str. 5 "Es ward die Stätte Licht"?
264.	Prolog zur Schillerfeyer. (Stanze 4. "Und so geschahs." Vgl. Goethes Epilog zur Glocke. Der kleinliche Reminiszenzenjäger könnte auf diese Stelle deuten.)
270.	Ein Bild aus dem Dänenkrieg. / Ob der Eingang, so schön u. kräftig er ist, nicht aufzuopfern wäre? /
276.	Ein deutsches Schiff.
279.	Bei Vilagos.
304.	Auf der Jagd.
310.	Eine Waldblume. (Nach meinem Gefühl dürfte der Anfang von No. IV, die erste Seite, etwas mässiger gehalten seyn.)
324.	Die Mohrin. c Str. 1, "Die Fächer schwirren gl [änzen] u. modern"? − Auch stört die zufällige Ähnlichkeit des Reimes in diesen 4 Zeilen. − Str. 5 "Die Sehnsucht nach jenen goldnen Körnern" befremdet immerhin etwas an dieser Stelle. Str. 6 "der Peitsche klatschen − Belachen"??
328.	Ein Stück Bühnenleben. c "das Auge, scheingebrochen, festgeschlossen"? Die beiden Prädikate scheinen einander auszuschliessen.
340.	Wär' Dir ein leichter. c "Dein Forschen nenne nicht Erfüllung der ewig göttlichen Gewalt"?
354.	Wir werden nimmer uns verstehen!
359.	Laß uns die herbstlich schönen Tage. c "das rechte Wallen pflegen"?
363.	Reimsprüche durchaus. c No. 16 "Selbsttäuschung − kniest" damit ist der Gedanke wohl nicht ganz richtig ausgedrückt. /

126

Einzelne Bedenken
(zweifelhafte Metaphern, Gleichnisse und Anderes)

S. 298.   *"Er schlägt sein Geld aus seiner Stirne Schweiß".*

304.   *"Stand er vor mir als wie ein längst verkl* [ungen] *Unheimlich Hel-*
        denlied".

322.   *"der Hahn die Morgenfanfare kräht".*

129.   *"schwere Tropfen, wie v. Thränen, hör ich – fallen."*

301.   *"dumpfhingrollend"* als Epitheton zu dem allgemeineren Begriff Ge-
        witternacht erscheint zu momentan malend.

234.   In dem Persischen Klaggesang eine allzu starke Häufung der Epi-
        theten, besonders der Participialform. Dies einigermaßen auch in
        dem Stücke S. 185.

122.   *"wenn die Sonne sank, wie manche Thränen".* Die Wiederholung
        dieser Worte könnte den Schein des Preciösen haben. Ähnlich S.
        296: *"Ihr stammt aus einem Lande".*

304.   *"Und bot ihm an".* Diese Art, im Anfang einer Erzählung statt des
        bestimmten Subjekts schlechthin das Pronomen personale zu ge-
        brauchen, ist ausnahmsweise wohl einmal zu gestatten; sonst
        däuchte sie mir allzu kostbar modern.

152.   *"Der Chor der Alten, der – zu der Orchestra aufwärts steigend"?*

155.   *"Und werden stillen Glücks nie müder Schanzer"?*

Sprachlich wäre anzufechten;

61.   *"einen Sarg verhämmern"*

85.   *"wenn ich müssig hingestreckt"*

92.   Str. 2 *"Am Strand – fern gerückt".*

126.   *"Vorbei als an dieß Eiland".*

283.   *"ein wechselnd Schwanken"; pleonastisch.*

In den Distichen wäre mehr Wechsel der Verfüße durch haeufigere Spondeen
wohlthaetig. Die Anfänge sind fast durchweg dactylisch; eine Ausnahme bei
No. 24; *"Lang schon".* In No. 4 fällt der 2 malige falsche Dactylus *"in deinen*
Ästen", "in deinem Schatten" allzu stark auf. In No. 8 ist der Spondeus der 2ten
Hälfte des Pentameters wehthuend. Ebenso in No. 12 der Hiatus; *fühle entsa-*
gend".

Sollte ich bei der nächsten Auflage eins und das andre Stück ganz mißen, so
dürften es vielleicht die Gedichte S. 47–54, und S. 234 seyn.

[Eduard Mörike]

127

Mörike's critical comments are not extensive. It is characteristic of him to be very reticent in his literary commentary. How carefully he chooses his words when taking a critical stance was once shown by Ulrich Hötzer in connection with comments Mörike made regarding his reading of Goethe's poems. In a case where he considered Goethe's violation of good usage and other liberties in the use of poetic diction, he used the elegant phrase "grata negligentia."[22] Loewe's slips and liberties, on the other hand, elicit from him the relatively severer comment: "einzelne Bedenken." Mörike's procedure in his comments on Loewe can be divided according to the following four categories: (1) A selection process (2) Sense or logic of the lyric expression (3) "Echo" of other poets and (4) Aspects of style and usage.

(1) A selection process. First, his listing and commentary represents a selection, possibly for an anthology or, as already indicated, for a third edition which did not materialize. That his procedure pursues this end rather than a reading for pure personal pleasure can be seen by the systematic, chronological listing of titles and first lines starting with page 9 and concluding with page 363. Also, such notations as "besonders" for a number of couplets, as well as the summary comment, "in den Stücken aus Venedig vieles Bedeutende und Schöne," points to an outside addressee for such a selection procedure. Also, and this surely is the most telling comment, Mörike finally alludes to a possible third edition, "bei der nächsten Auflage," for which, presumably, his corrections and selection criteria were to have been considered.

Another aspect of the selection procedure is a kind of intensification as the commentary proceeds, almost as if Mörike was changing his mind in the very process of his critical reading from a willing acceptance in the beginning to a qualified rejection at the conclusion of his reading. At first he only uses an occasional questioning mark; that is to say, he questions an occasional wrong sound, choice of words, or a simile such as in the poem "Gebirgsmorgen" (p. 55), the line "gleich den flammigen Lavaflüssen," where the neologistic adjective is somewhat awkward especially because of the incongruous rhyming with "schlammigen Regengüssen" in the subsequent line of the same stanza. Toward the end of the Loewe volume, especially pages 247–363, Mörike's critical comments become more frequent and explicit. Thus, for example, on p. 363ff., Mörike specifically questions the formulation in "Reimspruch No. 16:"

Selbsttäuschung ist das schlimme Kind,
Vor dem du vaterselig kniest,
Das du, für Wahrheit taub und blind,
Dir selbst zur Strafe auferziehst.

Mörike's reference to the first two lines, "Damit ist der Gedanke wohl nicht ganz richtig ausgedrückt," is as severe as his critical commentary will ever get throughout his commentary. No doubt Mörike saw in this formulation a gross oversimplification, because self-deception (Selbsttäuschung) is not as easily identified and objectified in the figure of a bad child (schlimmes Kind) as Loewe implies.

(2) Logic of the lyric expression. As a second general criterion Mörike questions several instances of Loewe's logic of lyric expression. In regard to his comment to Loewe's "Ein Stück Bühnenleben," in the section entitled "Buch der Betrachtung" (pp. 335–363), the context is the following stanza:

Braut von Messina! – Auf der Bahre lag
Don Manuel, vom Trauertuch umflossen;
Bleich war sein Antlitz wie ein Wintertag,
Das Auge, scheingebrochen, festgeschlossen.
An seine Brust warf sich ein jammernd Weib
Und schrie zum Himmel so gewalt'ge Klagen,
So wahre, als ob wirklich einst ihr Leib
Den da Erschlagnen muttertreu getragen. (p. 328ff.)

Mörike dryly ascertains: "'Das Auge, scheingebrochen, festgeschlossen?' Die beiden Prädikate scheinen einander auszuschließen." Indeed, if the actor playing the slain Don Manuel in *Die Braut von Messina* has his eyes closed (festgeschlossen), he cannot simultaneously appear to project an open-eyed death stare (scheingebrochen). As an additional note of sarcasm, Mörike mockingly echoes "scheinen" in his critical comment. Mörike points to another instance of faulty use of logic of lyric expression in the poem "Pan schläft"

129

(Sonet No. 7 of the larger section "Sonette und Distichen," pp. 143–161):

Pan schläft! In allen Wipfeln Mittagsstille!
Man hört des Gottes Athemholen;
Die jungen Blätter flüstern wie verstohlen
Und nur in langen Pausen zirpt die Grille.

Im Schlummer liegt der hohe Götterwille
Und hat zu feiern der Natur befohlen,
Die Stunden schleichen wie auf Blumensohlen;
Pan schläft! in allen Wipfeln Mittagsstille!

Ein sonnig Netz umschlingt mit goldnen Ringen
Die weite Flur und hält den Bach gefangen,
Bis seine muntern Wellen sanfter klingen;

Den Rosenbusch nur regt ein schüchtern Bangen,
Sehnsüchtig duftet er nach holdem Singen
Der Nachtigall und bebt voll Thauverlangen. (p. 149)

Mörike's critical comment, "Die viertletzte Zeile will mir nicht ganz einleuchten," refers to the line "Bis seine muntern Wellen sanfter klingen." "Muntere Wellen" is a visual as well as an auditory image, but its source of lively (munter) sound is quite independent of the time of day (Mittagsstille) and therefore cannot be subject to the sun (sonniges Netz). The criticism also contains another subtle and ironic wordplay by Mörike: The logic of light controlling sound cannot "einleuchten." Both instances of faulty lyric logic and the manner in which Mörike casts his criticisms suggest that his comments were probably addressed not to Loewe directly but to some third reader/editor.

(3) "Echo" of other poets. In a third aspect of his selection process, Mörike points to a possible plagiarism which, so he warns, could be found by a "kleinlichen Reminiszenzenjäger." This is in references to Loewe's "Prolog zur Feier des hundertjährigen Geburtstages Friedrich Schillers" in the section "Gestalten:"

Und so geschah's! — von heil'ger Glut durchdrungen,
Schritt er die Bahn des Ruhmes ohne Halt.
Wie stolz hat er sein Saitenspiel geschwungen,
Wo es der Menschheit höchste Güter galt!
Wie sprach er kühn mit donnerlauten Zungen
Das Urtheil der despotischen Gewalt!
Und wußte doch der Liebe zaubrisch Walten
In reinster Mädchenblüthe zu entfalten. (Stanza 4, p. 265)

Mörike who knew Goethe's poetry by heart warns Loewe of the echo in the first line which indeed occurs in Goethe's "Epilog zur Glocke:"

Und so geschah's! Dem friedenreichen Klange
Bewegte sich das Land, und segenbar
Ein frisches Glück erschien: im Hochgesange . . .[23]

Mörike confined himself to pointing out one echo, even though he could have added that the type of stanza as well as the overall number of stanzas (thirteen) and the rhyme scheme (ab ab ab cc) are also in imitation of Goethe's poem. On the other hand, and in defense of Loewe, these similarities may have been specifically intended by him as a way of paying tribute to both Schiller and Goethe. Nevertheless, this is a clear indication of Mörike's extreme sensitivity toward reminders of antecedent lyric expressions which he, as we have seen in his own work, is not always able to suppress.

Under the heading "sprachlich wäre anzufechten," in which Mörike limits himself to five brief questionable uses of diction, he does not list any additional, general selection criteria. In the second to the last section which deals exclusively with matters of prosody, Mörike limits himself to a comment about the section "Sonette und Distichen" (p. 143—161), specifically to No. VIII:

Zagend erblickst du den Berg, den felsgezackten, gewalt'gen,
Und dich befällt schon im Thal Furcht vor Schwindel und Müh'.
Wage dich muthig empor, dort wehen erquickende Lüfte,
Freier erscheint dir die Welt, trittst du dem Riesen auf's Haupt.

Mörike's criticism contains the barb of a "painful" allusion to Loewe's lyric thought and expression when he laments the break in rhythm in the second half on the last line, "trittst du dem Riesen auf's Haupt," by mockingly lamenting: "der Spondeus der 2ten Hälfte des Pentameters [ist] wehtuend."

In the brief concluding comment, Mörike, for the first time, suggests a total elimination from a possible "nächste Auflage." His pagination would exclude the poems "Frühlings-Telegramme" No. 1–4 (p. 47–54) and "Persischer Klaggesang" (p. 234). There are definite similarities in both poems that have to do with the notion of "treiben:" "Frühlings-Telegramme" opens with the couplet:

> Es trieb Prinz Lenz mit starker Hand
> Den König Winter aus dem Land.

"Persischer Klaggesang," in turn, begins:

> Der die zahllose Völkerheerde
> Trieb auf die hellenische Erde,
> Über des Pontus zürnende Wogen
> Ufer-verbindende Joche gebogen . . .

This poem concludes after numerous stanzas with the lines:

> Länderbeherrschendes Persien, zage!
> Hingewürget sind deine Söhne.
> Durch das brechende Susa töne
> Nimmer verhallende Todtenklage.

It is a commonplace in Mörike scholarship to point to Mörike's aversion to "forciren."[24] This is true, as we have seen above in his criticism of young poets who want to force their creative powers into yielding to demands for fame, as well as in the present instances, where it is a matter of the right theme and tone. The notion of force, forcing, of a driving force represented in the verb "treiben" predominate in both poems. Thus, it comes as no surprise that Mörike reserves his sharpest critical rebuke for these two poems by suggesting total exclusion from further consideration.

If there is a unifying, critical approach to Loewe's poems in these brief comments, it is Mörike's "Gefühl" for "mäßigeren Ausdruck." Indirectly, this gentle but firm demand is repeated by Mörike in his selection procedure in regard to the poems "Ein Bild aus dem Dänenkrieg" and "Eine Waldblume." In the case of the former, the context of the opening lines of this hyper-patriotic poem is:

> Die Zeit des Waffenstillstands ist vorbei;
> Auf's neu erhebt der Däne sein Geschrei,
> Nicht trotzig pochend auf sein gutes Schwert,
> O nein − auf's Meer! Das Meer ist uns verwehrt!
> Drum höhnt der Zwerg den Riesen tief ergrimmt,
> Weil ihm die Schiffburg auf den Wellen schwimmt!
> Allein, Gott Lob, bald fertig liegt die That,
> Der langen Spaltung ruhmvoll Ende naht,
> Der Tag, wo deutsches Tuch im Winde bauscht,
> Die deutsche Flotte durch die Meere rauscht
> Und prahlend trägt in aller Länder Kreis
> Die deutsche Tapferkeit, den deutschen Fleiß (p. 270)

Mörike's reticent comment in regard to these lines is a masterpiece of diplomatic understatement: "Ob der Eingang, so schön und kräftig er ist, nicht aufzuopfern wäre?" For the latter poem, "Eine Waldblume," No. IV, the context is as follows:

> O sei mir willkommen viel tausendmal
> In meinem Schlosse, im schimmernden Saal,
> Wo die Ahnenbilder mich rings umstehn,
> Doch nicht eine dabei so schön zu sehn
> Von allen den Frauen in fürstlicher Pracht,
> Wie du in der schlichten wollenen Tracht!
> Ihr Diener herbei! den Lüster beflammt!
> Bringt rauschende Seide, bringt starrenden Sammt,
> Und flechtet der Herrin um's goldige Haar
> Zu den Perlen des Meeres den Demant klar! (stanza iv, p. 317)

Mörike's comment, "Nach meinem Gefühl dürfte der Anfang von No. IV, die erste Seite, etwas mäßiger gehalten seyn," is related to his aversion toward too much forcefulness in tone and subject in the context of a lyric poem. Any "Waldblume" could hardly help from wilting in embarrassment at being assailed by so much loud and heated avowals as the lyric-dramatic persona projects in these ten opening lines.

In conclusion, we could also become guilty of excess in reading into this limited number of concrete notations by Mörike an entire set of aesthetic principles of how Mörike viewed lyric production. On the other hand, there are only Mörike's brief and more general comments in letters which give us tenuous sign posts regarding his critical estimate of the work of other contemporary writers. The larger picture of Mörike's critical work is still forming and has to await the appearance of the remaining letters and the Mayer/Waiblinger *Bearbeitungen*. But here in these critical comments, in a concrete document, Mörike's own lyric work is also reflected, especially in his demand for precision of the lyric expression as well as his characteristic plea for a moderate tone as part of his late creative period. Mörike's poems "Erinna an Sappho" and "Bilder aus Bebenhausen", written in 1862–63, marked the last high point of his lyric creativity; this creativity found a remarkable, critical echo in the "Bemerkungen zu Loewes Gedichten" which in all probability stem from the same period.

Notes – Chapter IV

1 Renate von Heydebrand, *Eduard Mörikes Gedichtwerk*. J.B. Metzler: Stuttgart, 1972.
2 Hans-Ulrich Simon, *Mörike Chronik*. J.B. Metzler: Stuttgart, 1981.
3 As part of the 24 volume critical-historical edition in progress in Marbach since 1967, a separate volume of Mörike's *Bearbeitungen anderer Dichter* (vol. 9, editor: Ulrich Hötzer) is planned.
4 Located in the manuscript catalogue of SNM/Deutsches Literaturarchiv, Marbach. Listed under: "E[igenhändige] Bemerkungen zu F. Loewes Gedichten," SNM 4575, category "Verschiedenes."

5 Cf. Franz Brümmer, *Lexikon der deutschen Dichter und Prosaisten vom Beginn des 19. Jahrhunderts bis zur Gegenwart*, 8 Bände, 6. Auflage, Reclam, 1913. This compendium lists only a second edition (1860) of the first edition of the poems. This second edition also never seems to have been reprinted.

6 Cf. Eduard Mörike, *Unveröffentlichte Briefe*, ed. Friedrich Seebaß. Stuttgart, 1945. The dates of the four extant letters are: Jan. 2, 1862; Nov. 6, 1862; April 9, 1865 and Dec. 30, 1874. The only letter by Loewe to Mörike which is known is an unpublished one, dated Oct. 30, 1873, located in SNM, Mörike Archiv, No. SS Ba 8.

7 Seebaß, *Unpubl. Letters*, p. 337.

8 Seebaß, *Unpubl. Letters*, p. 571.

9 Simon, *Mörike Chronik*. More than a dozen meetings, visits and mentions of Loewe in letters to others are listed for the years 1860–74.

10 Seebaß, *Unpubl. Letters*, p. 571.

11 Seebaß, *Unpubl. Letters*, p. 312. Mörike promises Cotta "tätige Teilnahme mit Freuden" on the journal *Morgenblatt* which Cotta publishes.

12 Cf. Gerhard Storz, *Eduard Mörike* (Stuttgart: Ernst Klett, 1967), p. 370. Also, a number of public honors were bestowed on Mörike during this period. In 1862 he received the Maximilian Order from the King of Bavaria, followed by "Ritterkreuz Erster Klasse des Friedrich Ordens" awarded by the King of Württemberg. There also took place in Mörike's last creative phase a number of celebrated visits and correspondences with established writers such as Storm, Geibel, Heyse, Turgeniew and others.

13 Seebaß, *Unpubl. Letters*, p. 329.

14 Seebaß, *Unpubl. Letters*, p. 327.

15 Seebaß, *Unpubl. Letters*, p. 328. "Timor est emendator acerimus" (fear is the keenest source of improvement).

16 Seebaß, *Unpubl. Letters*, p. 330.

17 Seebaß, *Unpubl. Letters*, p. 479. Mörike reports in his letter to Luise Walther, June 18, 1874: "Von Hemsen hab ich einen angenehmen Brief und eine belebende Lektüre: den 4. und 5. Band von Eduard Devrients Geschichte der deutschen Schauspielkunst, ein ganz vortreffliches Buch . . . Von Feodor Loewe heißt es: 'Der junge Mann empfahl sich durch Bildung und Verstand, auch durch poetische Fähigkeit, sein energieloses und nüchternes Darstellertalent ließ ihn ungefährlich für Moritz [Heinrich Moritz was Loewe's predecessor at the Hoftheater whom he replaced] erscheinen. Er wurde es aber in andrer Weise, indem er sich mit Amalie Stubenrauch verschwägerte, und je mehr sich so der Boden unter seinen Füßen befestigte, lockerte sich der seines Beschützers'." Devrient accuses Loewe here of advancing his career on the basis of social connection rather than professional skill.

18 Cf. Simon, *Mörike Chronik*, p. 135.

19 Seebaß, *Unpubl. Letters*, p. 279. Mörike writes Pressel: "Die mir bezeichneten Artikel aus der Augsburger Zeitung und sonst sind uns noch nicht zu

Gesichte gekommen." To this Seebaß in his notes adds: "Gemeint sind wohl die ausführlichen Besprechungen der bei Cotta erschienenen Gedicht-sammlungen von H. Lingg, F. Löwe, J.G. Fischer, A. Knapp in der Beilage zur Augsburger 'Allgemeinen Zeitung' vom 11.10. und 27.10.1854.

20 Anonymous, Supplement to No. 300 of the *Allgemeine Zeitung*, Oct. 27, 1854.

21 In transcribing Mörike's handwritten notations, I proceeded as follows: The manuscript itself is untitled, its present title, assigned in the archive, is set in square brackets. All of Mörike's quotes of either first lines or titles of poems have been compared with the poems in print of the edition of Loewe's *Gedichte*, Stuttgart: Cotta, 1860. In some cases Mörike's no-tations are reproduced, including the peculiar letter c with which Mörike preceded several of his critical comments. All of Mörike's writings is set in italics. Additionally, those comments which can be considered critical in one way or the other are underlined. In the first part of the selection list in the ms Mörike had underlined several of the titles which he lists in pp. 9 through 363. Since these titles are part of the favorable selection, these underlinings have not been reproduced in the transcription. The signature of Mörike's name at the conclusion of the ms is not by him.

22 Ulrich Hötzer, "'grata negligentia' — 'ungestiefelt Hexameter,' Bemerkun-gen zu Goethes und Mörikes Hexameter," *Der Deutschunterricht*, vol. 16 (1964), H. 6, pp. 86–108.

23 *Goethes Werke*, 8. Auflage, ed. Erich Trunz (Hamburg: Christian Wegner, 1966), vol. 1, p. 256.

24 "*Nur nichts forcieren*, so hieß die selbstgeprägte Devise, nach der er leben mußte, ob er wollte oder nicht." Cf. Hans Egon Holthusen, *Eduard Mörike in Selbstzeugnissen und Bilddokumenten* (Hamburg: Rowohlt, 1971), p. 116.

Chapter V

The Process of Reading as Marginalia: Mörike's Extant Library

The task of reconstructing Mörike's library is an ongoing process. In the following discussion, compilation and transcription steps in the direction of a possible outline of this task are taken. One has to start with what has survived the ravages of time and is located in the various archives and libraries where an active attempt at collecting Mörike manuscripts and books from his personal possession was made. There are basically three *Nachlaß* collections. The most comprehensive is the Schiller-Nationalmuseum / Deutsches Literaturarchiv in Marbach (SNM), where the critical-historical edition of Mörike's works has been in progress since the late 1960's. This is also the only one of the three repositories where an active program of acquisition of Mörike materials continues today. The orther two collections (*Teilnachlaß*) are the Goethe und Schiller Archiv, part of the Nationale Forschungs- und Gedenkstätten der klassischen deutschen Literatur in Weimar (GSA), and the Fritz Kauffmann Sammlung in the Wilhelmspalais in Stuttgart (Stadtarchiv). As indicated in *Part A*, a few works are in private collections.

In the three archives I have also recorded all legible notes, corrections and marginalia and other evidence of active reading and perusal in all books which have been authenticated to have been in Mörike's possession. The actual extent of Mörike's personal library was of course larger than the fifty plus items listed below. The most conspicuous gap is the missing Schlegel-Tieck translation of the Shakespeare edition (for a discussion of this, see Chapter II above). A number of other important works which have evidence of Mörike's ownership and use in them and which are now either in private hands or described in auction catalogues should be mentioned as complimentary to the extant list:

(1) *Affenheimische Nebenstunden*, Neuntes Stück, enthaltend Caspari Sagittari Hallensem. Schwabach, 1746.

(2) G.C. Lichtenberg, *Vermischte Schriften.* Wien, 1817.

(3) G. Reinbeck, *Mythologie für Nichtstudierende.* Wien, 1817.

(4) H. Heine, *Alamansor* (aus Tragödien), Berlin, 1823.

(5) *Deutscher Musenalmanach auf das Jahr 1834,* hrsg. A.V. Chamisso und G. Schwab. Leipzig, 1834.

(6) F.T. Vischer, *Über das Erhabene und Komische.* Stuttgart, 1837.

(7) D.F. Strauss, *Zwei friedliche Blätter.* Alt., 1939.

(8) W. de Wette, *Kurzgefasstes exegetisches Handbuch zum Neuen Testament,* 2 vols. Leipzig, 1839–41.

(9) C.B. Stark, *Quaestionum Anacreonticarum* . . . Lipsiae, 1846.

(10) J. Munder, *Die Glocke. Histor. Unterhaltungsbuch.* Stuttgart, 1849.

(11) Paul Heyse, *Novellen und Terzinen.* Berlin, 1867.

Additionally, for his own works and translations Mörike consulted a large number of works. An instructive contribution in this respect was made by Ulrich Hötzer who in the process of editing Mörike's translations of classical Greek and Roman poets, indicated Mörike's actual use of existing "Textvorlagen" of more than sixty (!) works (See list of sources for *Classisches Blumenlese,* p. 21–22; *Theokritus,* p. 371; and *Anakreon,* p. 463–467 in *Eduard Mörike, Werke und Briefe.* Übersetzungen, critical-historical edition, vol. 8, part 3). However, most of these works Mörike could not afford to own and had to borrow in cumbersome communications with sources in Stuttgart and Tübingen.

Given these indications and other hints to lost items mentioned by Mörike collectors (including Hermann Hesse), the overall size of Mörike's library was at least twice the size listed below in *Part A.* Even at that, however, it was a library of modest size. Nevertheless, Mörike's library is of a sufficient size to give us definite clues as to the manner of his reading such as *concentration* and *focus.*

The first aspect has been dealt with in the previous chapters. Whereas the emphasis in those discussions was on Shakespeare, Mörike's main preoccupations also included two other major poles of orientations: Goethe and Lichtenberg. As to the way in which Mörike read, as it is reflected in the marginalia reproduced below, his brief notes in D.F. Strauss' *Kleine Schriften* (Item No. 51) may serve as a representative example. Typically, Mörike's focus is a dual one. On the one hand, on a kind of pictorial level, his imagination is open to richness in the constellation of characters and images. Here, he is thrilled by Strauss' evocation of the figure of Christ as child ("Der Erlöser als Kind"). Side-by-side with such inner-eye reading, the marginalia exhibit Mörike's other focus based on a kind of word and language sensitivity in which he notes many instances of usage, lyrical logic, obtrusive neologisms and matters of prosody. (Here, Mörike notes the right and wrong use of the word "beispielsweise.") In this latter respect, Mörike is clearly text oriented. That is to say, even for the lyric poem, he sees his corrective contribution as leading to some presumed, final perfect form.

In reproducing Mörike's notations, I proceeded as follows. *Part A* lists the actual works from Mörike's possession. The bibliographical data includes page numbers (including prefatory pagination) in most cases, as well as the location and the archival designation and numbering system. In both *Part A* and *Part B* Mörike's notes are represented in italics. As in the previous chapters, the italics indicate Mörike's handwriting and heretofore unpublished notations. Notations by others, mainly limited to dedications, are identified accordingly. Additional words or letters which were added to clarify Mörike's abbreviations are bracketed. Wherever necessary sufficient original printed text and context to which Mörike's notations refer have been provided to clarify such notations and critical commentary. Words which Mörike crossed out are in double italic parentheses: *(( ))*. To represent Mörike's own underlining, italics are underlined. Mörike's spelling has been retained throughout, including certain abbreviation: His abbreviation for "nicht" is o̅; the abbreviation for "Christ" — either by itself or in adjectives and compound nouns — is a capital C. The letter combination "tzt" or "tz" Mörike almost always shortened to zt and z respectively. The abbreviation "pp" stands for etc. Mörike also uses the abbreviation "NB" from the Latin *nota bene*. To indicate elipses or breaks in the text from which he quotes himself, Mörike uses dahes. Asterisks indicate addition or correction by Mörike to his reading text.

Part A lists all books of the extant works and reproduces Mörike's notations with it for most items. For eleven items (No. 2, 3, 12, 27, 29, 36, 41, 45, 53a, and 53b) these notations are too extensive to be listed with the main entry; they are listed separately and constitute *Part B* of the Annotated Bibliography of Mörike's Extant Library.

Part A: Annotated Bibliography of Mörike's Extant Library

1. Bauer, Ludwig. *Alexander der Große. Karaktergemälde in drei Abtheilungen.* Stuttgart: Hallberg'sche Verlagsbuchhandlung, 1836. (383), SNM, I: Mö 6A/Bau. On the front endpaper Mörike signed: *Ed. Mörike.* In addition to handwritten corrections of printing errors there are occasionally underlined passages without comments or notations.

2. *Briefwechsel zwischen Schiller und Goethe: In den Jahren 1794 bis 1805,* zweite, nach den Originalhandschriften vermehrte Ausgabe. Stuttgart und Augsburg: J.G. Cotta'scher Verlag, 1856. (Bd. 1, 432) (Bd. 2, 470), SNM, I: Mö 6A/Schil. In the first volume on the front endpaper Mörike signed: *Ed. Mörike,* and in the second volume: *Mörike.* There are many inserts, amendations and corrections in both volumes. Complete Notations follow this list in *Part B* under No. 2.

3. *Conversations-Lexikon: Allgemeine deutsche Real-Enzyklopädie für die gebildeten Stände,* 12 Bände, 8. Original Auflage. Leipzig: F.A. Brockhaus, 1833–1837. (Bd. 1, 971) (Bd. 2, 988) (Bd. 3, 768) (Bd. 4, 1050) (Bd. 5, 852), (Bd. 6, 804) (Bd. 7, 948) (Bd. 8, 1000) (Bd. 9, 916) (Bd. 10, 864) (Bd. 11, 858) (Bd. 12, 647), SNM, Leihgabe des Stadtarchivs. In all volumes Mörike signed his name as either *Ed. Mörike* or *Eduard Mörike.* In the fifth volume he added the year *1836* under his name. All volumes contain small additions, reading marks and dates; the latest date indicated is *1860.* Complete notations follow this list in *Part B* under No. 3.

4. Conz, Carl Philipp. *Ueber den Geist und die Geschichte des Ritterwesens aelterer Zeit, vorzueglich in Ruecksicht auf Deutschland.* Gotha: Carl Wilhelm Ettinger, 1786. (144), SNM, I: Mö 6A/Con.

5. *Deutsche Kinder-Reime und Kinder-Spiele aus Schwaben,* aus dem Volksmunde gesammelt und herausgegeben von Ernst Meier. Tübingen: Verlag von Ludw. Friedrich Fues, 1851. (xiv, 153), SNM, I: Mö 6A/Mei. On the front endpaper Mörike wrote: *Eduard Mörike / Geschenk des Hrs. Verf.* [Herausgeber Verfassers]. Cf. Mörike's "Worterklärungen" to his story "Das Stuttgarter Hutzelmännlein," where he acknowledges using several of Meier's Kinder-Reime.

6. *Deutscher Jugendkalender. Geschichten und Reime von Robert Reinick,* hrsg. von R. Reinick und H. Bürkner, mit Holzschnitten nach Zeich-

141

nungen von Dresdner Künstlern. Leipzig: Wigand, 1847–1854. Several beginning pages are missing. SNM, I: Mö 6A/Deut.

7. *Eßlinger Bibel*, Eßlingen: G.A. Bonacker, 1748. On the front endpaper, not in Mörike's handwriting, but presumable in that of his great grandfather's (on his mother's side), there is the following signature: "Johann Adam Beyer / 5. Jan. 1733." Private possession of the widow of Rev. Walter Hagen, Marbach. This Bible passed on to Mörike after his mother's death on April 26, 1841. Cf. letter to Hartlaub, May 21, 1841 in *Freundeslieb' und Treu*: "Heute stand ich einmal in Gedanken vor meinem Bücherschrank, sah meiner Mutter Bibel (die ich nur wenige Tage vor ihrer Krankheit neu hatte binden lassen) und schlug sie um irgendein Wahrzeichen auf. Da stand oben in der Ecke rechts die Stelle Psalm 40, 3." Verse 4 of Psalm 40 concludes: "und hat mir ein neues Lied in den Mund gegeben." In an additional fanciful postscript to this letter Mörike suggests to Hartlaub that the newly written poem "An Philomele" was directly inspired by the reading of his mother's Bible and by a nightingale which he overheard the next day while reading this same Bible.

8. *Fünf Bücher deutscher Lieder und Gedichte, von A. Haller bis auf die neueste Zeit. Eine Mustersammlung mit Rücksicht auf den Gebrauch in Schulen.* Hrsg. Gustav Schwab. Leipzig: Widmann'sche Buchhandlung, 1835. (xiii, 737), Stadtarchiv. This anthology contains a total of thirty major and minor poets of the eighteenth and early nineteenth century. Mörike is represented with only one poem, "Mein Fluß."

9. *Fünf Bücher deutscher Lieder und Gedichte, von A. Haller bis auf die neueste Zeit.* Hrsg. Gustav Schwab, fünfte neu vermehrte Auflage besorgt von Michael Bernays. Leipzig: S. Hirzel, 1871. (xviii, 849), Stadtarchiv. On the front endpaper is the following dedication by Gretchen Mörike: "Rich. Kauffmann zu Weihnachten 1880 von Frau Professor Mörike." In addition to "Mein Fluß" of the first edition of this anthology in 1835, the following five poems by Mörike were included: "Im Frühling," "An die Geliebte," "Agnes," "Schön-Rohtraut," and "Die Geister am Mummelsee." Mörike pencilled in two significant changes in the printed text of his poem "Mein Fluß," essentially bringing it into conformance with his final authorized edition of his poems. On page 489, in the first stanza, line 5, he changed the word "kühlt" to *fühlt*. Secondly, on page 490, in the last two lines of the last stanza Mörike crossed out the wording: "Die lieben Sterne führe du / zu ihrer Mutterquelle!" and substituted the wording *Nach tausend Irren kehrest du / Zur ew'gen Mutterquelle!*

10. Geibel, Emanuel. *Neue Gedichte*. Stuttgart und Augsburg: J.G. Cotta'scher Verlag, 1857. SNM, I: Mö 6A/Gei. In front on the endpaper Mörike wrote: *Fanny Mörike. Geschenk des Verf*. On the inside back cover Mörike noted additionally: *S. 213, VI Reim, 216 XV, 217 XVIII, 236 XLVI, 228 L*. On page 222 in the section "Distichen," XXXII, Mörike wrote *Jean Paul* next to the following poem:

Witz ist ein schelmischer Pfaff, der keck zu tauschendem Ehebund
Zwei Gedanken, die nie früher sich kannten, vermählt,
Aber der nächste Moment schon zeigt dir im Hader die Gatten,
Und vor dem schreienden Zwist stehst du betroffen und – lachst.

11. Goedeke, Karl. *Goethe und Schiller*, zweite durchgesehene Auflage. Hanover: Verlag von Louis Ehlersmann, 1859. (viii, 431), GSA. Mörike signed on the front endpaper: *Mörike*. On the inside of the back cover he noted: *Goethes Mutter S. 113, An den Mond 89, S. 88 Elpenor mit Iphigenie wetteifern konnte*. The only other significant marginalia besides numerous corrections of printing errors are on page 248, where Mörike notes: *Über die Beziehung der 17 Sonette auf Minna Herzlieb vergleiche man die Schrift: Das Frommannsche Haus u. seine Freunde pp. Jena 1872*.

12. Goethe, Johann Wolfgang. *Goethe's sämmtliche Werke*, 40 Bände, vollständige, neugeordnete Ausgabe. Stuttgart und Tübingen: J.G. Cotta'scher Verlag, 1840. (Bd. 1, viii, 322) (Bd. 2, x, 363) (Bd. 3, 350) (Bd. 4, xii, 340) (Bd. 5, 300) (Bd. 6, xii, 444) (Bd. 7, 370) (Bd. 8, 372) (Bd. 9, 388) (Bd. 10, 314) (Bd. 11, 207) (Bd. 12, 310) (Bd. 13, 398) (Bd. 14, 274) (Bd. 15, 313) (Bd. 16, 339) (Bd. 17, 404) (Bd. 18, 344) (Bd. 19, 412) (Bd. 20, 260) (Bd. 21, 288) (Bd. 22, 414) (Bd. 23, 404) (Bd. 24, iv, 332) (Bd. 25, 268) (Bd. 26, 346) (Bd. 27, 520) (Bd. 28, xvi, 387) (Bd. 29, x, 443) (Bd. 30, 480) (Bd. 31, 446) (Bd. 32, viii, 459) (Bd. 33, vi, 350) (Bd. 34, 368) (Bd. 35, vi, 458) (Bd. 36, vi, 446) (Bd. 37, xx, 370) (Bd. 38, 248) (Bd. 39, viii, 468) (Bd. 40, viii, 552), GSA. Mörike requested these twenty double volumes from his publisher, Cotta, as initial payment for the second edition of his poems and received them in June 1847. Each of the double volumes contains the signature *Mörike* on the front endpaper. Also on the first double volume Mörike wrote: *Dies Exemplar der Goetheschen / Werke soll, wegen der am Schluß / der einzelnen Baende von mir gemachten Bemerkungen, nicht / veräußert werden, sondern in meiner Familie erhalten bleiben / Ed. Mörike*. Complete notations follow this list in *Part B* under No. 12.

13. *Goethe's Sprüche in Prosa*. Zum ersten Mal erläutert und auf ihre Quellen zurückgeführt von G. Loeper. Berlin: Gustav Hempel, 1870. (259), Stadtarchiv. On the front endpaper there is the following dedication:

"Dem theuren Freunde E. Moerike zum Willkommen bei der Rückkehr von Bebenhausen 1. August 1874. W. Hemsen." On the back endpaper Mörike noted the numbers and brief subject indications of some of his favorite passages in Goethe's works. He was particularly interested in Goethe's views about art, poetry and about some of his own favorite authors such as Lichtenberg, Shakespeare and Schiller. The following are Mörike's notations in their entirety. (The numbers refer to the specific aphorisms in the text.) *Vorbemerkungen des Herausgebers S. 3–16. 34, 35, 40, 123, 173 Shakespeare. 290, 332 Bibel. 333, 334ff, 341 Mad[ame] Roland. (ella sera unlogisch) 345ff. Napol[eon]. 349, 363 Schiller u. G[oethe], 396 Man weicht der Welt – d[urch] die Kunst 569–71, 576 Geduld. 629 Mystis. Anmerkg. 634. Menschenverstand 644, 808, 810 das Phänomen ist eine Folge ohne Grund 868 u. 869: Anmerkung Mathemat. 871, 872 Lichtenberg, Anmerkung. 903 Erfinden, Entdecken 904. 927 Behauptung des Unwahren Anmerkung. 978ff Gesezliches im Object u. Subject. 981–82 Darwin. 1001 Anmerkung Frauenhofer. 1019 Anmerkung.* Mörike's notation "Anmerkung" refers to the editor's copious notes. Mörike's characteristic attitudes are reflected in many of these passages from Goethe's works. Aphorism No. 396 may serve as an example: "Man weicht der Welt nicht sicherer aus als durch die Kunst, und man verknüpft sich nicht sicherer mit ihr als durch die Kunst." Perhaps most remarkably, as revealed by the date of the dedication and Mörike's subsequent notes, he was intensely preoccupied with Goethe throughout his life until days or weeks before his own death in June 1875.

14. *Hausbuch aus deutschen Dichtern seit Claudius. Eine kritische Anthologie.* Hrsg. Theodor Storm. Hamburg: Wilhelm Mauke, 1870. (xx, 714), SNM, I: Mö 6A/Sto. On the front endpaper is the following dedication in Storm's handwriting: "Eduard Mörike mit herzlichem Gruß. Husum 10. November 1870 / Th. Storm." Below this Mörike wrote: *Marie Mörike von ihrem Vater zu Weihnachten 1871.* Storm had selected the following thirteen poems by Mörike for inclusion in this anthology: "Schön Rohtraut," "Früh wenn die Hähne krähn," "Rosenzeit, wie schnell vorbei," "Früh im Wagen," "Die Soldatenbraut," "Wie süß der Nachtwind nun die Wiese streift," "Peregrina," "An meinen Vetter," "Ach nur einmal noch im Leben," "Der alte Turmhahn," "Lose Ware," "Denk' es, o Seele," and "Erinna an Sappho." On page 439 there is the following printed footnote by Storm: "Es kann noch immer nicht stark genug betont werden, daß Mörike's Gedichte in keiner Bibliothek fehlen dürfen, in der unsere poetische Literatur wenn auch nur andeutungsweise vertreten ist." This tribute in 1870 to Mörike constitutes the first acknowledgement of Mörike as a poet of national stature and precedes

Storm's other, better-known tribute, the essay, "Meine Erinnerungen an Eduard Mörike" in *Westermanns Monatshefte* by some seven years.

15. Hebbel, Friedrich. *Gedichte. Gesammt-Ausgabe*, stark vermehrt und verbessert. Stuttgart und Augsburg: J.G. Cotta'scher Verlag. 1857. SNM, I: Mö 6A/He. On the front endpaper Mörike wrote: *E. Mörike / Geschenk des Verf*[assers]. On the back endpaper Mörike added his judgment, *verfehlt*, next to listing the following two titles of poems: *289 Das abgeschiedene Kind an seine Mutter, 294 Prolog zu Goethes 100 j*[ähriger] *Geb*[urtstagsfeier]. Next to the notation *194* referring to Hebbel's poem "Ein Geburtstag auf der Reise," Mörike added: *pers*[önlich] *rührend wahr*. The notations of *S. 271/181* are listed by Mörike without additional comment.

16. Heyse, Paul. *Meleager. Eine Tragödie*. Berlin: Verlag von Wilhelm Hertz, 1854. (112), Stadtarchiv. On the front endpaper is the following dedication by Mörike's wife Gretchen: "Rich. Kauffmann / Geschenk von Margarethe Mörike."

17. Heyse, Paul. *Neue Novellen*. Stuttgart und Augsburg: J.G. Cotta'scher Verlag, 1858. (356), SNM, I: Mö 6A/Hey. On the front endpaper Mörike wrote: *Ed Mörike / Geschenk des Verf.*

18. Heyse, Paul. *Thekla. Ein Gedicht in neun Gesängen*. Stuttgart und Augsburg: J.G. Cotta'scher Verlag, 1858. (176), SNM, I: Mö 6A/Hey. On the front endpaper Mörike wrote: *Ed. Mörike / Geschenk des Verf. / seiner lieben Tochter Fanny zum 12. April 1872.*

19. *Historische Antiquitäten. Oder auserlesene Denkwürdigkeiten aus der Menschen-Völker-Sitten-Kunst- und Literaturgeschichte der Vorwelt und des Mittelalters*, zweiter Teil, hrsg. A.F. Rittgräff. Wien: Carl Gerold, 1815. (172), SNM, I: Mö 6A/Rit.

20. Hölderlin, Friedrich. *Aus Hölderlins Hyperion*, Bd. 2, Tübingen: Cotta, 1799. (Bogen C, 33–48), SNM, I: Mö 6A/Höl. The title to this excerpt was added by Mörike with calligraphic handwriting.

21. Hölty, Ludewig, Heinrich, Christoph. *Gedichte*, besorgt durch seine Freunde Friedrich Leopold Graf zu Stolberg und Johann Heinrich Voß. Frankfurt & Leipzig, 1772. (xxviii, 190), SNM, I: Mö 6A/Hoel. Apparently this book passed through several hands before Mörike sent it to Georg Scherer as a gift. On the front inside cover, not in Mörike's handwriting is the following notation: "Dein B. er grüßt dich hier / Und schenkt den Hölty Dir." Below this is the additional comment: "Geschenk Ed. Mö-

rikes / Georg Scherer." On the back endpaper Mörike added Hölty's poem "Auftrag." Additionally, on page 24, in connection with Hölty's poem "Mailied" Mörike corrected and commented on someone else's correction: Hölty's printed text of lines 5–6 of the third stanza of this poem is: "Küßt ihn, Brüder küßt, / Weil er küßlich ist!" In another handwriting someone who must have owned the book prior to Mörike noted: "N.B. Küßlich ist nicht Deutsch." Mörike, in turn, crossing out this note responded: *Alter Kanzleihengst! Durch Hölty ist das Wort klassisch.*

22. Hölty, Ludewig, Heinrich, Christoph. *Gedichte, nebst Briefe des Dichters,* hrsg. Karl Halm. Leipzig: F.A. Brockhaus, 1869. (xx, 266), Stadtarchiv. On the front endpaper there is a dedication to Mörike: "dem theuren Freunde / Eduard Mörike / ein Maien-gruß / 1872 W[ilhelm] H[emsen]." Mörike crossed three poems: p. 37, "Das Feuer im Walde" in the section "Idyllen;" p. 103, "Der Bach" in the section "Oden;" and p. 130, "Mailied" in the section "Lieder und Vermischte Gedichte."

23. Kauffmann, Ernst Friedrich. *Lieder und Gesänge von Kauffmann für eine Singstimme mit Begleitung des Pianoforte,* Hefte I–XVI. Stuttgart: Ebner [no date], (58). On the front endpaper Mörike signed: *Ed. Mörike.* A second booklet attached to this collection is entitled: Lieder und Gesänge für eine Mezzo-Sopran oder Bariton-Stimme mit Begleitung des Pianoforte komponiert von Kauffmann, Heft 1. Berlin: Bote & Bock [no date]. (6), Stadtarchiv. Among the poems / Lieder by Heine, Beck, Lenau, Geibel and Kerner, Mörike is represented with six: "Um Mitternacht," "Lammwirts Klagelied," "Peregrina," "Schön-Rohtraut," "Lied vom Winde," and "Der Gärtner."

24. Kerner, Justinus. *Die Dichtungen,* 2 Bde., dritte Auflage. Stuttgart und Tübingen: J.G. Cotta'scher Verlag, 1841. SNM, I: Mö 6A/Ker. In both volumes Mörike wrote on the front endpaper: *Ed. Mörike.* In the second volume he added below his signature: *Geschenk des Verfassers d. 19. Oct. 41.* In volume one Mörike added the following notes on the back endpaper: *non placent 307* [Verjüngung], *310* [Arzt und Pferd], *322* [Bittre des Erdballs], *336* [Glut des Herzens], *342* [An Dieselbe], *121* [An Marie von Hügel], *288f., 120* [Der Mutter Grab], *110* [Was sie als meinen], *358* [Nr. 5, Des Bruders Tod], *189* [Abschied], *140* [Der Zopf im Kopfe], *43 Metall u. Glas.* Mörike apparently considered these poems to be unpleasant. The German equivalent of the Latin *non placent* is "ungefällig, nicht schön."

25. Kielmeyer, Carl Friedrich. *Über die Verhältnisse der organischen Kräfte unter einandͤr in der Reihe der verschiedenen Organisationen, die Gesetze*

28

Dieß hängt mit einer Menge ähnlicher Vorfälle in meinem Leben zusammen. Ich bin sehr abergläubisch, allein ich schäme mich dessen gar nicht, so wenig als ich mich schäme zu glauben, daß die Erde stille steht. Es ist der Körper meiner Philosophie, und ich danke nur Gott, daß er mir eine Seele gegeben hat, die dieses corrigiren kann.

Bei meiner Nervenkrankheit habe ich sehr häufig gefunden, daß das, was sonst bloß mein moralisches Gefühl beleidigte, nun in das physische überging. Als jemand einmal sagte: „mich soll Gott tödten," wurde mir so übel, daß ich dem Menschen auf eine Zeit lang die Stube verbieten mußte.

Es schicken wohl wenige Menschen Bücher in die Welt, ohne zu glauben, daß nun jeder seine Pfeife hinlegen oder sie anzünden würde, um sie zu lesen. Daß mir diese Ehre nicht zugedacht ist, sage ich nicht bloß, denn das wäre leicht, sondern ich glaube es auch, welches schon etwas schwerer ist, und erkennt werden muß. Autor, Setzer, Corrector und Censor mögen es lesen, vielleicht auch der Recensent, wenn er will, das sind also von tausend Millionen gerade fünfe.†

Wenn nur der Scheidepunkt erst überschritten wäre! Mein Gott, wie verlangt mich nach dem Augenblick, wo die Zeit für mich aufhören wird, Zeit zu sein; wo mich der Schooß des ewigen Alles und Nichts wieder aufnehmen wird, in dem ich damals schlief, als der Haynberg*) angefüllt wurde, als Epikur,

*) Ein bekannter Berg bei Göttingen.

29

Cäsar, Lucrez lebten und schrieben, und Spinoza den größten Gedanken dachte, der noch in eines Menschen Kopf gekommen ist.

Seit einigen Tagen (22. April 1791) lebe ich unter der Hypothese (denn ich lebe beständig unter einer), daß das Trinken bei Tisch schädlich sei, und befinde mich vortrefflich dabei. Hieran ist gewiß etwas Wahres, denn ich habe noch von keiner Änderung in meiner Lebensart und von keiner Arznei so schnell und handgreiflich die gute Wirkung empfunden, als hiervon.

Es gibt für mich keine gehässigere Art Menschen, als die, welche glauben, daß sie bei jeder Gelegenheit ex officio witzig sein müßten.

Man ist nie glücklicher, als wenn uns ein starkes Gefühl bestimmt, nur in dieser Welt zu leben. Mein Unglück ist, nie in dieser, sondern in einer Menge von möglichen Ketten und Verbindungen zu existiren, die sich meine Phantasie, unterstützt von meinem Gewissen, schafft. So geht ein Theil meiner Zeit hin, und keine Vernunft ist im Stande, darüber zu siegen. Dieses verdiente sehr auseinander gesetzt zu werden. Lebe dein erstes Leben recht, damit du dein zweites genießen kannst. Es ist im Leben, wie mit der Praxis des Arztes, die ersten Schritte entscheiden. Das ist doch unrecht irgendwo, in der Anlage oder im Urtheil.

Als ich am 18. Dec. 1789 in meiner Nervenkrankheit die Ohren mit den Fingern zuhielt, befand ich mich sehr viel besser, nicht allein, weil nun mein Nervensystem weniger Stöße bekam, sondern auch, weil ich nun das kränkliche Sausen in den Ohren

und Folgen dieser Verhältnisse. Eine Rede den 2. Februar 1793 am Ge-
burtstage des regierenden Herzogs Carl von Wirtemberg . . ., neuer un-
veränd. Abdr. Tübingen: Christian Friedrich Osiander, 1814. (48), SNM,
I: Mö 6A/Kie.

26. Lenau, Nicolaus. *Gedichte.* Stuttgart und Tübingen: J.G. Cotta'scher Buchhandlung, 1832. (viii, 272), SNM, I: Mö 6A/Len. The handwritten
dedication on the front endpaper is to Mörike, and is probably in his
sister Clara's writing: "Eduardem zum Geburtstage."

27. Lichtenberg, Georg Christoph. *Vermischte Schriften*, Bd. 1–8 in 4 Doppelbänden, neue Original Ausgabe, hrsg. Chr. W. Lichtenberg. Göttingen:
Verlag der Dieterischen Buchhandlung, 1867. (Bd. 1–2, xxviii, 572)
(Bd. 3–4, iv, 616) (Bd. 5–6, iv, 868) (Bd. 7–8, viii, 688), SNM, I: Mö
6A/Lich. On the front endpaper of the first of these four double volumes
is the following dedication: "dem theuern Freunde Eduard Mörike / zum
Willkomm bei der Rückkehr / von Bebenhausen, 1. August 74 / W. Hemsen." This edition of Lichtenberg is one of at least two that were in Mörike's possession. The first edition was published in 1799. Ther is evidence
as late as June 1932 that Mörike also owned the 1817 edition at one
time which disappeared with the auction in 1932 (Vgl. H.W. Rath's
auction catalogue, "Mörike und der schwäbische Dichterkreis," in
SNM). According to Rath, the 1817 edition contained a notation by
Mörike dated "Köngen, 19. Sept. 1827." The 1867 edition contains
many signs of Mörike's reading. On page 28 and 29 of volume one he
wrote the following poignant comment: *Und eben jezt, den 5. August
1874, Abends 4½ Uhr steckte ich mir eine Zigarre an, um diese Blätter,
vielleicht zum fünftenmal in meinem Leben, und zum ersten mal in dieser
neu geschenkten Ausgabe mit neuer Lust zu lesen! M.* Complete notations folow this list in *Part B* under No. 27.

28. *Magikon. Archiv für Beobachtungen aus dem Gebiete der Geisterkunde und
des magnetischen und magischen Lebens, nebst andern Zugaben für
Freunde des Innern als Fortsetzung der 'Blätter aus Prevorst,'* hrsg. Dr.
Justinus Kerner, erster Jahrgang, drittes Heft. Stuttgart: Ebner und Seu-
bert, 1840. SNM, I: Mö 6A/Magi. On the front endpaper Mörike noted:
Eduard Mörike / Geschenk desgl. Herausgeber.

29 Mayer, Karl. *Gedichte*, zweite, sehr vermehrte Ausgabe. Stuttgart und Tübingen: Verlag der Cotta'schen Buchhandlung, 1839. (xiii, 465), SNM,
I: Mö 6A/May. On the front endpaper Mörike wrote: *Eduard Mörike /
Geschenk des Verf. / Schenkts seiner 1. Schwester Clara d. 21. Dez.
1871.* Mörike's many letters to Mayer and to others reveal his extensive
editiorial advice and help to Mayer. For one of Mörike's selections of his

favorite poems by Mayer based on this second edition and now contained in the mss folder "Abschriften fremder Werke" kept at SNM, see notations in *Part B* under No. 29.

30. Mayer, Karl. *Gedichte*, dritte, verbesserte und vermehrte Auflage. Stuttgart: Verlag der J.G. Cotta'schen Buchhandlung, 1864. (xxx, 556), SNM: 75.596. On the front endpaper is the following dedication: "Dem 1. Ed. Mörikschen Hause von K.M."

31. Moreto, Don Augustin. *Donna Diana. Lustspiel in drei Akten.* Stuttgart: Verlag der Expedition der Freya (Carl Hoffmann), 1868. (78), SNM, I: Mö 6A/Mor. The dedication on the front endpaper seems to be a playful attempt on Mörike's part to disguise his handwriting. He wrote: *Der lieben Clara zur freundlichen Erinnerung an Richard Larkens als Perin gedacht, Stuttgart d. 9. Spt. 1874.*

32. Mörike, Johann Christian Ludwig. *Zum Andenken Luthers: Aus Gelegenheit eines noch vorhandenen Familien-Bechers von dem Großen Manne. Ein Vermächtnis für meine Kinder.* Stuttgart: August Friedrich Macklot, 1802. (83), SNM, I: Mö 6A/Mör. This work is an attempt by the brother of Mörike's grandfather (1743−1820) to prove that Martin Luther was his ancestor. Some of the notes on the back endpaper are not by Mörike. The following biographical data is in Mörike's handwriting: *D. Luther war Student zu Erfurt anno 1502. Und Magister daselbst anno 1503. Professor zu Wittenberg anno 1504. Doctor Theol. daselbst anno 1512. Widersprecher des Papstischen Ablasses anno 1517, nach Worms gefordert anno 1521. Seine Lehre in der Augsburgischen Confession vorgetragen, dem Kaiser und Reich anno 1530. Er hatte das erste mal die Verdeutschung der Bibel drukken lassen anno 1534. Dieselbe auf das Neue zum Druk versorget anno 1541. Er ist begraben zu Wittenberg in der Schloß-Kirche, nachdem er zu Eisleben, anno 1546,d. 18. Febr. seines Alters im 63ten Jahre gestorben war.*

33. Mörike, Johann Christian Ludwig. *Meine Abstammung von Dr. Luther und sein Tischbecher, bekannt gemacht aus Veranlassung des dritten Reformations-Jubiläums. Ein Nachtrag zu meinen schon 1802 herausgegebenen Schriften* [including a genealogical chart]. Stuttgart: Verlag der J.D. Sattler'schen Buchhandlung, 1817, (29), Stadtarchiv. On the front endpaper Mörike wrote in red pencil: *Dr. Mörike.* Below this is a dedication by the author: "Dr. Hochwürden / Herrn Prälat, Oberhofprediger u. Oberconsist. Rath / von d'Antel / übergibts Ehrfurchtsvoll / der Verfasser."

34. Mörike, Karl Friedrich. *Philosophische Studien meines Sel. Vaters Dr. K. Mörike.* [1811], SNM, Heimatmuseum. The title to this manuscript as well as the following preface was added by Mörike: *Dieses Heft, so wie das beiliegende lateinische Manuscript (Systema Medicinae Fragment nebst der Abhandlung über Nervenfieber) soll von meinen Kindern als Probe des großnatürlichen Fleißes sorgfältig aufbewahrt werden – nachdem die übrige Masse seiner schriftlichen Privatarbeiten, wohl 10 mal so viel als hier erhalten ist, verloren gegangen. Stuttgart / d. 18. Nov. 1869.* Attached to this manuscript are other philosophical and medical writings by Mörike's father consisting of the following six parts:

(1) "Erfahrungen und Bemerkungen über das Nervenfieber (Typhus nervosus) und besonders über das ansteckende Nervenfieber (Typhus contagius)" (64). Below the title, possibly in Clara Mörike's writing is the following comment: "Zur Erinnerung an den lieben Vater Carl Mörike Dr. in Ludwigsburg."

(2) "Über den Verlauf des 1811. Jahrgangs in Rücksicht der in diesem Jahr im Ludwigsburger Amt epidemisch geherrschten Ruhrkrankheit" (88).

(3) "Bruchstück eines wissenschaftlichen Werkes" (30), SNM 2937.

(4) "Bruchstück verschiedener Arbeiten philosophischen und medizinischen Inhalts, meist in lateinischer Sprache" (554).

(5) "Bruchstück einer Arbeit über philosophische Fragen in lateinischer Sprache" (8).

(6) "Systema Medicinae Philosophicis Exstructum" (88).

35. Mörike, Eduard. "Mozart auf der Reise nach Prag," *Morgenblatt für gebildete Leser.* (40), (Nr. 30, 22, Juli 1855) (Nr. 31, 29. Juli 1855) (Nr. 32, 5. August 1855). SNM, Heimatmuseum. These copies of the journal in which Mörike first serialized his novella bear several corrections and changes by him and were later included in the book version. The four installments are also prefaced by mottos from Goethe, Horace, Shakespeare and Alexander Oulibicheff. For certain characterizations of Mozart to which Mörike is clearly indebted, see: Alexander Oulibicheff, *Nouvelle Biographie de Mozart suivie d'un apercu sur l'histoire générale de la musique et de l'analyse des principales oeuvres de Mozart.* Moscouw 1843. Translation into German by A. Schraishuon, 3 vols., Stuttgart, 1847.

36. *Mozins kleines, deutsch-französisches und französisch-deutsches Hand-Wörterbuch,* durchgesehen und verm. von C.G. Holder, Stuttgart und Augsburg: J.G. Cotta'scher Verlag, 1855. (768), SNM, I: 6A/Moz. On the front inside cover Mörike wrote: *Mörike. Stuttgart.* Additionally, Mörike penciled in many new entries in both sections of the dictionary. Complete notations follow this list in *Part B* under No. 36.

37. Müller, M.I.G. *Deliciae Hortenses. Blumen-Arzney-Kuechen-Baum-Gartens-lust.* Stuttgart: Johann Benedict Metzler, 1745. (496), SNM, I: Mö 6A/Mül. On the back cover Mörike affixed a lable with the incription: *Das Lieb u. schmackhaft Gartenbüchlein von Müllern.* On the inside front endpaper Mörike wrote: *In Pfarrgarten zu Cleversulzbach gehörig 1835.* On page 148, where a discussion of the planting and care of citrus-fruit trees begins, Mörike wrote into the margin: *April / 1855 für Mozart / gelesen.* This refers to Mörike's novella, "Mozart auf der Reise nach Prag," in which an orange tree and its fruit play an important part. Complete notations, including other bucolic delights such as Mörike's "Storchen-Kalender," follow this list in *Part B* under No. 37.

38. *Neue Rothenburgische Seelen-Harfe* (352), *und D. Joh. Ludwig Hartmanns sel. geistreiches Gebet-Büchlein* (24), *Episteln und Evangalia* (103). Rothenburg ob der Tauber: Georg Christian Holl, 1767/1768. SNM, 49. 770. On the front endpaper of this three-part work Mörike's sister Clara signed her first name. In the back, on the endpaper, Mörike wrote the first stanza of his poem "Gebet:" *Herr! schicke was Du willt, / Ein Liebes oder Leides! / Ich bin vergnügt, das beides / aus Deinen Händen quillt.*

39. Nordstern, Cornelius. *Digitus Dei. Oder die ernsthaffte und wunderbare Drau-Warnungs und Straff-Hand Gottes an Himmel, Luft, Wasser und Erden* . . . Nürnberg: Leonhard Loschge, 1682. (122), Stadtarchiv.

40. *Poetae Lyrici Graeci.* Recensuit Theodor Bergk. Leipzig und London: Reichenbach und Williams & Norgate: 1853. (109), Stadtarchiv. This anthology of Greek poetry, including the title page, the preface and the editorial notes, is written entirely in Latin. On the front endpaper Mörike wrote a dedication to his friend Julius Klaiber: *Ingenioso Poeta-rum Graecorum interpreti / Carissimo amico / Julio Klaiber / memori mente tradidit hunc thesaurum / Stuttg. m. Oct. MDCCCLXIV / Ed. Moerike.*

41. Sachs, Hans. *Etzlich schön lehrreiche / Dichtwerk von Hanns Sachs / Schu-stern und Meistergängern. / von Nuerenberg. / Enhaltend / Lehren von Tugend u. Laster. / Lust und Trauerspil. / Allerley weltlich History.* SNM, 48675. The ficticious title in parody of Hans Sachs was supplied by Mörike in decorative writing. The actual title of this fragmentary volume of the first edition of chronicles and historical poems by Sachs is missing. The title should read: Das Ander Buch. Sehr herrliche schöne, artliche und gebundene Gedicht, etc., Nürnberg: Christoff Heussler, 1560. Mörike further embellished the title page with several small figures and one large one sitting on a bagpipe. Under the bagpipe, again in

imitation of Sachs, Mörike wrote: *Ein großer gewülkähnlicher Dudel-sack so von selber spilt wann sich der schwer Genius drauf setzet.* Follo-wing the title page Mörike added a page on which he wrote the dedica-tory poem, *Zueignung an Herrn Doctor Albrecht* [sic] *Zellern.* Mörike's dedicatory poem alludes to the Hamlet-Chronicle poem, "Historia / Fengo ein fuerst in / Itlandt Erwuerget / sein Bruder Horwendillum," page CCIIff. This is Hans Sachs' version of the chronicle of "Amplet" (Hamlet), based on Saxo Grammaticus' work, *Gesta Danorum.* Mörike sent this work and the dedicatory poem as gifts to the psychiatrist Al-bert Zeller whom Mörike had consulted in connection with the psycho-logical action and motivation in his novel *Maler Nolten.* For full annota-tions and discussion see Chapter III and *Part B* following this list under No. 41.

42. Schmid, Johann Christoph. [two excerpts of] *Lebenserinnerungen des Hanss Ulrich Kraft.* The first printed excerpt consists of pages 651 through 744 along with two handwritten pages by Schmid. SNM 10432. A second 3-page handwritten excerpt (SNM 10433) contains the following reconstructed title by Mörike: *Hans Ulrich Kraft. Nach einer Handschrift dessen (vom 16. Jahrh.) worin er für s. Familie sein Leben beschrieben. Hier bearbeitet von Joh. Chr. v. Schmid, wirtemb. Prälaten, mit der spä-teren Revision von dessen eigener Hand.* Mörike also subsequenty added the following comment on the second excerpt: *Aus dem Nachlaß des Prälaten Joh. Christoph v. Schmid (Verf. des Schwäb. Wörterbuchs). Die Revision dieser Arbeit, zum Behuf eines Wieder-Abdrucks, der wie es scheint unterblieben ist v. seiner Hand. Ich erhielt die Blätter von seiner Tochter zum Geschenk. M.*

43. [Schummel, Johann Gottlieb.] *Spitzbart. Eine komi-tragische Geschichte für unser pädagogisches Jahrhundert.* Leipzig: Weygandschen Buchhand-lung, 1799. (425), SNM, I: Mö 6A/Schu. To this anonymously published work Mörike added the name of the author and a dedication on the front endpaper: *Johann Gottlieb Schimmel Professor zu Liegnitz. / Seinem verehrten Freunde Herrn Dr. Wilh. Hemsen / Dies nicht ganz unschmack-hafte Schinklein / zum Gruß von Ed. Mörike / Stuttgart 12. März 65.*

44. Secundus, Johannes. *Küsse,* aus dem Lateinischen übersetzt von Franz Passow. Leipzig: Gerhard Fleischer, 1807. (775), Stadtarchiv. On the front endpaper there is a dedication to Mörike: "dem theuren Freunde Eduard Mörike im Sommer 1872 / W.H." Below this is the following acknowledgement of receipt by the Mörike biographer Julius Klaiber: "Zum Andenken an Eduard Mörike (4. Juni 1875) von Gretchen und Clärchen Mörike / am 4. Juli 1875 in Untertürkheim erhalten / J. Klai-ber." On the back endpaper there are the following notations in Mörike's

writing: *Bas. V/VI. Majestas, – das Unendliche? Vielmehr: die unbe-schränkte Macht.* The context of "Basium VI" (in the German trans-lation: Sechster Kuß, p. 18–23), line 16 of the actual printed text in Latin, is: "Majestas domui convenit illa Jovis." This is translated by Passow: "Denn das Unendliche wohnt herrschend in Jupiters Haus." Apparently dissatisfied with the repeated occurrence of this translation, Mörike wrote above "das Unendliche" in the text: *die Allgewalt.*

45. Simrock, Karl. *Altdeutsches Lesebuch in neudeutscher Sprache, mit einer Übersicht der Literaturgeschichte.* Stuttgart und Tübingen: J.G. Cotta' scher Verlag, 1854. (viii, 531), SNM, I: Mö 6A/Sim. On the front end-paper Mörike signed his name: *Ed. Mörike.* Mörike also left numerous penciled-in changes, additions and corrections in this book. He also seemed to have "censored" several explicit passages of Hartmann von Aue's "Der arme Heinrich," by bracketing and changing the more erotic passages of the text. He used this anthology extensively while teaching literature to young women at the Katherinenstift in Stuttgart from 1851 to 1866. Complete notations follow this list in *Part B* under No. 45.

46. Storm, Theodor. *Sommer Geschichten und Lieder.* Berlin: Verlag von Alex-ander Duncker, 1851. Stadtarchiv. On the front endpaper in Mörike's writing: *Gretchen Mörike.*

47. Storm, Theodor. *Ein grünes Blatt. Zwei Sommergeschichten.* Berlin: Ver-lag von Heinrich Schindler, 1855. (72), SNM, I: Mö 6A/Sto. On the front endpaper there is a dedication by Storm to Gretchen Mörike: "Frau Gretchen Mörike vom Verf."

48. Storm, Theodor. *Gedichte,* zweite vermehrte Auflage. Berlin: Verlag von Heinrich Schindler, 1856. (vi, 190), SNM, I: Mö 6A/Sto. On the front endpaper Mörike wrote: *Gretchen Mörike.* On the back wrapping Mörike noted the page numbers of some of his favorite poems by Storm: *S. 3* [Abseits] / *S. 57* [Gote Nacht] / *S. 68 von Katzen.* Cf. Mörike's letter to Storm, May 26, 1853.

49. Storm, Theodor. *Auf der Universität.* Münster: Verlag der E.C. Brunn' schen Buchdruckerei, 1863. (128), Stadtarchiv. On the front endpaper there is the following printed dedication to Mörike: "Eduard Mörike / in alter Liebe und Verehrung / zugeeignet."

50. Storm, Theodor. *Zerstreute Kapitel.* Berlin: Verlag von Gebrüder Paetel, 1873. (188), SNM, I: Mö 6A/Sto. On the front endpaper Storm wrote the following dedication: "Seinem alten lieben Mörike / Husum, 12. Febr. 1873 / Th. Storm." The sole reading mark in the text is on page

90, where the penciled-in emphasis was probably made by Mörike next to the following passage from the story "Eine Halligfahrt:" "Auch die Natur, von welcher, gleich der Rose, sie nur ein Theil ist, vermag uns nichts zu geben, als was wir selber ihr entgegenbringen."

51. Strauß, David Friedrich. *Kleine Schriften, biographischen, literar- und kunstgeschichtlichen Inhalts.* Leipzig: F.A. Brockhaus, 1862. (x, 450), SNM, I: Mö 6A/Stra. On the back endpaper Mörike left the following notations: *S. 164 der Erlöser als Kind / 166f. Religiöse Malerei / "beispielsweise" richtiger Gebrauch dieses Worts S. 415 ob. unrichtig S. 272.* Page 164 refers to Strauß's Chapter VI (p. 122–184), entitled, "August Wilhelm Schlegel und Schlegels Abhandlung 'Über das Verhältnis der schönen Kunst zur Natur.'" In this connection Strauß observes about Schlegel: "Tiefer als in seiner literarischen finden wir Schlegel in seiner Kunstkritik von den Vorurtheilen der romantischen Schule befangen. Dahin rechnen wir nicht die schöne Äußerung: 'Ich sehe den Erlöser der Welt am liebsten als Kind. Das Geheimnis der Vermischung beider Naturen scheint mir in dem wunderbaren Geheimniß der Kindheit überhaupt am besten gelöst, die so grenzenlos in ihrem Wesen wie begrenzt ist.'" Possibly stimulated by this image, Mörike, in turn, achieved an almost perfect balance of divinity and nature in his poem "Schlafendes Jesukind" which was published that same year as Strauß's work.

52. Uhland, Ludwig. *Ludwig Uhland. Eine Gabe für Freunde zum 26. April, als Handschrift gedruckt.* Stuttgart: Buchdruckerei der J.G. Cotta'schen Buchhandlung, 1865. (479), SNM, I: Mö 6A/Uhl. On the front endpaper Mörike wrote: *Eduard Mörike / Geschenk der Frau Emilie Uhland.* In the back, on the inside cover, there are the following notations: *S. 103 Uhl an s. Mutter / 104 ihre Antwort / 115. 117 / S. 432 Humbold usw. / 338.* On page 219 there is the following printed editorial note: "Uhland hatte seine Antrittsrede an der Universität Tübingen lange verschoben . . . So war seine Antrittsrede — eine eigene Ironie des Zufalls — Uhlands letzte akademische Thätigkeit. Deshalb sagte er später: die obligate Musik dabei habe ihm 'abgeblasen'." To this note Mörike added the clarifying comment in the margin: *(Das Trauerblasen vom Stadtthurm).* This collection of letters from and to Uhland also contains the exchange between Jakob Grimm and Uhland in 1847 in which Mörike is being recommended for the Tiedge poetry prize for his "Idylle am Bodensee." Mörike made no changes in or additions to the text of these letters.

53. a. Vischer, Friedrich Theodor. *Aethetik oder Wissenschaft des Schönen.* Erster Theil: Die Metaphysik des Schönen. Reutlingen und Leipzig: Carl Mäckens Verlag, 1846. (viii, 489), SNM, I: Mö 6A/Visch. On the front endpaper Mörike signed: *Eduard Mörike.* There are numerous no-

tations and reading marks in the text, especially in connection with Vischer's discussion of the concept of catharsis. Complete notations follow this list in *Part B* under No. 53. a.

53. b. Vischer, Friedrich Theodor. *Aesthetik oder Wissenschaft des Schönen. Dritter Theil. Die Kunstlehre, zweiter Abschnitt, Die Künste.* Stuttgart: J.G. Cotta'scher Verlag, 1857. (xiii, 314), SNM, I: Mö 6A/Visch. On the front endpaper Mörike wrote: *Mörike / Geschenk des Verfassers.* The second part of the *Aesthetik* is missing from among the works in Mörike's possession. The pagination in vol. 1 concludes with page 489 and vol. 3 continues with p. 1160. There are several notations by Mörike in this vol. 3. Complete notations follow this list in *Part B* under No. 53. b.

54. Waiblinger, Wilhelm. *Gesammelte Werke, mit des Dichters Leben.* Bd. 2, 3, 5, 6, 8, 9 (in drei Doppelbänden), hrsg. H. v. Canitz, rechtmäßige Ausgabe letzter Hand. Hamburg: Heubel, 1839–40. (Bd. 2, 296) (Bd. 3, 261) (Bd. 5, 274) (Bd. 6, 276) (Bd. 8, 312) (Bd. 9, 280). In private possession of Frau Walter Hagen, Marbach. These three double volumes Mörike apparently gave to his wife-to-be, Gretchen. In the first volume he wrote: *Gretchen v. Speeth;* and in the third volume: *Gretchen Speeth.* There are many minor corrections and changes which are in part incorporated in the anthology of selected poems by Waiblinger which Mörike edited and published in 1844. Volume 9 of the *historisch-kritische Gesamtausgabe, Eduard Mörike: Werke und Briefe*, in progress, is intended to account for Mörike's revisions of Waiblinger's poems.

55. *Wuertembergisches Gesang-Buch.* Enthaltend / eine Sammlung / reiner und kraeftiger / Lieder / welche ein Herzogl. Synodus / zum Gebrauch der Gemeinden aus / dem heutigen Ueberfluß erlesen und / angewiesen. Stuttgart: Christoph Friedrich Cotta, 1779. (380), Stadtarchiv. On the back endpaper Mörike noted: *Das walt Gott / die Morgenröthe S. 257 / (tumm v. 2) / (was alls v. 3).* Because of Mörike's particular affinity for the mood of the early morning hour before sunrise in his poems, I reproduce here the context of the first three stanzas of this fifteen (!) stanza hymn from the section "Morgenlieder" (p. 254–260), to which his notes refer:

[1]

Das walt Gott, die morgenröthe
Treibet weg die schwarze nacht,
Und der tag rückt an die stätte,
Der da alles munter macht:
Drum so muntre ich mich auf,

Und mein herz gedenket drauf,
Wie ich dir, mein Gott! lobsinge,
Und dir dank und ehre bringe.

[2]

Loben doch bald mit dem morgen
Dich die kleinen vögelein;
Eh sie für das futter sorgen,
Muß es erst gesungen seyn:
Sollt ein tummes thierlein nun
Mir hierinn zuvor es thun?
Nein, das singen, loben beten,
Hab ich mehr, als sie vonnöthen.

[3]

Wann ich könnte übersehen,
Was alls für gefährlichkeit
Ich gehabt hab auszustehen
Meine ganze lebens-zeit;
Ja, was noch für ungelück
Alle stund und augenblick,
Und so lang ich werde leben,
Über meinem haupte schweben.

Part B: Additional Notations in Items No. 2, 3, 12, 27, 29,
36, 37, 40, 45, 53 a, and 53 b.

2. *Briefwechsel zwischen Schiller und Goethe.* 2 vols.

Mörike did careful editorial work in his two volumes of the *Goethe-Schiller Briefwechsel*, by correcting the wording, revising the dating and sequence of the letters, by adding explanatory notes and adding missing passages. Thus, Mörike created a definitive text for himself. As his notes indicate, he collated his two printed volumes with the original manuscripts at the publisher, Cotta in Stuttgart.

He may also have intended his changes and additions for a collaborative contribution to the philological work of the brothers Grimm and Michael Bernays on Goethe as he implies in an unpublished letter to Cotta, March 9, 1866. (See *Eduard Mörike. Gedenkausstellung, 1975. Katalog*, p. 402.) In the double volume I and II of *Goethes sämmtliche Werke*, Mörike intended his notations: *theilweise für die Brüder Grimm u. M. Bernays.* (see below, notations and discussion regarding item No. 12.) Apparently this collaboration did not get beyond the planning stages and Mörike's own prodigious note taking.

Unlike those on his other reading material, Mörike's corrections in the *Briefwechsel* are very clean and legible, as if his notes were to serve as additional correction sources for subsequent editions by Cotta. Most of those corrections can now be traces in the text and *Lesarten* of later editions. No attempt is made here, however, to ascertain systematically whether and in which later editions corrections were incorporated which correspond to Mörike's corrections and notes. Mörike's notations are discussed in greater detail in Chapter I in connection with his reading of Goethe.

In volume I, consisting of the letters written between 1794 and 1797, Mörike corrected as indicated:
P. 1, letter No. 1 (S. to G.) Jena, June 13, 1794:

Hier in Jena haben sich die H.H. Fichte, Woltmann und von Humboldt
zur Herausgabe dieser Zeitschrift* vereinigt . . .   *mit mir*

P. 3, Jeder Schriftsteller von Verdienst hat in der lesenden Welt seinen eigen-Kreis, und selbst der am meisten gelesene hat nur einen* Kreis in derselben. *größern

P. 7, letter No. 4 (S. to G.) Jena, Aug. 23, 1794:

Aber diese logische Richtung, welch der Geist * der Reflexion zu nehmen genöthigt ist, verträgt sich . . . *bei

P. 28, letter No. 24 (S. to G.) Jena, No. 16, 1794:

Herr v. Humboldt wird auf den nächsten Sonnabend seine Reise nach * Frankfurt antreten. *Erfurt

P. 45, letter No. 44. Apparently, letter No. 44 is part of letter No. 43 (G. to S.) Weimar, Jan. 27, 1795. Mörike crossed out No. 44 and added: *Ist nur Anhang zum Vorhergehenden.*
P. 58, letter No. 60. Here Mörike added: *steht im Original auf dem selben Blatt wie Nr. 58* [S. to G., Jena, March 19, 1795.] *und ist Postscript nach dem Eintreffen von Nr. 59* [G. to S., Weimar, March 19, 1795.] P. 77, letter No. 82 (G. to S.) Carlsbad, July 8, 1795:

Als berühmter Schriftsteller bin ich übrigens recht gut aufgenommen worden, * wobei es doch nicht an (wunderlichen Verwechslungen) gefehlt hat; z.B. sagte mir ein allerliebstes Weibchen: sie habe meine letzten Schriften mit dem grössten Vergnügen gelesen, besonders habe sie (der Ardinghello) über alle Massen interessirt. Sie können denken dass ich, mit der grössten Bescheidenheit, mich in Freund (Heinse's Mantel) einhüllte, und so meiner Gönnerin mich schon vertraulicher zu nähern wagen durfte. Und ich darf nicht fürchten, dass sie in diesen drei Wochen aus ihrem Irrthum gerissen wird.

Goethe hatte ursprünglich geschrieben: "wobei es doch nicht an Demüthigungen gefehlt hat." sodann: "besonders habe sie Giaffer der Barmecide über alle M." und weiter: "dass ich — mich in Klingers vollständige arabische Garderobe einhüllte." Bei der gegen das Ende der zwanziger Jahre unternommenen Redaction des Briefwechsels unterdrückte G. die ursprüngliche Lesart aus Schonung für seinen noch lebenden Landsmann und Jugendfreund Kl. der erst 1831 in St. Petersburg starb. — Heinse starb 1803.

Mörike's note on page 77 is written on a separate piece of paper and glued into the book. The parentheses in the excerpt are Mörike's. Because of the potential confusion of his own wording and commentary with that of the letters Mörike hit upon a practical solution: His own commentary he wrote in Latin handwriting and the Goethe − Schiller text he wrote in Sütterlinschrift.
P. 78, letter No. 84 (S. to G.) Jena, July 20, 1795:

> Der Ihrige hat mich sehr erfreut, und ich wünsche herzlich, dass Ihnen die *((Heinse))** sche Maske recht viele freundliche Abenteuer zuwenden möge. Ich halte es für gar nichts schlechtes, sich unter (einer solchen)** bei Damen wohl aufgenommen zu sehen, denn das schwierigste ist alsdann schon abgethan.
>
> **(Klinger')*   ***(einen solchen Namen)*

P. 109, letter No. 123 (G. to S.) Weimar, No. 21, 1795: This note by Mörike is also written on a separate piece of paper and glued into the book.

> *Nr. 123. Hier ist der unter Nr. 127 folgende Brief einzuordnen, dessen zweite Hälfte die gegenwärtige Nummer ausmacht. Der erste Theil brach mit den Worten ab − "was denken Sie wie es dem armen" −*
>
> *In einem im Besitz der Verlaghandlung befindlichen mit handschriftlichen Bemerkungen, wahrscheinlich von Dr. H. Hauff, versehenen Exemplar des Briefwechsels ist zu Nr. 123 bemerkt, auf dem betreffenden Blatte des Originalmanuscripts stünden noch vor dem Abgedruckten folgende Worte: "Roman gehen werde? Ich brauche die Zeit indessen wie ich kann, und es ist bei der Ebbe zu hoffen, daß die Fluth wiederkehren werde." Es ist klar, daß, nachdem G. so weit geschrieben hatte, der Brief Schillers vom 20. Nov. eintraf, der das Beileid des Freundes über den Tod des Goethe am 1. Nov. gebornen Knaben aussprach, daher G. nun fortfuhr: "Ich erhalte Ihren lieben Brief..."*

P. 114, letter No. 127 (G. to S.) Weimar, 1795: At the conclusion of this letter, ending with the words. "was denken Sie wie es dem armen," the editor had written "Unvollendet." This was crossed out by Mörike and substituted with the words: *Fortsetzung s. bei Nr. 123.*

P. 163, letter No. 180 (S. to G.) Jena, July 2, 1796:

> Ruhig und tief, klar und doch unbegreiflich wie die Natur, so wirkt es und so steht es da, und alles, auch das kleinste Nebenwerk, zeigt die schöne *
> *((Gleichheit))* des Gemüths, aus welchem alles geflossen ist.   *Klarheit*

P. 214, letter No. 216 (G. to S.) [no other date or place besides] 1796:

> *Nr. 215 Am Schlusse des Briefes war im Original noch beigefügt: "Auf Hero und Leander habe ich große Hoffnung: wenn mir nur der Schatz nicht wieder versinkt."*

P. 254, letter No. 254 (G. to S.) Weimar, Dec. 9, 1796:

> Der Wunsch Ihres Schwagers der anfangs abgelehnt worden war, kommt wieder und zwar durch den Herzog von Weimar * zur Sprache.
>   *Meiningen*

P. 257, letter No. 256 (G. to S.) Weimar, Dec. 10, 1796:

> Für das übersendete Exemplar zweiter Aufgabe * danke ich schönstens . . .
>   *Auflage*

On page 265, between letters No. 265 (G. to S.) Leipzig, Jan. 1, 1797 and letter No. 266 (G. to S.) Jan. 11, 1797, Mörike glued in two pages of commentary, in which he further fills in details about a literary feud between Schiller and Reichardt into which Goethe was also drawn:

> *Vor Nr. 265 ist ein noch ungedruckter Brief Goethes zu stellen, welcher den Handel zwischen Schiller und dem durch die in den Xenien erfahrenen Angriffe aufs äußerste erbitterten Componisten Reichardt betrifft. Letzterer hatte durch eine im zehnten Stück seines Journals "Deutschland" veröffentlichte "Erklärung des Herausgebers an das Publicum über die Xenien im Schillerschen Musenalmanach 1797" seine "herzliche Verachtung gegen Schillers nichtswürdiges und niedriges Betragen" ausgesprochen, und ihn als Herausgeber des Almanachs aufgefordert "den Urheber der Verleumdung anzugeben, oder falls er sich selbst dazu bekennt, seine*

Beschuldigung öffentlich zu beweisen. Kann er diess nicht, so ist er für ehrlos zu achten. Ehrlos ist jeder Lügner; zwiefach aber der feigherzige, der sich und die Beziehungen seiner Injurien nicht einmal ganz zu nennen wagt."

Schiller war durch diese maßlosen Invectien aufs höchste aufgeregt; er wollte eine "schnelle und entscheidende Replique," und sandte Goethe mit dem Brief Nr. 264 das Concept einer Gegenantwort zur Prüfung. Aus den Briefen 265, 267, 268, und 269 geht hervor, daß Goethe dem Freund abzukühlen und dessen in der ersten Aufregung vermutlich gereizt ausgefallene Erwiderung dadurch zu verhindern unternahm, daß er versprach selbst ein "Gegenmanifest" auszuarbeiten und den Gegner abzufertigen. Schiller ergab sich "mit Freuden" in den Rath des Freundes, und beruhigte sich, und wohl in Folge gemeinschaftlichen Einverständnisses wurde dann die Sache ganz fallen gelassen. Da im Briefwechsel nach dem Briefe vom 25. Dec., womit das Schreiben aus Leipzig vom 1. Jan. 1797 folgt, worin Goethe schon auf sein Versprechen der Abfassung einer Gegenerklärung Bezug nimmt, so mußte, weil zwischen dem 25. Dec. und dem 27sten, dem Tag der Abreise Goethes nach Leipzig, ein mündlicher Verkehr beider Freunde nicht stattgehabt, der Brief in welchem eben Goethe die Ausarbeitung eines Gegenmanifests versprochen hatte, d.h. das Schreiben, dessen Eingang Schiller in seinem Kalender unter dem 29 Dec. anmerkte, als verloren betrachtet werden. Dieser anscheinend zu Verlust gegangene Brief hat sich in dem der Cottaschen Verlagshandlung gehörigen Collationsexemplar der Schiller-Goetheschen Correspondenz abschriftlich vorgefunden.

Am Anfang desselben zeigt G. den Empfang der Sendung Schillers an, erklärt, er sei zur Zeit äußerst zerstreut und könne daher die Sache weder, wie sie es verdiene, überdenken, noch darüber etwas beschließen. Er wolle indeß seinem Freunde, der ja nichts übereilen möge, vorläufig seine ungefähre Meinung sagen. Sie beide dürften, da kein Termin sie zwinge, den Vortheil der reifsten Überlegung nicht leidenschaftlich aus der Hand geben. Diesselbe sei um so nöthiger, als die Sache prosaisch verhandelt werden sollte und das erste Wort von der größten Bedeutung sei. Die Prosa müßte so ästhetisch als möglich sein, "ein rednerischer, juridischer, sophistischer Spaß, der durch seine Freiheit und Übersicht der Sache wieder an die Xenien selbst erinnerte." Schiller Aufsatz sei "zu ernst und gutmüthig." Der Freund steige freiwillig auf einen Kampfplatz, der dem Gegner bequem sei; er contestire litem, und lasse sich ein, ohne von den so schon bei der Hand liegenden Exceptionen Gebrauch zu machen. Er (Göthe) sehe die Sach so an: ein ungenannter Herausgeber von zwei Journalen greife einen genannten Herausgeber eines Journals und eines Almanachs deßhalb an, weil er in einigen Gedichten verleumdet und als Mensch angegriffen wor-

den sei. Man müsse nun den Gegner aus seinem bequemen Halbincognito heraustreiben, und zuerst von ihm verlangen, daß er sich auf seinen Journalen nenne, damit man doch auch seinen Gegner kennen lerne. Dann müsse man von ihm verlangen, daß er die Gedichte wieder abdrucken lasse von denen die Rede sei. Diese beiden Präliminarfragen müßten erst erörtet sein, ehe man sich einlasse, sie incommodirten den Gegner aufs äußerste, und er möge sich benehmen, wie er wolle, es werde Zeit gewonnen; gelegentlich erschienen noch mehrere Gegner, denen man beiher etwas abgeben könne, das Publicum werde gleichgültig, und sie Beide seien in jedem Sinn im Vortheil. Er (Goethe) finde auf seiner Reise gewiß so viel Humor und Zeit um einen solchen Aufsatz zu versuchen, auch wolle er sich mit Freuden, die sich für sie interessirten, berathen pp.

P. 298, letter No. 304 (S. to G.) Jena, April 25, 1797:

Zwischen Nr. 301 und 304 ist ein noch ungedruckter Brief Goethes einzureihen, worin er an Schillers Ausführungen über Natur und Wesen des epischen Gedichts anknüpft und interessante Andeutungen giebt über das von ihm projektirte epische Gedicht "die Jagd." Sein neuer Stoff — schreibt er — habe keinen einzigen retardirenden Moment; es schreite alles von Anfang bis zu Ende in einer geraden Reihe fort; allein er habe die Eigenschaft daß große Anstalten gemacht werden, daß man viele Kräfte mit Verstand und Klugheit in Bewegung setze, daß aber die Entwicklung auf eine Weise geschehe, die den Anstalten ganz entgegen sei, und auf einem ganz unerwarteten, jedoch natürlichen Wege. Nun frage es sich ob man einen solchen Plan auch für einen epischen ausgeben könne, oder ob man ein derartiges Gedicht nicht zu einer subordinirten Classe historischer Gedichte rechnen müsse.

In volume II, consisting of the letters written between 1798 and 1805, Mörike corrected as indicated:

P. 44, letter No. 431 (G. to S.) [no place designation, probably written between the 14. and the 18. of February, 1798:]

Ich bitte Sie um gefälligen Beistand, durch Einstimmung und Opposition: die letzte ist mir immer nöthig, niemals aber mehr als wenn Ich * das Feld der Philosophie übergehe, weil ich mich darin immer mit Tasten behelfen muss.   *in

P. 101, letter No. 484 (S. to G.) Jena, July 11, 1798:

((*Geist*)) * schickte mir so eben ein mächtig grosses Gedicht aus Desden, das mir halb so gross noch einmal so lieb wäre. **Gries*

P. 154, letter No. 545 (G. to S.) Jena, No. 16, 1798: On a separate piece of paper glued into the book, Mörike had written the following:

> *Nach Nr. 545 fehlt ein zur Zeit nur in dem Manuscr. vorhandenes Schreiben Goethes vom 24. Nov. 1798 worin er sagt, er werde da der viele Schnee ihn nicht zum besten tractire, zu hause bleiben, bis ihn der "Lodersche Wagen zum Feenpalast der Literatur" hinführe; zugleich bittet er den Freund, ihm "die Geschichte der Attande" zu schicken da 'so eine hypothetische Lectüre' nach Tische nicht übel sei. Nr. 546 ist Schillers Antwort darauf.*

P. 170, letter No. 562 (G. to S.) Weimar, Dec. 25, 1798:

> Viel Glück zu der abgenöthigten Vollendung der Arbeit.

At the conclusion of this letter, Mörike wrote: *Hieher das eingelegte Schreiben.* On a separate piece of paper, which is glued into the book, Mörike reproduced the following letter by Goethe:

> *Überbringer dieses stellt ein Detachement Husaren vor, das Order hat, sich der Piccolominis, Vater und Sohn, wie es gehen will, zu bemächtigen, und wenn es derselben nicht ganz habhaft werden kann, sie wenigstens stückweise einzuliefern. Euer Lieb' [illegible] werden ersucht, diesem löblichen Vorhaben allem möglichen Vorschub zu thun.*

> *Die wir uns zu allen angenehmen Gegendiensten erbieten, – Melpomenische zum Wallensteinschen Unwesen gnädigst verordnete Kommission.*

> *Weimar den 27. Dec. 1798   Goethe und Kirms.*

P. 282, letter No. 726 (G. to S.) Oberrossla, March 6, 1800:

> Von Ihrer neuesten Arbeit * hoffe ich sehr viel Gutes.
>
> **(Jungfrau v. Orleans)*

P. 346, letter No. 821 (S. to G.) Weimar, June 28, 1801:

> Für Cotta habe ich indess doch eine Ballade, "Leander und Hero," wirklich zu Stande gebracht, nebst noch einigen kleinern Gedichten, was ich Ihnen bei Ihrer Zurückkunft vorzutragen hoffe. Das Schauspiel * fängt an sich zu organisieren, und in acht Tagen denke ich an die Ausführung zu gehen.
>
> *Braut v. Messina*

p. 382, letter No. 862 (G. to S.) Jena, June 8, 1802:

> Die Gelegenheit der abgehenden Boten kann ich nicht versäumen und melde mit wenig Worten dass meine Arbeit gut von statten geht. * Ich habe . . .
>
> *Hier herein gehört das Billet Nr. 914*

P. 404, letter No. 896 (G. to S.) Weimar, March 22, 1903. The following represents the entire text of the letter:

> Hierbei das gerettete Venedig. Wenn Sie Zeit haben, so sehen Sie es durch und wir sprechen heute Abend davon. Mich verlangt sehr Sie zu sehen. Die verwünschte Acclamation neulich hat mir ein paar böse Tage gemacht.*
>
> * s[iehe] *Nr. 909*

P. 412, letter No. 909 (S. to G.) [no date and place.] The following represents the entire text of the letter:

> Cotta wollte Ihnen um zwölf Uhr aufwarten. Wenn Sie aber um diese Zeit spazieren fahren wollen, so können Sie ihm eine Zeit bestimmen, oder er wird Ihnen nach Tische aufwarten. Er bleibt bis zum Abend. Wegen des Bewussten habe ich ihn vorbereitet.
>
> *(Vom 26. Apr. – Gehört nach Nr. 896)*

P. 413, letter No. 912 (S. to G.) [no date and place] :

> Es kommen mir heute so viele dringende Briefexpeditionen zusammen, dass ich vor neun Uhr nicht fertig werden und also nicht kommen kann . . . *(Dies Billet ist vom 12. Sept. und wäre nach Nr. 915 einzureihen.)*

P. 414, letter No. 914 (S. to G.) [no date and place.] The following represents the conclusion of the letter:

Weil wir jetzt drei Schauspieler mehr haben, so rieth' ich die drei mitspre-
chenden Statisten, nämlich den Croat, den Schwitzer und den zweiten
Cuirassier, mit unsern drei neuen Schauspielern zu besetzen so kann das
Stück durchaus frisch weggespielt werden.

In der Komödie sehe ich Sie heute wohl?

*(Für diesen Brief ist das Datum des 22sten Mai 1802 ermittelt worden, wo
Nathan gegeben wurde.)*

This concludes Mörike's notes on the letters. In addition, on the back
endpaper of Volume II, there are the following notations by Mörike:
He is particularly interested in Goethe's views on the nature of
poetry and the unconscious element of the creative process:

*Über das Wesen der Poesie S. 282 folg. Göthe. Über das Bewußtlose der
künstlerischen Production S. 338. Eleg. u. Idyll Goethes S. 365 No. 170.
"Der Sammler" S. 208. Bemerkg. bei der Bilder Ausstellg. S. 251.*

The most important reference here in connection with our knowledge of Mörike is the reference to artistic production. P. 282 refers
to a letter (G. to S.) Oberoßla, March 6, 1800, [related April 3,
1801, in *Goethes Briefe*, vol 2. ed. Karl R. Mandelkow. Hamburg:
Christian Wegner. 1962–67.] in which Goethe discusses what at the
conclusion of the letter he refers to as his "Glaubensbekenntniß".
The entire letter deals with the process of artistic creativity which
interested Mörike intensely throughout his life. The following
represent the opening lines of the third paragraph of Goethe's
letter:

Was die Frage betrifft die Ihr letzter Brief enthält, bin ich nicht allein
Ihrer Meinung, sondern ich gehe noch weiter. Ich glaube, daß alles was das
Genie als Genie thut, unbewußt geschehe.

3. Conversations-Lexikon. 12 vols.

Vol. I (1833), p. 300, Mörike corrected the following entry:

Antigone, Tochter des Königs Ödipus (s.d.) von Theben und seiner Tochter * Jokaste . . .   *Mutter

Vol. I, p. 746, Mörike furthermore added as follows to the entry: "Beireis, Gottfr. Christoph (1730—1809)," *Vgl. Göthes Tag u. Jahreshefte.* The entry records some of the legends surrounding the eccentric Beireis. Beireis claimed to have been in possession of a 6400 Carat diamond, and he supposedly had a secret recipe for vinegar, for which he would demand large sums of money from those who would acquire the rights of production. This figure seems to have been Mörike's model for his own creation of the vinegar-maker, Präzeptor Ziborius in his dramatic poem, "Häusliche Szene."

Vol. II (1833), p. 669, Mörike heavily underlined two pages of description under the entry: "Cid." He seemed particularly interested in the sentence: "Aus diesen Romanzen "Poema del Cid el Campeador" (und wahrscheinlich aus der Sammlung des Escobar) hat Herder seinen 'Cid' (Tübingen, 1806) 70 übersetzt."

Vol. III (1833), p. 302, Mörike corrected a couplet by Schiller, which was erroneously cited. It was listed under the entry: „Distichon:"

Im Hexameter steigt des Springquells *((silberne))* * Säule
Im Pentameter drauf fällt sie melodisch herab.   *flüssige*

Vol. IV (1834), p. 415, Mörike added to the entry, Friedrich Wilhelm III, *gest. 1840.*

On page 518, for the entry, "Gassner, Johann Joseph (1727—1799)," the controversial catholic priest-healer, who practiced exorcisms on a large scale in Germany, there is a note in what seems to be Mörike's wife's handwriting: "Ist authentische Unwahrheit!" Also on page 577, under the entry, Gelübe, she added: "ja, ja der aufgeklärte Gottesverehrer!" Also on page 769 under the entry, "Golgatha," she added: "welch rühmlicher Glaube!" In this connection it has to be remembered that Margarete Mörike was a staunch, polemical Catholic. Here she takes issue with the commentary by the editors of the encyclopedia, whom she must have considered too protestant or secular for her own taste.

On page 691, Mörike supplies an entirely new entry: *Geuling (Arnold) s. Occasionalismus.*

Vol. V (1834), p. 14, Mörike added to the entry, Hahn (Phil Math.)* mechanisches Genie und Pfarrer . . .   *Siehe Uhr.*

Vol. V, p. 151, under the entry, "Hegel," Magarete Mörike added another comment. The dicussion of Hegel and the short sketch of his ideas concludes with the statement: "Hegels System zu prüfen, ist hier nicht der Ort" To this Margarete Mörike had added: "und der Mann dazu schon gar nicht!"

Vol. V, p. 369, under the entry, "Hölderlin (Friedr.)," Mörike added as follows:

> . . . ein durch sein unglückliches Schicksal wie durch die großartige Erscheinung seines ursprünglichen Talents merkwürdiger Dichter, wurde * zu Neislingen im Würtembergischen, nach Anderen zu Lauffen geboren. Nachdem er in Tübingen seine theologischen Berufsstudien . . . vollendet hatte begab er sich nach Frankfurt am Main, wo er Hauslehrer wurde. Hier fesselte ihn eine höchst unglückliche Neigung zu der Mutter seiner Zöglinge ** einer Frau von schwärmerischer Phantasieglut . . .
>
> *d. 20. März,   **Gattin des Kaufmanns Jac. Fried.*
> *Gontard, Susette, geb. Borkenstein aus Hamburg*

Vol. VI (1835), p. 50, under the the entry, "Kant, Immanuel," Mörike corrected several misspellings in a summary of a review of Kant's philosophy by Reichardt, which first appeared in the almanac *Urania*, 1812.

Vol. VI, p. 403, under the entry, "Kupferstechkunst," Mörike added the name, *Joh. Fried. Rause.*

Vol. VI, on the back endpaper, Mörike noted the names: *Langendijk and Lemnius.* Langendijk, Pieter (1683–1756), is described in the encyclopedia as the "einzige wahrhaft komische Dichter Hollands." Lemnius, Simon (1510–1550), is described as an "Epigrammatist und beißender Satiriker," who attacked his contemporary Martin

Luther in many satirical tracts. Mörike's notations of these two names is one more indication of his fondness for satire and humor in literature.

Vol. VIII (1835), p. 29, under the entry, "Magie," Mörike corrected as follows: . . . das ((Versprechen)) des Blutes *das Besprechen

Vol. VI, p. 321, under the entry, "Metaphysik," Mörike added as follows: "Den griechischen Namen soll diese Wissenschaft zufällig erhalten haben; gewiß ist es aber, daß Aristoteles in den Büchern, welche später die Überschrift erhielten, aus welcher durch Zusammenziehung dieser Namen entstanden ist * auch diejenigen Gegenstände behandelt . . ." *μετὰ τὰ φυσικά'* sofern dieser Theil der Philosophie des Arist. seine Stelle nach seiner Physik zufällig erhielt.

Vol. VII, p. 888, under the entry, "Nordische Mythologie," Mörike underlined several pages of information, and he corrected and added as follows: "Dieser [Bor] nahm zum Weibe Belsta*, Tochter des Riesen Bergthrir, und hatte zum Sohne Odin, Wili und We."** *Bestla, **Nach andrer Angabe. Odin, Honir u. Loki. On page 890, Mörike adds in this connection: Die Wanen sind eigenes Göttergeschlecht welchem Niordr mit seinen Kindern Freyr und Freya angehört.

Vol. VIII (1835), p. 324, under the entry, "Paskewitch, Fürst von Warschau," Mörike added: gest. 1855.

Vol. VIII, p. 630, under the entry, "Pluto," Mörike corrected as follows: ". . . eigentlich bloß ein Beiname Hades . . . war des Kronos oder Uranus* und der Rhea . . ." *Saturnus. On the back endpaper of vol. VIII, Mörike noted: Poularden. On the back endpaper of vol. IX, Mörike noted: A.W. Schlegel.

Vol. X (1836), p. 574, under the entry, "Stuttgart," Mörike bracketed the following description of the castle Solitude and commented as follows: (". . . der prächtige Lorbeer- und Concertsaal, der neue Marstall, das ansehnliche Gebäude der von hier verlegten Militärakademie, das Opernhaus, der Lustgarten, die Thiergärten das chinesische Gebäude, der Orangeriegarten und die Plantagen . . .") diese existieren längst nicht mehr.

Vol. XI (1836), p. 233, under the entry, "Thränen," Mörike added to the following passage about the elimination of tears:

"Wird aber ihr Übergang aus dem Auge in die Nase zerstört und verhindert, z.B. durch Verstopfung oder Verwachsen des Thränenkanals etc. . . . eine Operation nöthig macht, durch welche ein neuer künstlicher Kanal gebildet wird, damit die Thränen in die Nase gelangen können."* *Meine Thränle gehen net weg! Marie. taeglich. 1860.

Vol. XII (1837), p. 30, under the entry, "Waiblinger, Wilhelm," Mörike added the following to the list of Waiblinger's publications: die "Blüthen der Muse aus Rom" (Berl. 1829).

Vol. XII, p. 42 and 43, a great deal of the information under the entry, "Walhalla," Mörike underlined.

Mörike's final notation in this twelve volume encyclopedia, in vol. XII, is the correction of the birthdate of Friedrich, Crown Prince of Württemberg, from, "24. Aug. 1823" to: 4. März 1823.

12. *Goethes Sämmtliche Werke.* 40 vols.

In the table of contents of the double volume I–II Mörike crossed almost half of all the represented poems. Below the word "Inhalt," p. IV, he had written: *Auswahl zur Anthol.* Next to the printed category "Antiker Form sich nähernd" he had written *davon etwa 30*. At the end of the six pages, p. VIII, of the table of contents, he wrote: *folglich zu viel*. Mörike had apparently planned to edit a small anthology of Goethe's poems and had abandoned the project after selecting too many "must" poems for the inclusion into the anthology.

No other edition by any author occupied Mörike more than this Goethe edition. His numerous marginalia are concerned with several areas. First he noted all those ideas or concepts which he found interesting under the category *interessante Stellen*. Secondly he noted matters of style, diction, grammar and prosody under various headings. Thirdly he was apparently accumulating what he considered to be Goethe's contributions to the German language. These would include newly coined words and Goethe's idiosyncratic use of language. Mörike had apparently planned to submit his findings to Jakob Grimm's etymological *Wörterbuch*, for which work had begun in the 1840's. The heading Mörike used for this philological bracket was *Grimm*. One further category within the marginalia is Mörike's critical commentary. Though small in number these short interpretive comments are – besides occasional comments in letters – our only concrete source of Mörike's views of Goethe's works.

On page 63, vol. I, in the poem "Vom Berge," line 4, Mörike noted as follows:

Fänd' ich hier und fänd' ich dort mein Glück?
alte Lesart: War', was war mein Glück?

On page 67, vol. I, in the poem "Herbstgefühl," line 6, Mörike noted as follows:

Schneller und glänzend voller! *alte Lesart: glänzet voller*

On page 80, vol. I is Goethe's later version of "An den Mond," which begins, "Füllest wieder Busch und Thal." Here Mörike glued in a slip of paper, on which he wrote Goethe's earlier version of "An den Mond" in its entirety. This version begins, "Füllest wieder's liebe Thal." Under the title Mörike noted: *(Aus Goethes Briefen an Frau von Stein. Band I, S. 155. Januar 1778.)* Mörike's handwritten copy of the poem contains two slight variations from the text as it is represented in the Hamburg (1964) edition. Line 15 Mörike reproduces as follows: *Bei des Frühlings Lebenspracht.* In the Hamburg edition this line is rendered: "Und bei Frühlingslebens Pracht." In line 21 Mörike has a singular form: *Was dem Menschen unbewußt*; the Hamburg edition has the plural variation: "Was den Menschen unbewusst." In the Weimar edition of 1887, vol. I, p. 393, edited by Gustav von Loeper et al., Mörike's version of the poem with the two variations is listed as "Einzelhandschrift g, Beilage des Briefes vom 19. Febr. 1778 an Frau von Stein."

On page 141, vol. I, in the poem "Ballade vom vertriebenen und zurückkehrenden Grafen," in the seventh stanza Mörike added as follows:

Der Alte wandelt nun hier und bald dort, ? *der Alte nun wandelt bald hier*

On page 151, vol. I, in reference to the printed poem, "Der König in Thule," Mörike glued in a slip of paper, on which he wrote the following note:

In der 2ten Sammlung "Volks- und andere Lieder p." Musick von Siegmund v. Seckendorff; Dessau 1782 steht "Der König von Thule aus Goethes D. Faust" – und lautet die erste Strophe:

"Es war ein König in Thule,
Ein goldenen Becher er hätt'
Empfangen von seiner Buhle
Auf ihrem Todesbett."

On page 255, vol. I, beside the printed title "Euphrosyne," Mörike noted: *1797 Christiane Neumann.*

On page 117, vol. II, beside the printed title "Erklärung eines alten Holzschnittes / vorstellend / Hans Sachsens poetische Sendung," Mörike noted: *1774 (nicht 76)*.

On page 166, vol. II, beside the title "Der Wandrer," Mörike added: *1772.*

On page 218, vol. II, in connection with Goethe's poems entitled "Drei Palinodien," Mörike glued in a slip of paper with the following handwritten note:

> *Im Katalog der Berliner Goetheausstellung von 1861 ist zu diesem Gedicht (No. 33 der Handschriften) bemerkt: Eigenhändig datirt W. d. 3. Nov. 1813. – Voran steht von Goethes Hand eine "Fabel" von Haug: "Der Irisbogen rief verwegen" (aus dem Morgenblatt 1813 No. 270). Das hierauf folgende Goethesche, in den Werken als "Palinodie" (No. 3) bezeichnete Gedicht hat hier die Überschrift: "Gegenfabel." – Auch die vorhergehende Palinodie (No. 2) "Geist und Schönheit im Streit" scheint sich auf Haug zu beziehen, wenigstens verweist Musculus unter dem Worte "Haug" auf das Gedicht und den darin vorkommenden "Herr Hauch" –*

On the back endpaper of double volume I and II are many notes and abbreviations apparently written at various times in both ink and pencil. These notes refer back to the texts with titles, words and page number. Line numbers were not used in any of the twenty double volumes. Mörike gave all of these notes a general heading: *Kritische Bemerkungen eines müßigen Grammatikers, theilweise für die Brüder Grimm u. M. Bernays.* Specific headings given by Mörike are: *Sprachlizenzen, Druckfehler, Eigenheiten, u. dgl.* and *Prosodie.* Under *Prosodie* Mörike lists the following:

> *Bd. 1 S. 292 No. 96 uns eině Fl.*
> *271 Z. z. Antwŏrt*
> *311 No. 61 Kunstwěrk*
> *313 No. 81, 82 Vorthěil*
> *308 No. 30 Es versengt*
> *263 N. 7 von unt. Freundschäft*
> *264 N. 4 von ob. Dăs*
> *277, 9. Sĭe begraben*
> *278, 13 – vielfăchen*
> *279, 20 überăll*
> *280, 24 samt*

```
291, 92 – Wintĕr
291, 96 – ĕinĕ
246 unt. Zu bereiten
226, oben Sie erscheinet
```

Mörike's reference all accurately refer to a given line or word. Thus, for example, his reference Bd. 1, 311 No. 61 Kunstwerk, refers to the 61. distich of the poem "Vier Jahrszeiten" on page 311 of volume I, where Mörike finds the particular stress on the second syllable of the word "Kunstwerk" worth recording:

> Fortzupflanzen die Welt sind alle vernüft'gen Discurse
> Unvermögend; durch sie kommt auch kein Kunstwerk hervor.

Under the category *Sprachlizenzen,* Mörike lists the following: *Wandrers Nachtl* [ied]: *Beispiel Goethescher grata negligentia: "Alles Leid u. Schmerzen." "Was soll all der Schmerz u. Lust." Von Matthisson in der Anthol*[ogie] *corrig* [iert]. *Ein Gleiches S. 57 "Lag im Mondenschein" pp Bd. I, 63 "So gold du bist."* This latter reference is to Goethe's poem "Auf dem See," line 11, "Weg, du Traum! so gold du bist:"

Under the category *Eigenheiten* Mörike lists three instances: *Bd. 2, 324 geklirrlos.* This word refers to Goethe's translation from *Manfred* by Byron. The following are the pertinent lines (67–70) of the poem:

> Bannfluch
>
> Schau! der Zauber wirkt umher dir,
> Dich geklirrlos fesselt Kette;
> Ueber Herz und Hirn zusammen
> Ist der Spruch ergangen – schwinde!

The second instance of what Mörike considered Goethe's *Eigenheiten* is: *338 unt. glimmern.* This occurs in Goethe's poem "Neugriechische Liebe – Skolien", in the fourth stanza:

> Seh' ich doch das Lämpchen schon
> Aus der Hütte schimmern,

Lass um deinen Wegenthron
Alle Sterne glimmern.

The third instance of Goethe's *Eigenheiten* is listed by Mörike as: *2, 344 unt.* *"ermudigt."* This word occurs in Goethe's poem "Hochländisch."

In the second double volume 3 and 4, on page 151, Mörike wrote the following note under the title, "Maximen und Reflexionen / in sieben Abtheilungen." *Hiezu vergleiche man.* *"Goethes Sprüche in Prosa" zum erstenmal erläutert u. auf ihre Quellen zurückgeführt von G. v. Löper. Berlin 1870."* Several maxims are crossed-heavily, such as the following:

Wie kann man sich selbst kennen lernen? Durch
Betrachten niemals, wohl aber durch Handeln.
Versuche deine Pflicht zu thun und du weißt
gleich was an dir ist.

On page 159 Mörike noted: cf. Lichtenberg under the following reflection by Goethe:

Der Aberglaube gehört zum Wesen des Menschen und flüchtet sich, wenn man ihn ganz und gar zu verdrängen denkt, in die wunderlichsten Ecken und Winkel, von wo er auf einmal, wenn er einigermassen sicher zu seyn glaubt, wieder hervortritt.

On page 162 Mörike added as indicated: "Ein in natürlicher Wahrheit und Großheit, obgleich wild und unbehaglich ausgebildetes* Talent ist Lord Byron, und deßwegen kaum ein anderes ihm vergleichbar.

vielmehr durch grenzenlose Eitelkeit verschrobenes

On page 220 Mörike added the following commentary: *Diese 9 genau zusammenhängenden Sätze nahm Goethe aus einer latein. Übersetzung der Enneaden des Plotinus. s. "Goethes Sprüche in Prosa, erläutert pp von G. v. Löper" Nr. 678—686.* Mörike is here referring to nine maxims, which he crossed, starting on page 220 with "Da wir überzeugt sind, dass derjenige, der . . ." and concluding on page 222 with "aus welchem die Natur bestehet und wonach sie

174

handelt." In an earlier handwriting Mörike wrote on the back end-paper of this volume: *Bd. 3, 220 "Da wir überzeugt sind" bis 220 – schön wie aus einem platonischen Dialog.*

At the end of the seventh maxim on page 221 there are further marginalia by Mörike. The context is: "Denn nicht die Urmusik macht den Musiker, sondern die Musik, und die übersinnliche Musik bringt die Musik im sinnlichen Ton hervor." *Unmusik, wie G. richtig schrieb im Latein. immusica im Original* ἀμουσία. *Der Satz "Nicht die Urmusik sondern die Musik macht den Musiker" würde dagegen die Ansicht Goethes ausdrücken, der hier indessen das Wort nicht führt.*

On the back endpaper of this double vol. III and IV Mörike continued his collection of Goethe's noteworthy idiosyncracies in prosody, diction and usage. Noteworthy ideas are always listed separately. There is only one reference here to one of Goethe's "ideas." *Bd. 3 S. 173 "Alles Lyrische."* This refers to Goethe's maxim, "Alles Lyrische muss im Ganzen sehr vernünftig, im Einzelnen ein bisschen unvernünftig seyn." Under the headings *Gr*[imm] and *Sprache* Mörike listed: *4, 213 unt. "ob nur gleich."* This refers to Goethe's "Noten und Abhandlungen zu besserem Verständnis des West-östlichen Divans." In these notes the following sentence occurs: "Unsere heiligen Bücher liegen auch dort, ob nur gleich legendenweis, zum Grund."

In vol. V of the double volume V and VI Mörike crossed and underlined many lines of "Hermann und Dorothea," "Achilleis" and "Reineke Fuchs." There is, however, only one short comment in the text itself: On page 193 of "Reineke Fuchs," "Sechster Gesang," Mörike adds scanning marks to the following line:

Mir beim Bischŏf, Hĕrrn Ohnegrund wērdĕn, zürnte nicht etwa

Under this line Mörike wrote: *(defect.)*

On the back endpaper of double volume V and VI there are several critical comments in reference to the texts. In connection with "Hermann und Dorothea" Mörike noted: *S. 38 "Daß dir werde die Nacht" p. – ob im Munde der Mutter zulässig?* This refers to the following lines in the "Euterpe; Mutter und Sohn" section of "Hermann und Dorothea:"

Da antwortete drauf die gute Mutter verständig:
Sohn, mehr wünschest du nicht die Braut in die Kammer zu führen
Daß dir werde die Nacht zur schönen Hälfte des Lebens,

In a second reference to "Hermann und Dorothea" Mörike wrote: *Nicht ganz angemessene Sprache in "Hermann und Dorothea" S. 68 "Laß mich reden mein Kind." Die thätige Mutter belebt im Ganzen d[ie] W[irtschaft].* This refers to the "Erato; Dorothea" section of "Hermann und Dorothea."

On the back endpaper there are three further comments referring to "Hermann und Dorothea" under the heading *Gr*[imm] : *5 Bd. S. 82 Im Trübsal die Hoffnung.*" This refers to the line: "Diesem stärkt es zu künftigem Heil im Trübsal die Hoffnung." The second reference is: *5 Bd. 61 unt. Weibe der Jugend.* This refers to the following context:

Heil dir, junger Mann! Dein treues Auge, dein treues
Herz hat richtig gewählt! Glück dir und dem Weibe der Jugend!

In connection with "Achilleis" Mörike noted: *Bd. 5 Achilleis unhomerische Züge S. 99 unt: "Und muß davon der Zither —* This refers to the following lines of the text:

Doch was kümmert es mich! Wer Waffen schmiedet, bereitet
Krieg und muss davon der Zither Klang nicht erwarten.

Mörike lists three further examples under *Unhomerisch: S. 100 Reizend ermattet pp Ibid. So gleitet er herrlich pp Ibid mit dem Ernste des ersten pp.* This refers to fourteen lines in "Achilleis" beginning with "Reizend ermattet, als hätte die Nacht . . ." concluding with:

Nur zu Kronion trat Ganymed, mit dem Ernste des ersten Jünglingsblickes
im kindlichen Auge, und es freute der Gott sich.

S. 101 ihn o̅ sprechen. This refers to the line: "Ja, ich mag ihn nicht sehn, nicht sprechen."

S. 107 mit Adel. This refers to the line: "Aber Ares versetzte darauf mit Adel und Ehrfurcht:"

176

The following is written separately from the category *"unhome-risch." S. 110 schrecklich blicket pp (An sich sehr schön).* This note refers to the line: "Schrecklich blicket ein Gott da wo Sterbliche weinen," of "Achilleis."

In another separate comment Mörike noted: *Homers ganz würdig: 105 Und stand wie ein Berg* — This refers to the lines:

> ... da riss die göttliche Here
> Schnell vom Sitz sich auf und stand, wie ein Berg in dem Meere steht.

In three further comments referrring to "Achilleis" Mörike notes unusual usage under the heading *Gr*[imm] :

S. 117 unt. Ungramm. Verflechtet. This refers to the lines:

> Und so freut es ihn auch, den holden Sänger zu denken,
> Der des Gesanges Kranz mit seinem Namen verflechtet;

S. 116 herrlich gr. Loos. This refers to the line: "Aber keinem steht ein herrlicher grösseres Loos vor."

Bd. 5 180 "Da erblickt' ich — sich schleichen" ungramm. This refers to lines in "Achilleis vierter Gesang:"

> Da erblickt' ich den Vater aus einer Ritze sich schleichen,
> Zwischen den Steinen kam er hervor und stieg aus der Tiefe.

There is only one comment in the text of volume VI and no notes on the back endpaper. Volume VI contains "Alles an Personen und zu festlichen Gelegenheiten Gedichtete enthaltend." On page 150 in the section "Pilgernde Könige" under the footnote 50: "Im Wandersinne zu einem alten Manuscript der heiligen drei Könige-Legende" Mörike added: *in der Bearbeitung von G. Schwab.*

In the text of volume VII of the double volume VII and VIII Mörike added a correction to the direction of the play *Die Mitschuldigen.* On page 105 Mörike put parentheses around "Sophie erstaunt." He then added: *Alcest fährt fort.*

On page 223 of volume VII in "Götter, Helden und Wieland" Mörike corrects Euripedes' speech: "Du fühlst nichts, da du in den ((Gasthof)) Admeteus trittst? *gastoffenen Hof.* The only comment on the back endpaper is in connection with this correction on page 223: *Bd. 7. S. 223 statt Gasthof — gastoffener Hof, Schlimmbesserung von Seiten eines Revisors.*

There are only two notations on the back Endpaper in which Mörike refers to volume VIII: *Bd. 8 S. 56* z[weiter] *T*[eil] *v*[on] *u*[nten.] *"Wirst Du, was wirst Du gewinnen? cf. "Aus meinem Leben: Bd. 22 S. 355: "War', was war' mein Glück."* The reference to vol. VII is to the following lines in the play "Claudine von Villa Bella" in which Claudine says: "Schone mein Blut! / Wirst du, was wirst du gewinnen?" In the second reference Mörike is referring to *Dichtung und Wahrheit.*

The final reference on the back endpaper in Volume VII is: *S. 117 "Flohene Freuden" (Aus dem ersten Entwurf beibehalten.)* This refers to a line in the monologue of Elmire in the sixth entrance of "Erwin und Elmire. Ein Singspiel": "Flohen Freuden / Ach, säuseln im Winde."

In volume IX of the double volume IX and X, which contains *Götz von Berlichingen, Egmont, Clavigo, Stella* and *Die Geschwister,* it is *Götz von Berlichingen* which bears particularly heavy reading marks. Some of these reading marks are of a peculiar nature. Mörike bracketed passages that contain overtly erotic and earthy language. On page 35, Act I; Jagsthausen, Maria and Weislingen, Mörike put brackets around the following partial statement by Maria: "Ihr scheint aber schon von dem Besitze nehmen zu wollen, was nur unter Bedingungen euer ist." Still in the same scene, Mörike further bracketed: "Sie hatte geliebt, und durfte reden." Further below, after Franz, Weislingens Bube enters the scene, part of his speech is also bracketed: ". . . Ich hätte mein Vermögen gegeben, die Spitze ihres kleinen Fingers küssen zu dürfen! Wie ich so stund, warf der Bischof einen Bauern herunter, ich fuhr darnach und rührte im Aufheben den Saum ihres Kleides, das fuhr mir durch alle Glieder."

In the second act, which opens with a song by Liebetraut, while the Bischof von Bamberg and Adelheid play chess, Mörike altered the second stanza of the song in the following way:

Da fand er die (Busen) *Schönen*
Ach leider so bloss   ("bloss" changed to "loss")

Sie nahmen so willig
Ihn auf den Schoss.

On page 49 of the second act, scene: "Bamberg. Zimmer der Adelheid," Mörike bracketed the following exchange after Liebetraut comes into her room and says: "Nun, gnädige Frau, was verdien ich?"

Adelheid: Hörner von deinem Weibe. Denn nach dem zu rechnen, habt Ihr schon manches Nachbarn ehrliches Hausweib aus Ihrer Pflicht hinausgeschwatzt.

Liebetraut: Nicht doch, gnädige Frau! auf ihre Pflicht, wollt Ihr sagen; wenn's ja geschah, schwatzt ich sie auf ihres Mannes Bette.

On page 70 of Act 3; Jagsthausen, the conclusion of Sickingen's initial statement is bracketed by Mörike:

Bei Mädchen, die durch Liebesunglück gebeizt
sind, wird ein Heiratsvorschlag bald gar.

On page 76 of Act 3; Wald an einem Morast, the following exchange between two soldiers is bracketed:

Erster Knecht: Was machst du Hier?

Zweiter Knecht: Ich hab Urlaub gebeten, meine Notdurft zu verrichten. Seit dem blinden Lärmen gestern abends ist mir's in die Gedärme geschlagen, dass ich alle Augenblicke vom Pferde muss.

On page 88 of Act 3, Jagsthausen, Mörike altered a comment by Sickingen in the following way:

$\bar{o}$ e[ine] *Stunde ruhn*
Ich will ((ihr Bette nicht besteigen)) bis ich euch
ausser Gefahr weiss.

On page 109 of Act 4; Adelheids Schloss, Franz tells Adelheid that he loves her. The second part of the statement is bracketed: "Mein Herz ist zu voll, meine Sinne halten's nicht aus."

Finally, on page 127 of Act 5; Adelheid's Schlafzimmer, Mörike bracketed part of the stage direction: ". . . die weinend ihn umhalst."

In the back endpaper there are only two references to volume IX: *Grimm 9. S. 43 unt.* *"Muthilich, männilich."* This refers to the diction of the first stanza of the song by Liebetraut with which the second act of *Götz von Berlichingen* opens:

Mit Pfeil und Bogen
Kupido geflogen,
Die Fackel in Brand,
Wollt mutilich kriegen
Und männilich siegen
Mit stürmender Hand.

The second reference to volume IX is: *Un-gramm*[atisch], *9, S. 262 ob. "– den er zu verbergen sucht, und ganz außer sich ist."*

There are no notations in the text of volume X, but on the back endpaper are the following notations: *Gr. 10 S. 43 ob. "Ohne Vorbewußt."* This refers to the third avt of "Der Gross-Coptha" in which the Domherr says: "Sie wünscht das kostbare Halsband, sie giebt mir den Auftrag, ohne Vorbewußt ihres Vaters."

A second notation refers to Goethe's grammar: *Un-gramm*[atisch] *10. S. 226 ob.* "Und sich – im Blute tauchen."

In the double volume XI and XII, which contains *Faust I* and *II* exclusively there are many underlinings and comments. Many comments in *Faust I* were first made in pencil and were unfortunately erased. In the text of *Faust I* there are again several changed and bracketed passages. On page 112 of the scene "Strasse," Mörike added as follows to alter the impact of Faust's words:

Wenn nicht das süsse junge Blut
Heut nacht* in meinen Armen ruht,   *noch*
So sind wir um Mitternacht geschieden.

Below this, in the same scene, the following couplet is bracketed:

Schaff mir ein Halstuch von ihrer Brust,
Ein Strumpfband meiner Liebeslust!

In the subsequent scene, "Abend," lines 2708 through 2716 in which Faust expresses his emotion as he stands in front of Gretchen's bed are also bracketed by Mörike.

On the back endpaper Mörike referred to *Faust I* in the following note: *S. 50 "Man sehnt sich nach des Lebens Bachen." Diese Vorstellung widerspricht nach meinem Gefühl dem übrigen Zusammenhang durchaus. Oder was sind denn hier des Lebens Bachen? – Ich fürchte sie sind nur durch d. Reim herbeigeführt.*

Under the general heading, *Sprachli*[zenzen], Mörike noted as follows in reference to *Faust II*:

Bd. 12 Sprachlich[es]	*S. 103 "Das bringt mich nicht."*
zwei Silben zu wenig.	*S. 103 "Der Zelten Trug."*
	S. 153 "Tüchtighaft" (!) (177 doppelhaft)
	163 "Weiteröffnen"
	165 "Betrete: st[att] *Betritt*
	166 "des Herren" (?)
	175 "unterschworen"
	205 "schweighaft"
	206 "zugeschaltet" – "heitert"
	206 "zirkt"
	243 "Schweigniß"
	266 "erlangt"
	268 "Lieber Kömmling" (!)
	276 "Wohngewinn"
	276 "Willens-Kur"
	299 unt. "Gemeindrang"
	301 "Dauerstern"
	304 "Zwienatur"

In the text of the double vol. XIII and XIV, *Iphigenie, Tasso, Elpenor* and *Werther* show particularly heavy evidence of Mörike's reading. The underlinings in volume XIII of *Iphigenie* and *Tasso* suggest recitation. There are no marginal comments, but there are many

181

lightly underlined words and passages. On page 65, for example, Mörike underlined as follows:

Nur *mich*, die Schuld ist mein, ich fühl' es wohl;
Da konnt' *ich anders nicht dem* Mann begegnen.

On page 74, Dritter Auftritt, Mörike adds as part of the directions to Iphigenie's fourth speech: *(erregt)*

In *Tasso*, page 101, Lenore's speech bears many underlinings, which also seem to indicate Mörike's oral delivery as well as an intense preoccupation with certain passages:

Wenn er in seliger Betrachtung sich
Mit *deinem* Werth beschäftigt, mag er auch
An meinem leichtern Wesen sich erfreun.
uns liebt er nicht, — verzeih' dass ich es sage! —

Aus allen Sphären trägt er was er liebt
Auf einen *Namen* nieder, den wir führen,
Und sein Gefühl theilt er uns mit; *wir* scheinen
Den Mann zu lieben, und wir lieben nur
Mit ihm das Höchste was wir lieben können.

In *Elpenor*, page 389, Act II, Mörike corrected as follows:

Polymetis: Als einen schmerzbeladnen ((Feind))* ernähre . . ."   *Freund*

In volume XIV, preceding Goethe's preface to *Werther* Mörike added the following note: *Die handschriftlichen Änderungen pp in dieser Ausgabe betreffend vergleiche man: Michael Bernays: über Kritik und Geschichte des Goetheschen Textes Berlin 1866.*

One of the variants in the text, which was merely a different "Lesart," Mörike noted on page 31 of volume XIV in *Werther*: "Am 21. Junius: Ich lebe so glückliche Tage, wie sie Gott seinen Heiligen *aufspart*;* und mit mir . . ."   *Göthe schrieb: ausspart.*

On page 66 of *Werther*, in the letter dated "Am 30. Aug., O Wilhelm! die einsame Wohnung einer Zelle, das härene* Gewand und der Stachelgürtel waren Labsale," (*Ursprüngliche Lesart "das härine."*)
     Vergl. Luther in Offenb. Joh. 6, 12.)

182

On page 145, Mörike added parentheses and amendations as follows: "Der Herausgeber an den Leser." "Alles das ist vergänglich aber keine Ewigkeit soll das glühende Leben auslöschen, das ich gesten auf deinen Lippen genoss, das ich in mir fühle! Sie liebt mich! Dieser Arm hat sie umfasst, diese Lippen (haben) auf ihren* Lippen gezittert, dieser Mund (hat) an dem ihrigen gestammelt. Sie ist mein! Du bist mein! ja, Lotte, auf ewig." *In der Orig. Ausg. fehlt hier, einer poetischen Licenz gemäß, das Hilfszeitswort.

In the back on the endpaper Mörike noted as follows under *Sprachliches* in reference to *Werther: Bd. 14 S. 10 15. Mai "ein j[unges] Dienstmädchen das ihr Gef[äss]" S. 31 unt. "zum Zwecke (Ziele) meiner Spaziergänge pp"* 21. Juni

In reference to "Briefe aus der Schweiz" in Volume 14, Mörike also noted under *Sprachliches*:

> *Bd. 14 S. 187, "Prätension an."* The context of the letter is: "man giebt da gern jede Prätension ans Unendliche auf."

> *Bd. 14 S. 190 "erschlafen – den Tag"*
> *S. 212 unt. "das Gebräude der Wolken"*
> *(S. 227 "Winweben")*
> *S. 252 "Es sind Leute, wo pp*

In the double volume XV and XVI, *Die Wahlverwandtschaften* and *Wilhelm Meisters Lehrjahre*, erster Teil, bear particularly heavy reading marks and notations. In the text of *Die Wahlverwandtschaften*, Mörike crossed the following paragraphs, which *all* refer to the physical setting of the novel: par. 3, 5, 9 of chapter 1; 19, 20 of chapter 2; par. 10, 11, 13, 22, 26 of chapter 3; par. 23 of chapter 6; par. 7, 8, 9, 11, 15, 16, 17, 23 of chapter 7; the third last paragraph of chapter 8 and the first paragraph of chapter 9.

In the back, on the endpaper, there is the following critical commentary: *15, 277 "Zum zweiten Mal" – ex. Beispiel der eigentlichen psycholog. Erscheinung, die ich u. einer meiner Freunde um sie kurz zu bezeichnen "Identitätsmomente" nennen. Goethe hat die Sache hier für s[einen] Zweck einigermaßen modifiziert. Es müssen ō immer bedeutende Augenblicke sein.* This comment refers to Ottilie's speech in par. 16, chapter 14 of *Die Wahlverwandtschaften*.

Mörike further notes:

Bd. 15 S. 94 "wobei er in der Unschuld s[eine]s Herzens" – obgleich unten "was an dieser Neigung strafbar seyn mochte." (S. 93 unt. und 94 oben. "Diese Selbstbeherrschung" pp. Bemerkungen die nicht in solcher Allgemeinheit gelten wollen, daher auch nicht so ausgedrückt seyn sollten.) S. 107 unt. "ja sie mußte" – bis zum Schlusse des Capit. nicht ganz natürlich.

Bd. 15 S. 133 unt. Die Bemerkung Ottiliens vom unmäßig. Weingenuß der Männer an dieser Stelle störend.

190 oben "Das Alphabet" pp (matter Witz)

(Unter den Aphorismen in Ott. Tagebuch ist mancher Sonderbare und Halbwahre.)

(S. 220 unt. "Es wandelt niemand ungestraft unter Palmen.")

225 mitt. "Ott. konnte es im Stillen ō finden."

234 mitt. "Sie erblickt – vieles gethan." st[att] Sie sieht wo sie auch hinblickt, vieles gethan.

Under a separate category Mörike wrote: *Zweifelhafte, oder (Ottil.) falsche Schönheiten pp.*

15 S. 50 die Geberde

51 unt. "Warf sich zu ihren Füßen" etc.

65 unt. Medaillon – "drückte es gegen die Stirn"

77 "die gold. Kette hingegeben

80 "Wie befehlen Sie die Einrichtg."

178 ob. "– ich wünsche, daß Sie sich – kennen lernen."

In volume XVI, *Wilhelm Meisters Lehrjahre*, erster Teil, in the text itself, especially in Book I, Mörike marked passages in three different ways. There are single vertical lines, double and triple vertical lines in the margins of certains passages. The last two sentences of the first paragraph of Chapter 9 of Book I is marked with a single line: "Seine reine Seele fühlte, daß sie [Mariane] die Hälfte, mehr als die Hälfte seiner selbst sey. Er war dankbar und hingegeben ohne Grenzen."

In Chapter 11 the second halves of the last two paragraphs are marked with double lines.

In Chapter 14 the following passage is marked with a single line: "Wer mit einem Talente zu einem Talente geboren ist, findet in demselben sein schönstes Daseyn!" The following passage in Chapter 14 is marked with triple lines: "Ein ganzer Roman, was er an der Stelle des unwürdigen morgenden Tages tun würde, entwickelte sich in seiner Seele, angenehme Phantasien begleiteten ihn in das Reich des Schlafes, sanft hinüber, und überliessen ihn dort ihren Geschwistern, den Träumen, die ihn mit offenen Armen aufnahmen und das ruhende Haupt unsers Freundes mit dem Vorbilde des Himmels umgaben."

In Chapter 16 the second half of the second paragraph and the following passage of the final paragraph are marked with a single line: ". . . wenn ich bald mit Fröhlichkeit der süssen Liebe an deinen Busen zurückkehre."

In Chapter 17, the final chapter of Book I, par. 19, the middle of paragraph 30 and the conclusion of paragraph 31 are marked with double lines.

On the back endpaper of this double volume XV and XVI there are several notations referring to *Wilhelm Meisters Lehrjahre*:

Bd. 15 S. 9 mitt. "'Was bringen Sie' fragte Mariane" – sonst immer Du.
Bd. 16. S. 32 "seine reine Seele" cf. – 222 "der Gräfin, deren reine Seele
– ō ohne sanften Tadel b[emerken] k[onnte.]"
Bd. 16 S. 65 "daß er mit der Gage" –"von Disproportion der w[öchentlichen] Gage." "Wobei denn doch"
Dieser letzte Saz hinkt sonderbar hinterdrein.
Bd. 16 S. 139 ob. "Nicht – durch Worte – seine Arbeit zieren" (!) überhaupt will diese theatral.
Belehrung ō viel heißen. Bedeutend ist was auf der folgenden Seite über das Schicksal gesagt wird.
Vergl. S. 78 unt. u.s.w. This last comment refers to par. 31 of Chapter 9 in Book I.
Bd. 16 S. 208 unt. "daß eine Theil den – einen leidenschaftlichen Vorzug gebe" wird kaum gesagt werden können. This comment refers to par. 7 of Chapter 8 of Book III.
Bd. 16 S. 235 "die Nativität stellen" paßt ō gut in diesem Fall. This comment refers to the following phrase in the 6th par. of the 12th chapter of Book III: "Unsere Schauspieler konnten sich also leicht die Nativität stellen."
S. 285 u. "Mit lebhaften Schritten nahte er sich der Besserung" – Die Besserung ist aber mit dem ersten Schritt schon da. This refers to the first sentence of Chapter 11 in Book IV:

In the double volume XVII and XVIII, containing *Wilhelm Meisters Lehrjahre*, Part Two, and *Wilhelm Meisters Wanderjahre* respectively, there are no notations in the text itself. On the endpaper in the back are the following notations by Mörike:

> Bd. 17, 74 "Gewisse Man[ieren] u. Redensarten – ausgeschlossen sein" – unverständlich.
> Bd. 17, 112 unt. ebenfalls? allenfalls?
> Bd. 17, 203 "in dieser Weste" st. "Welt" – ein lange Zeit durch alle Ausgaben fortgeführter Druckfehler, der nun erst durch Stieg [?] Bernays berichtigt worden ist.
> Bedenkliche Ansicht. Bd. 17, 221 m. daß eine Frau die das Hauswesen – gewiß sein könne." This refers to the phrase: "dass eine Frau, die das Hauswesen recht zusammenhalte, ihren Mann jede kleine Phantasie nachsehen und von seiner Rückkehr jederzeit gewiss seyn könne."
> Bd. 17, 263 mitt. "ein Talent – zu dem ich ō die geringste Anlage hatte."
> Vergl. S. 302 "den Trieb zu einem Talente, die Anlagen zu hundert Fähigkeiten."

In the text of *Wilhelm Meisters Wanderjahre* in vol. XVIII there is only one note in reference to the poem "Woher im Mantel so geschwinde," in Chapter 5 of Book I: *Vergl. die ursprüngliche Gestalt diese Stücks in den Gedichten 1. Bd. S. 167.*

On the endpaper in the back Mörike noted as follows:

> Bd. 18 S. 9 Wohlerhalten oder wohl/erhalten in 13 Zeilen 3 mal, u. abermals auf der folg. Seite.
> S. 60 Perfect m. Präsens im unmittelbaren Wechsel 3 mal.
> Bd. 18 S. 116 Zeile 9 von unten. unvollständiger Satz.
> Bd. 18 S. 175 ob. mitt. unt. "wunderlich- wunderlich- wundersam" auf derselben Seite. Auf der folg. "wunderbar."
> Bd. 18, 292 "ernst – lieblichen (st. "ernstlichen – was eine verdorbene, durch viele Ausgaben geschleppte Lesart ist) – "welchen jene Freunde – nun aber sich," etc. (unrichtige Satzconstruction)

On the endpaper in the back of the double vol. XIX and XX there are also extensive notes in connection with the remaining chapters of *Wilhelm Meisters Wanderjahre*. Mörike wrote the following summary commentary:

> Zusammengestoppelte Fetzen und höchst willkürl. Erzählungsform. Bd. 19, 104, 105, 106 oben.

186

Das heftige Auf u. Abgehn 3—4 mal 107 unt. 110, 112.
Als Beispiel des unerquicklichsten Gewächses in den Wanderjahren das
14. cap. Buch 3 Philine wird hier zur wahren Carikatur. Wie sehr muß man
wünschen, daß G[oethe] die kleinen anmuthigen Geschichten, geistrei-
chen Betrachtungen u. Ansichten die er in diesen Wanderjahren zusammen
verwob, lieber als einzelne Stücke mitgetheilt hätte! In seinen Briefen an
S. Boisseree sieht man recht, daß es ihm selbst nicht ganz wohl u. geheuer
bei dieser Behandlung war.

There is only one comment under *Gr*[imm] in reference to vol. XIX:
Bd. 9 S. 395 "jedem Wechsel unangetastet."

In the remainder of vol. XIX, which contains "Reise der Söhne
Megaprazons," "Unterhaltung deutscher Ausgewanderten," "Die
guten Weiber" and "Novelle" there is little evidence of Mörike's
reading.

Vol. XX, containing exclusively Goethe's autobiography *Dichtung
und Wahrheit*, Erster Theil, reveals repeated readings by Mörike. Mörike added a note on page 1 beside the second paragraph of the text.
This is part of the "Vorwort," beginning with the phrase "Wir haben,
theurer Freund, nunmehr die zwölf Theile Ihrer dichterischen Werke
beisammen . . . *Diese Zuschrift ist, wenigstens in gegenwärtiger Fassung, der ganzen Schreibart nach offenbar von Goethe selbst.*

On the back endpaper Mörike noted as follows in regard to *Dichtung und Wahrheit* of vol. XX:

> *Gr.* [imm] *Bd. 20 S. 6 "die Hausflur"*
> *S. 30—31 zu häufige Widerholung der Redeform "um*
> *so" "um desto" pp. (4 mal)*
> *S. 89 "oberwähnt"*
> *89 mitt "vorfallenden Auctionen"*
> *133 "nach den fortgeschafften Bildern"*
> *186 ob. "die Spatel"*

On the endpaper in the back of the double vol. XXI and XXII containing exclusively the remainder of *Dichtung und Wahrheit*, there
are the following notes, in which Mörike combines references to both
volumes.

> *Bd. 21 S. 212ff Häufung von Conditionalsätzen.*

Under the category *Bes*[onders] *interess*[ante] *Stellen*, Mörike notes:

> *Bd. 21 S. 56 ob.*
> *S. 212 unt.*
> *S. 213 ob. "Sehen wir – während unseres Lebensganges – fühlen."*
>
> *Bd. 22 S. 162 "Die wahre Poesie"*
> *S. 173 unt. "Die wahre Darstellung"*
> *S. 254 unt. u.s.w.*

Under a second category, Mörike wrote:

> *zweifelhafte Reflexionen. Bd. 22 S. 160 "Was aber –"*
> *S. 276 unt. "Denn daß Niemand pp*
> *(Die ganze Ausführung ist ō befriedigend.)*

In a third listing, which is not given a heading, but which apparently falls into his previous categories of *Grimm* and *Sprachlizenzen*, Mörike lists the following:

> *Bd. 21 S. 136 "unmustern" (verwandt mit d. schwäb. musper)*
> *Bd. 21 170 "verselbsten" – "entselbstigen"*
> *Bd. 21 227 ob. Mittgott.*
> *Bd. 21 S. 230 "Wechselnichtigkeit"*
>
> *Bd. 22 S. 30 "vermannigfaltigen"*
> *Bd. 22 S. 81 unt. "Müthigkeit"*
> *Bd. 22 S. 84 ob. "vervollzähligen"*
>
> *Bd. 22 S. 91 ob. "sträcklings"*
> *Bd. 22 S. 200 ob. "Einbildisch"*
> *Bd. 22 S. 208 "verneuen"*
> *22 S. 297 mitt. "Misstage" "Peinen"*
> *S. 297 "kindhaft"*

In the double vol. XXIII and XXIV containing "Die Italiänische Reise," the only notation in the text itself is on page 13 in reference to the entry "Neapel, d. 27. Mai 1787: Das sehnliche erwartete Schächtelchen war* auch dabei." *die R. priveligirten Blutreinigungspillen, denn Goethe litt damals sehr an Obstructionen. On the back endpaper there are extensive notes by Mörike, relating to form and content:

> Bd. 23 S. 123 Zeile 8 Hier könnte man meinen Göthe unterdrücke irgend einen ganz abscheulichen Zug des fragl. Gemäldes. Nach anderweitiger Beschreibung aber thun die beiden Engel nichts besonderes; sie beklagen den Leichnam Jesu auf eine ganz natürliche Weise. Offenbar stand der Gedankenstrich ursprünglich nicht in dem Brief, sondern irgend ein harter unchristlicher Ausdruck, welcher dem Gegenstand im Ganzen galt u. der vor dem Abdruck getilgt wurde, wodurch nun die Stelle zweideutig ist. This comment refers to Goethe's letter dated "Bologna, den 18. October 1786 Nachts."

> Bd. 23 S. 76 "was ein erscheinendes Daseyn hat" überraschender philosoph. Ausdruck v. Jahr 86.

> Bd. 23 228 oben der Satz: "Die Ufer – die Lusträume!" Ähnliches Pathos wie bei Plinius d.h. Item S. 258–590. [Neapel, Febr. 2, 1787]

> S. 234 "In der Kunst ist das Beste gut genug."
> 261 "– wie sich die übrige Welt pp" ist ein schiefer Gedanke.
> 335 Urpflanze – ("muß es geben – woran wurde ich denn sonst –"

The following commentary by Mörike is all listed under Grimm:

> Bd. 23, 77 "Nahen und Fernen" 155, "Fernen und Engen"
> 162 "Fördernisse"
> 173 "zum Freuen"
> 182 "sich verhalten"
> 194 "nach verlesenen einigen lat. Gedichten"
> 205 "anerkennen thun wir"
> 214 "des Tags über"
> 230 "zerlästert"
> 234 "ward Rimini u. n[aheliegende] Orte"
> 245 "zunächst des Meeres" Item 252, 384
> 253 "bei Erblickung"
> 277 "von nichts weniger" st[att] "v[on] nichts geringerem"
> 284 "einem zu gute gehen lassen"
> 349 "Nachfahr"
> 373 "in die Höhe steilen"

Bd. 23,390 "entgottesdienstet"
395 "Ergötzlichkeit" im obsoleten Sinne.
– – "beufert"

Bd. 24   9 "Abwürdigung"
92 "Ebnermassen"
104 "ich werde mühen"
182 "das Recht und Pflicht"

In the double volume XXV and XXVI, containing Goethe's letters, only vol. XXVI shows notes in the text itself: on page 67 in the letter dated "Stuttgart den 30. August 1797," Mörike noted in the margin to the second paragraph: *An Schiller benutzt.* Also in regard to this letter, after the sentence: "Er hat ein historisches Bild vor, aus der Messiade, da Maria sich mit Porcia der Frau des Pilatus, von der Glückseligkeit des ewigen Lebens unterhält und sie davon überzeugt,"* Mörike noted: *Heutzutage bei Frau Legationsrath Reuß zu sehen.* Also in reference to this letter, after the sentence: "Er verlangt für die beiden grossen und drei oder vier kleinen 500 Ducaten,"* Mörike noted: *Als Isopi einst in Gegenwart eines Fremden eine grosse Summer Gold einnahm und dieser sich darüber verwunderte sagte der Meister in seinem gebrochenen Deutsch: Lern Sie Du was Reks, dann krieg Sie auch. M.*

In reference to the letter on page 84, dated "Stuttgart 4. Sept. 1797 after the sentence concluding "aber unendlich lieblich,"* Mörike noted: *noch gegenwärtig (1866) bei Regier. Rath Abel (dem Sohn des vorigen) zu sehn.*

On the back endpaper of double vol. XXV and XXVI there are many notes under four general headings: *Bedeutende Stellen, Angenehme u. heitere Partien,* and *Sprache* and *Gr*[imm].

Under *Bedeutende Stellen* Mörike listed:

Bd. 25 S. 190/99 (aus Anlaß der Sammlung des Hemsterhuis)
Bd. 25 S. 150 Zwischenrede
Bd. 26 S. 316/99

Under *Angenehme u. heitere Partien* Mörike noted:

Bd. 25 S.   *16 "und fragte in Ihro lakonischen Art"*
        51 Rollerfund
        59 Kanonenfieber
        82 Witterung des Schweinebratens, 93 Ähnliches: malerisch
        101 Das Wiederfinden Pauls
        111 Als vorgeblicher Schwager des Königs
        201 "Umstände jedoch die für das neue Theater" – freudige Theilnahme" (Bedenklich od. sehr der Mißdeutung ausgesetzt)
        213 ob. "Mit aber einigen Trost *– zu verschaffen suchte ich diesen Ungeh[euern] eine heitere S[eite] a[bzugewinnen.]" (Hat das innere Wahrheit?)*
        241 unt. Spaßhaftes 79 unt. deßgleichen 26, 215

Under the heading *Sprache und Styl* Mörike added the following notes:

Bd. 25 S.   *76 "bevorsahen"*
        171 oben "deutsamen Meister" (falscher Ausdruck, deutsam wäre eigentlich das object)
        194 ob. "bald auf Geist" (das 2te bald ist ausgeblieben)
        194 unt. "das ich – dürfte und das für mich."
        195 mitt. "brachte zur Sprache, daß er – welche beinah nun befremden aussah' (vergangene Zeit und gegenwärtige confundirt)
        214 "ich ergötzte mich an *einer heimlichen Schadenfreude" (statt in heimlicher)*

Bd. 26 S.   *8 unt. "das Chor"*
        26 "verstellt sie"
        37 unt. "einmals anders als Waare betrachten."
        65 oben "Diese Bilder – ist dennoch"
        188 m. "Äußerst merkwürdig" pp (Ideale Anwandlung der Gegenstände)

Under the reading *Grimm* Mörike added the following notes:

        Specif. Goethesche, etwas manierirte Redeweise
Bd. 25, 20 mitt. "den er aber aufzunehmen keinen Beruf empfand."
        S. 69 mitte "sich – hierüber verloren"

Bd. 26, *83 ob. "ober"*
   128 "von der Seite mit meinem Fürsten – geduldet zu haben."
   129 unt. "derbständig"
   151 unt. "selbstbeliebig – Unterbewußtseyn"
   162 ob. "zufrieden von"
   212 "mit lästigem Ungethüm"
   235 ob. "als auf solche – der begierigste" Nicht ohne Weiteres
      zu verwerfen
   287 unt. "aufgeordnet"
   305 mitt. "hervorgefordert"
N.B.   *311 mitt. "Auch fand man – aufgestellt wurden" scheint etwas*
      ausgefallen (in der Abbildung üben od. dergl.)
   316 "Kaiserling"
   338 ob. "aus dem Kummer," "veroffenbart"

In the double vol. XXVII and XXVIII, containing "Annalen" and "Benvenuto Cellini" respectively, there is only one indication of Mörike's reading in the text itself in vol. XXVII, page 73 under the date 1799:

Tieck las mir seine Genoveva vor, deren wahrhaft poetische Behandlung mir sehr viel Freude machte, und den freundlichsten Beifall abgewann.

This passage is unusually heavily underlined and marked with an exclamation mark and a question mark.

On the endpaper there are notes under the headings *Sprachlizenzen, Interessante Stellen* and *Gr*[imm].

Under *Sprachlizenzen*, Mörike noted as follows:

Bd. 27, *13 "einen so glücklich geborstenen Schafs-schädel, der mir"*
   14 "auch noch da – wenn er"
   14 "die Freigelegenste Wohnung"
   27 "Gemüths freunde" ?
   47 "Fichtens Absicht – mußte empfinden"
   51 "sein ins Ganze rege Geist"
   (52 mitt. Herder fühlt sich v. einiger Entf. p.)
   57 "Es bleibt daher dieses / Werk /"
   (59 mitt. "der König v. Pr., bei einiger Veranlassung)
   60 ob. "gab beliebige Kenntniß"
   (64 ob. "Da sich – ließe, so sey" p.)
   87 unt. "in weniger aber abgeschl. Ung."

Bd. 27,162 "Beschäftigung geschwiegen"
Gr[imm] *(163 "schreckhaft (was eigentl. "zum Sckrecken geneigt" heißen*
dürfte) im Sinne von schrecklich.)
166 unt. "den er vermindert und uns" pp
184 mitt. "wodurch wir nicht anders als" pp
    Vgl. Bd. 32, S. 440
185 ob. "dieses Bild, das − ließ er daß auf ein dünnes Brett ge-
    malt" p.
203 unt. "das Verkehr"
215 "nach Sturm u. Ungethüm"
248 Nibelungen S. 171 ob. "Lust- u. Gefühlsspiele"
264 Zeil. 6 − "und ich dann" pp Item Bd. 28, S. 70 Zeile 3 von
    unten.
275 Zeile 13 − "worum"
383 "auf Ansuchen Londoner Freunde" falscher Genitiv des Prädi-
    cats (Anders wenn es z.B. hieße − "einiger Lond. Fr.")
503 unt. "Verwerfer"
511 oben "lasse sich − Fehler vermeiden"
515 Alt-Goethescher pretiös behaglicher Hofstyl auf seinem höch-
    sten Gipfel

There are two additional notes referring to Goethe's translation of
Benvenuto Cellini's autobiography in vol. XXVIII; these are prefaced
by *Gr*[imm] :

192 ob. "aus Druck" statt "Druckbarkt"
301 unt. "erstaunend"

Under *Interessante Stellen* Mörike listed:

Bd. 27, S. 5 mitte: "Da der Dichter durch Anticipation" p
    52 unt. "Herder war v. Natur − mitgeth. hatte
    78 Durchcomponiren der Lieder

Separately form this last category, Mörike noted: *Zur Frage über*
pros. Wohllaut. Beispiel des Gegentheils Bd. 27 S. 375 unt. "den er
schon − hatte."
    In the double vol. XXIX and XXX only "Diderot's Versuch über
die Malerei" and "Rameau's Neffe" in vol. XXIX show evidence of
Mörike's reading in the texts. On page 286 in "Rameau's Neffe,"

after the sentence, "Va-t' en voir s'ils viennent, Jeans."* Mörike
noted: *Vergl. Goethes Gedicht: "Offene Tafel." "Hänschen geh und
sieh dich um" pp.
On the back endpaper there are many notations. In one separate
comment, not listed under a heading Mörike wrote: *Der Artikel
über Musik S. 336 enthält die sonderbarsten Urtheile. Ebenso der
über Rameau.*
Under the heading *Interessante Stellen* Mörike listed the following:

> *Bd. 29 S. 16 ganz*
> > *S. 19 unt. 20 oben*
> > *S. 290 "den selbst das Schweigen –*
> > *S. 320 d'Alembert spricht ganz offenbar in Beziehung auf sich und*
> > > *seine naturwissenschaftlichen Bestrebungen.*
> *Bd. 30 15ff Schönheit*
> > *30 42 unt. "doch so kann man überhaupt jeden Menschen als vielsylbi-*
> > > *be Charade –*
> > *30 360 unt. pp "der Sammler" 6ter Brief*
> > *30 454 mitt. "sein Horchen – gegen das linke Ohr gehoben."*
> > > *Parallele bei Schwind – bei ungewisser Affection des Geruches*
> > *bewegt sich die Hand gegen die Nase.*

A separate column of Mörike's notations lists *Sprachliches* and
Gr[imm] on the endpaper of double volume XXIX and XXX:

> *Fehler Bd. 29 S. 290 "bald" – fehlt das 2te bald*
> > *29 S. 358 ob. "Abhänglinge"*
> *Bd. 30 S. 10 unt. "Wenn die gesunde Naturbewundern"*
> > *(Der Satz ist fehlerhaft u. doch ist ers auch ō)*
> > *30 S. 294 oben "Dabei etwas Beliebiges (!) denken"*
> > *30 S. 298 "Das Möglichst zu thun" (ist falsch, drückt eher*
> > > *das Gegentheil von dem aus was gesagt werden*
> > > *will. Das Mögliche wäre was am leichtesten gesche-*
> > > *hen kann.*
> > *30 S. 427 Neu: "heimatsüchtig"*

In the double vol. XXXI and XXXII there are no notes in the text
itself, but there are many comments on the back endpaper under
Interessante Stellen and *Sprachliches*. Under the first Mörike noted:

Bd. 31 S. 41 unt. "Bewegung einflößen" kann kaum gesagt werden.
    S. 46 "höchst verstandene Falten"
    S. 53 unt. "Schooß auf Schooß"
    S. 67 "Das Verlangen um"
    S. 188 "Machgewalt"
    S. 192 "Aufstechende" "Abgesondertheiten"
    192 unt. "Dargeben"
    S. 275 "vermenschen"
    S. 393 unt. "abzuholen stehen möchte"
    S. 396 "Halb- und Ganzfabeln"
<u>Gr</u> *S. 402 unt.* "und man könnte, daß" pp

Bd. 32 S. 122 ob. "schon schweben" Beispiel v. poetisch. Ausdruck in
    der Prosa, noch nicht geradezu pretiös.
    S. 125 ob. "Wohlbewegung:
    S. 141 ob. "Ein Ereignen"
<u>Gr</u> *S. 145* "liebehaft"
<u>Gr</u> *S. 145* "Der Einsehende"
    S. 195 "fuß u. bauchfällige Clienten"
    S. 220 "eingebildet" für in den Einbildung
    S. 236 ob. "Daher rühren weil" –
    S. 332 mitt. "wohlschaulich"
    S. 351 ob. "daß – desto besser wird es."
    S. 414 "Das Vergangste"
    S. 440 "erlangen"
    (S. 440 "Nichts anders als" eine v. Goethe selbst an anderen Orten
    ganz unbefangen gebrauchte und hier mit Unrecht verwor-
    fene Redensart)
    S. 447 "durchgemeinter Vortrag"
    S. 449 Tabelle Rubrik 2, 8. "tagtäglich" statt "alltäglich"
    S. 456 "vereinzelnen"

In a separate comment Mörike wrote: *Bd. 32 106 mitt.* "Wenn wir
uns ins Wissen pp" – Wie hängen Vordersatz u. Nachsatz folgerichtig
zusammen?

In the double vol. XXXIII and XXXIV there are the following
notes on the back endpaper: two separate comments are prefaced
with *NB:*

Bd. 33 S. 199 ob. Über eine Behandlungsweise des Märchens, "daß eine
    gewisse humoristische" pp

Bd. 33 S. 259 unt. Manzoni *"Überzeugung — daß ein Geisteswerk" pp*
und S. 224 oben "ebenso wünscht der Verfasser" pp

Under the heading *Interessante Stellen* Mörike noted:

NB Bd. 33 S. 234 oben: "für den Dichter ist keine Person historisch — zu
leihen.

The remaining comments in vol. XXXIII and XXXIV are not given a
particular heading but appear to be part of the categories *Grimm,*
Sprachliches and general critical commentary:

Bd. 33 S. 107 "Lebendigung"
Bd. 33 S. 197 "so dürfte er jener grenzenlosen Lebhaftigkeit — als anheim-
gegeben erscheinen." (üble Construction)

Grimm S. 267 ob. "bepurpurend"
S. 349 "sein Amt — verübend"?

Bd. 34 S. 69 "Selbstgelassenheit"
S. 121 "Wen alles"
S. 125 unt. "stürm, stürm, Winterwind" (Shakesp.)
S. 177 ob. "Das er schon eh besaß" statt zuvor mit Recht, so auch
anderwärts.
S. 236 "flohene Freunde"

In the double vol. XXXV and XXXVI there are no comments in the
text itself except for the following commentary on the back endpaper:

Geschichte v. Göthes botanischen Studien Bd. 36 S. 67
Liebenswürdige Eitelkeit Bd. 36 S. 114ff
Widerwärtige Erfahrung des Autors Bd. 36 S. 102 mitt
Verstäubung bei Insecten Bd. 36 S. 139

Götz v. Berl. Unbegreifliche Verpfuschung des Stücks.
S. 127 Die vier Boten des heiml. Gerichts deuten das Vorhaben gar zu
schwach an. Vollends unverständlich ist S. 133ff. Man bleibt ungewiß
über Adelheids Tod. Das Mahnsbild des Mörders neben dem Wirklichen
— eine ganz ungeschickte Erfindung.

Grimm Wortbildung pp Bd. 35, 192 "Das Recht – das Reich dir anzuma-
grammat[isches]   *ßen (Widerspruch)*
                              Bd. 35, 378 "alles Dreyes"

Bd. 36 S. 77 unt. "fortwährendes Verkehr"
*   S. 78 mitt. st. "erheiterten" wahrscheinlich "erweiterten"*
*   S. 89 ob. "unörtlich"*
*   S. 137 "veredlend"*
*   S. 351 m. "eine auf und hinterwärtse"*

In the double vol. XXXVII and XXXVIII there are the following
notations on the back endpaper:

Lustige, heftige, treffende Stellen gegen Newton

Bd. 38 S. 88 par. 178
*   S. 156 par. 391*
*   S. 209 (569-591)*
*   S. 232 fg.*
*   S. 358 fg.*

Under a separate heading Mörike noted:

(Bd. 37 XIX "um derentwillen")
Bd. 37 S. 12 "Größtens"
Bd. 38 par. 247 Z[eile] *3 v. unt. S. 4 "Vorwortlich"*
Bd. 38 S. 8 "Zwischenrede"

In the final double vol. XXXIX and XL there are the following
notations on the back endpaper:

Interess[ante] *An*[führung] *von Stellen*

Bd. 39 S. 444 "meine Bewunderung nicht entziehen konnte."

Bd. 40 S. 126 unt. "eine dankbare Empfindung zu hegen geneigt seyn"
*   S. 130 "Die Briefe welche hierauf" pp komischer Ernst Altgöthi-*
*   scher Redeweise*
Opposition gegen die neueren geolog. Ansicht. Bd. 40 S. 293
Heftige Äußerung S. 296
Merkwürdige Concession Bd. 40 S. 302 unt.
Bd. 40 S. 401 Über das Sehen

Under *Sprachliches* Mörike commented:

Bd. 39 S. 146 unt. "Gesinnungen" statt Meinungen oder Ansichten.
Kleine Ungenauigkeiten im Ausdruck. 39 Bd. S. 240 Linie 8 von oben
und Linie 10 von unten (Die Frage: "Inwiefern" wird mit Ja beantwor-
tet.
Bd. 40 S. 301 mitt. "die kein Auge – vernommen hat."
Bd. 40 S. 399 unt. "wenn es zu thun ist"
Bd. 40 S. 505 "Dem Nachdenken angeeigneter"

In a separate comment on the endpaper of volume XXXIX and XL
Mörike wrote:

Neumann Bd. 40 S. 38
S. 41 Nr. 20 Le Prince
S. 485 unt. Eine falsche Hypoth.

27. G.C. Lichtenberg. *Vermischte Schriften.*

There are also extensive notations in the texts of these four double volumes. We can take Mörike quite literally, when he notes in the margin on page 28 of volume I, that he is perusing Lichtenberg for the fifth time in his life. On the back endpaper of the first double volume are extensive notations referring to the aphorisms contained here. Though no general heading or commentary was added by Mörike that would indicate a particular attitude toward Lichtenberg's ideas, it seems clear from the kind of aphorisms noted, that Mörike approved of the ideas expressed, and that he found much of what is characteristic of Lichtenberg. The following is a list of Mörike's notations; for each notation the context is indicated:

I, 243 xstl. Relig. [Christliche Religion.] This notation refers to one of Lichtenberg's aphorisms grouped under "7. Politische Bemerkungen" by his editor-sons: "Ich sehe darin nichts so sehr Arges, daß man in Frankreich der christlichen Religion entsagt hat. Das sind ja Alles nur kleine Winkelzüge. Wie wenn das Volk nun *ohne allen äußern Zwang* in ihren Schooß zurückkehrt weil ohne sie kein Glück wäre? Welches Beispiel für die Nachwelt, und welches kostbare Experiment, das man wahrscheinlich nicht alle Tage anstellt! Ja, vielleicht war es nöthig, sie einmal ganz aufzuheben, um sie gereinigt wieder einzuführen."

I, 278 Homer. This refers to a section of aphorisms entitled, "literarische Bemerkungen." This particular aphorism starts, "Mir ist es immer vorgekommen, als wenn man den Werth der Neuern gegen die Alten auf einer sehr falschen Wage wage, und den letztern Vorzüge einräumte, die sie nicht verdienen. Die Alten schreiben zu einer Zeit, da die große Kunst, schlecht zu schreiben, noch nicht erfunden war, und bloß *schreiben* hieß *gut schreiben* . . . Homer hat gewiß nicht gewußt, daß er gut schrieb, so wenig wie Shakespeare. Unsere heutigen guten Schriftsteller müssen alle die fatale Kunst lernen: zu wissen, daß sie gut schreiben."

II, 15/34. 20, 21 unt./9 Kunst des Schriftstellers. All of these references are to the section, "10. Ästhetische Bemerkungen." In the first reference on page 15, Lichtenberg again holds up classical writers as superior to modern writers. Horace is being used as an example. On page 94 Lichtenberg discusses suicide. He interjects half facetiously that suicide is a practical solution for superfluous characters in tragedies. On page 20 and 21 Lichtenberg deals with the test of time on good literature: "Kein Buch kann auf die Nachwelt gehen, das nicht die Untersuchung des ⸃vernünftigen und erfahrenen Weltkenners aushält." On page 9 Lichtenberg discusses choice of meter: "Die Versart den Gedanken anzumessen, ist eine sehr schwere Kunst, und eine Vernachlässigung derselben ist ein wichtiger Theil des Lächerlichen. Sie verhalten sich beide zusammen wie im gemeinen Leben Lebensart und Amt."

II, 93 Viele Kinder. This notation is to commentary under the section: "11. Nachtrag zu den witzigen und satyrischen Einfällen und Bemerkungen." Many witty sayings are included in this section, as, for instance, the one Mörike noted: "A. Der Mann hat viele Kinder. B. Ja, aber ich glaube, bei den meisten hat er bloß die Correctur besorgt."

II, 124 Prof. Meister. This notation refers to the section, "14. Zum Andenken von Verstorbenen:" "Am 18 Dezember 1788, starb mein vortrefflicher Meister. [Professor of Philosophy at Göttingen.] Allein, erst den 23. ward er, nach seiner Verordnung begraben . . . Er war ein Mann von den größten Fähigkeiten und einem Scharfsinn, der nicht seines Gleichen hat."

II, 133 unt. This notation refers to a maxim in the section, "15. Gute Ratschläge und Maxime:" "Es ist sehr gut, Alles, was man denkt, rechnet u. dergl., in besondere Bücher zu schreiben: dieß macht den Wachstum merklich, unterhält den Fleiß, und gibt einen Nebenbewegungsgrund, aufmerksam zu sein."

II, 156 Satyra. This notation, as well as the remaining seven notations in volume II, refers to the section entitled, "17. Allerhand." Here, in this particular aphorism, Lichtenberg writes in the vein of Juvenal: "Satyre ist am besten angebracht und am leichtesten geschrieben, wenn einige schlaue Betrüger ein ganzes Publikum geblendet zu haben glauben, und wenn man weiß, daß sie einen mit unter die Geblendeten zählen . . . Alsdann ist es schwer, *satyram non scribere.*"

II, 163 Feuerordnung. Lichtenberg here satirizes confusing and hence dangerous language of fire ordinances.

II, 168 Cicisbeat. "In Genua darf sich kein Mann bei seiner Frau auf der Straße oder sonst öffentlich blicken lassen; der Cicisbeat hat da die größte Höhe erreicht, und ein Mann, der nicht darauf achten wollte, würde verspottet werden und sich den größten Insulten des Pöbels aussetzen." The remainder of the commentary is devoted to a tongue-in-cheeck defense of this curious Italian custom.

II, 175 Weltmaschinen. "Es ist doch besonders, daß es in allen Ländern so viele Menschen gibt, die Weltmaschinen verfertigen . . . Einen läppischeren Gebrauch kann wohl der Mensch von seinen Seelenkräften nicht machen, als wenn er die Weltmaschine durch ein Räderwerk darzustellen sucht, das immer zur Familie der Bratenwender gehört und daran erinnert."

II, 184 Correspond. u. schöne Frau. "Es erleichtert die Correspondenz, wenn man weiß, daß der Correspondent eine schöne Frau hat."

II, 188 Musik f. Pflanzen. "Ob die Musik die Pflanzen wachsen mache, oder ob es unter den Pflanzen welche gebe, die musikalisch sind?"

II, 190 Sympathien. "Die Sympathien sind gewiß nicht alle zu verwerfen. Vielleicht finden wir einmal die Ursache dazu. Sie sind vielleicht Reste von den verlornen Wissenschaften einer andern Generation Menschen."

II, 194 Advocatenkniffe. "In England wird ein Mann der Bigamie wegen angeklagt, und von seinem Advocaten dadurch gerettet, daß er bewies, sein Client habe *drei* Weiber."

There are several minor corrections in the double volume III and IV, which are almost all "Druckfehler." On page 315 of the text, is a short critical comment by Mörike. This is in reference to the Lichtenberg-Voß feud, specifically to one of Lichtenberg's satiric-polemical articles, in which he attacks the German Homer translator J.H. Voß for his view that the German pronunciation of the Greek letter which had been traditionally rendered as "e" in such Greek proper names as Hera and Homer, should be ä or äh. Lichtenberg attacks Voß' recommendation vehemently with such derived forms as "to bäh or not to bäh." To this Mörike added on page 315 in vol. III: *Eigentlich aber doch abgeschmackt.*

In the double volume V and VI there are several printing error corrections and the following addition of page 128 of vol. V: Lichtenberg (under the pseudonym Emanuelem Candidum) wrote a lengthy satiric poem entitled "Schwimmende Batterien," which deals with the three year siege of Gibraltar by the French and Spanish, defended by G.A. Elliot, Lord Heathfield. Stanza 33 has a missing verse, which Mörike supplied: *Sein Pfeifchen an zu schmauchen.*

On the back endpaper are the following notations in reference to vol. V and VI:

V S. 364 Schnupftabak – Sprache
VI S. 348 Handel mit heil. großen Zehen
VI S. 400 Juvenal. Nihil est – summit

In the double volume VII and VIII, containing Lichtenberg's letters, there are also many signs of Mörike's careful perusal. He carefully amended printing errors, especially in the letters to Goethe. On the endpaper Mörike noted the following names and references to contents of letters by Lichtenberg. For each reference recipient and date are provided. The page numbers written by Mörike refer to vol. VII without a Roman numeral and to vol. VIII with Roman number II.

Anatomen, verliebt, II, 295	to Sömmering, June 2, 1786.
F. glaubt an Magnetismus II, 300	to Sömmering, Nov. 9, 1788.
Thümmel II, 308	to Sömmering, March 14, 1791.
Sömmering Ohr II, 309 u. fruher	to Sömmering, Apr. 20, 1791.
Embryo – Alexander II, 310, 312	same
Heirathen II, 308, 311	same
Guillotine 315	to Sömmering, June 5, 1795.
Ein etwas schimpfl. Friede	same
Die wahren Denker II, 319	to Sömmering, Sept. 22, 1795.
Rührung bei Gewitter 332	to Franz Ferdinand Wolff, July 21, 1783.

Volta II, 334	same
Ahnungen II, 333	to Wolff, Sept. 8, 1783.
Drachen II, 244	to Schernhagen, July 19, 1773.
Blizableiter auf das Gartenhaus II, 254	to Schernhagen, May 25, 1780.
Italien II, 282	Lichtenberg asks Sömmering to accompany him to Italy in 1785.
H. v. Weimar II, 259	Duke of Weimar visiting Lichtenberg, March 22, 1781.
Voss II, 90	to Nicolai, Febr. 18, 1781.
Wieland 67, 130 Holty	to Boie, Jan. 10, 1775 (praising poems.)
Gothiker II, 327	to Schernhagen, Febr. 1777.
Schiller 170	to Joh. Arnold Ebert, Jan. 8, 1795.
Bürger 73/204 II 267, 282	letters to Bürger and about Bürger.
Kant 72	to Bürger 1787 (defending Kant.)
Garrick 134, König v. E.	to Dieterich, Oct. 18, 1775 ("Vorgestern bin ich von einem Pagen des Königs Herrn Garrick vorgestellt worden.")
Forster II, 25, 221	to F.A. Lichtenberg, Apr. 3, 1788.
A. v. Humboldt II, 31 W. 32	to L.C. Lichtenberg, Sept. 16, 1788.
Lavater II, 150, 169 *Merk 32* *Bonaparte II, 61* *Chodowiecky II, 62*	Mörike here merely notes these names to ascertain Lichtenberg's view of each. same
Müller II, 76 Scherze	to J.G. Müller, 1785.
Ploquet II, 243	to Schernhagen, Aug. 1778.

Erstes Mon. 249	to G.H. Hollenberg, Oct. 12, 1777.
Glaube 200	to Joh. Georg Forster, Fall, 1787.
Galgen / unlog. Satz / 215	to Forster, Sept. 30, 1790.
Als Corrector II, 70f.	to Müller, March 31, 1785.

The following notes were difficult to identify and hence letter references are uncertain and have been left out of the listing:

Pfaff II, 104; Suttgarter II, 78; Hamburg 340; Bohnenberger II, 200; Portrait II, 91; Göppingen 286; Seine Frau II, 214, I, 320; Derbheit 199; Kanaan 273; Leichen-Anstaltung II, 249; Schmerz bei Todesf. II, 328; Mein Zustand 272; Gewitter 264, 216; Physikal. Versuche II, 145, 148; Physik, Hilfsm. f. d. Univers. II, 153.

29. K. Mayer, *Gedichte*, 2nd ed. 1839.

Attached to the second edition of Karl Mayer's poems is an undated manuscript listing selected titles and first lines of its content which Mörike compiled for an unknown recipient (SNM 75. 59613, "Aufzählung von Gedichttiteln"). At the conclusion of the listing Mörike added: *Viel eben so schöne stehn dazwischen und folgen nach.* The reason for Mörike's extensive editorial and critical assistance to Mayer has remained somewhat mysterious in view of Mayer's limited talent. The dedication which Mörike wrote in this work to his sister Clara and this attached selection of poems for which a copy may have been intended for her may provide a hint of an answer to this puzzle: Clara Mörike may have thought of Mayer more highly than her brother did. Mörike's persistent advice for and continued patronage of Mayer may have been one more element in the deep bond between him and his sister. (A similar situation may have existed in the case of Theodor Storm; judging from the dedication and notes, Gretchen Mörike may have had a greater affinity for the work of Storm than Mörike did.) *All* of the first lines in the following list (except for p. 62 and 283 which are full titles) are abbreviated by Mörike. This may contain another slight hint as to his reputed high esteem for Mayer: His own preference in his own poems is invariably for brief, precise titles and first lines.

S.   *8 Weiden laßt mich!*
    19 Mücken, Falter
    22 Sollt ich
    62 In einem Waldthale
    77 Nach Empfang eines Briefes
    91 Ach wie schallt
    135 Geflüchtet aus des
    283 Der stille Krieg
    302 O Glocke
      An dem Pfeilerkreis
    309 Unterm stillen
    314 Aus grüner Linden.
    321 Sonnengrün
    324 Durch der Zweige
    335 Stets ein liebl.

36. *Mozin's kleines, deutsch-französisch und französisch-deutsches Hand-Wörterbuch*

Mörike continually added new definitions and lexical items in both sections of this dictionary. In the first part, German-French, Mörike added the following items:

p. 29 *Ausschneiden – blagner.*
p. 41 Ausstellen (Waaren) – *etaler Ausstellung v. Waaren etalage, m.*
p. 128 *Brüssel – Bruxelles.*
p. 262 *krepieren (verrecken; platzen) – crever.*
p. 298 *Nachtvogel – oiseau de nuit*
p. 299 Addition under "Nadel" *Nadelholz*
p. 333 *Szepter, der – sceptre, m.*
p. 353 *schwarzgelb – jauneautre. Vergl. S. 155 gelblich.*
p. 360 *das Sieden – la cusson.*
p. 372 stecken *– etre reste court.*
p. 396 *türkiss – turguoise.*
p. 403 *Ungarn (Land) – La Hontrie (der U.) Hongrois.*
p. 419 verrauchen *– detrose, entorse.*

There are also many printing error corrections in both sections of the dictionary. In cases where the lexical item is not italicized, it indicates that Mörike merely added a new definition. In the French-German section he added as follows:

p. 23 Au-dela – *darüber hinaus*
p. 32 *blaguer (popular) – aufschneiden – hablar*
p. 68 *coucher en joe – das Gewehr anschlagen*
p. 86 *La-dessus – hinrauf*
p. 111 *Escapade – Bubenstreich*
p. 114 Etreindre – *Umarmung*
p. 139 *Guignon, m. – Unglück, bes. im Spiel; (famil.)*
p. 149 *Inert – unthätig, schwerfällig wie ein Klotz, ohne Leben und Regsamkeit.*
p. 158 *Lamproi marinee – die Brücke / Stuttg. d. 22. Dez. 1869.*
p. 160 *La libelule – die* Wasserjungfer [not Mörike's handwriting]
p. 180 *La nostalgie – das Heimweh.*
p. 204 *potpouri – Topf mit einem Gemengsel wohlriechender welker Pflanzen.*
p. 208 *gotteaux, arth. – ist gichterisch, spasmod. convuls. gichterisch.*

p. 217   *Raccommoder – ausbessern, ein Kleid.*
p. 250   *Sigisbee – der Cicisbeo.*
          Sigisbeisme – das Cicisbeat.
p. 251   soireee – *A-gesellschaft.*

37. M.I.G. Müller, *Deliciae Hortenses*, 1745.

On two pages of the back endpaper of this garden almanac Mörike carefully wrote a calendar, in which he recorded the behavior of storks in his town of Cleversulzbach where he lived from 1834 to 1843:

Storchen – Kalender

1835. kamen die Storchen in Kleversulzbach am 1. April an.
1836. zeigte sich einer am 2. März und ging wieder. am 9. März, Nach-
mitt[ag]s 2 Uhr kam ein Storch (wahrscheinlich derselbe vom
2. Mrz.) und stellte sich sogleich aufs alte Nest auf Schlegels
Scheuer.
  16. Mrz kam, wie behauptet wird, der Herr mit der Madam, nachdem
längere Zeit keins von beiden zu sehen gewesen.
  25. Aug. Von den 3 Storchen, (Vater Mutter + Kind) ging Eines noch
vor dem 25sten. die übrigen an gedachtem Tage.
1837. zeigte sich einer am 7. Mrz. flüchtig
  12. Mrz. flog einer aufs Nest
  18. Mrz. kam auch das Weibchen.
Anfangs April, bei eingetretener winterlich[er] Witterung ver-
schwanden die Storche und blieben etwa acht Tage aus ohne daß
man hätte denken können, wo sie sich indessen aufgehalten haben
mochten.
Sie kamen noch einige Mal, besahen das Nest, das ihnen ō gefiel,
da man eine Veränderung damit vorgenommen.
Endlich blieben sie gar aus.

41. Hans Sachs. *Etzlich schöne lehrreiche / Dichtwerk.*

This fragment of an enormous and original 1558 volume "das ander buch," containing three parts of Hans Sachs' works, is of special importance to Mörike's work. First, Mörike inadvertently had discovered in it a German version of the story of Hamlet in Sachs' *Historia / Fengo ein Fürst in Itlandt Erwürget sein Bruder Horwendillum.* This Hans Sachs version and its relation to Mörike's reading of Shakespeare is discussed above in Chapter III. Secondly, this fragmentary volume contains on the reverse side of the added title page a handwritten, narrative, dedicatory poem by Mörike. Thus, this volume constitutes a unique species of a manuscript, without which the whole body of Mörike's manuscripts, which serves as the basis for the new historical-critical edition, would be incomplete. How this particular poem fits into the larger context of Mörike's lyric production in connection with Mörike's own habits of selecting from his poems works for his last edition, is discussed by H.H. Krummacher in his article, "Zu Mörikes Gedichten, Ausgaben und Überlieferung," in *Jahrbuch der Deutschen Schillergesellschaft*, V, 1961, pp. 267–344. A different and incomplete version of this poem under the title, "An einen Freund," is included in Mayne, *Werke*, vol. I. The complete and original version of this poem in its spontaneous, delightful imitation of Sachsian verse has never been fully accounted for and it is here transcribed in its entirety:

> *Zueignung an*
> *Herrn Doctor Albrecht Zellern.*
>
> *Jüngst ich in eines Kaufherr Kram,*
> *Ein Pfund Toback zu holen, kam;*
> *Die Ladendirne jung und frisch*
> *Bescheidentlich stund hinterm Tisch*
> *Und wog mir in bedächt'ger Ruh*
> *Mein braun süßduftend Kräutlein zu,*
>
> *Derweilen schaut ich gähnend stumm*
> *So rings mich im Gewölbe um;*
> *Da auf ei'm Kistel konnt ich sehn*
> *Alt halbzerfazt ein Volumen,*

Dergleichen wohl zum Packen und Wickeln
Die Krämer blätterweis' zerstückeln.
Mit Andacht grüßt' ich alsogleich
Hanns Sachsens holde Musenstreich.

O schad' um so viel ed'le Reim!
In Staub verschütt't so güldnen Honigseim!
Verkauft mir die Schnurrpfeiferey.
Sie lächelt schalkhaft für sich hin,
Ob ich auch wohl bey Sinnen bin?
Dann lugt sie treu mir in die Augen:
Was mag Euch doch die Waare taugen?
Das ist ja Quark, Herr, mit Vergunst,
Doch steht's Euch an, habt ihrs umsunst.

Das war mir eben kein Verdruß,
Hätt gern gedanket mit ein'm Kuß,
Ich schlepp' den Schatz heim unter'm Arm,
Und gleich drauf los weil ich noch warm.
Da war denn viel und allerley
Im goth'schen Schnitt Mythologey,
Comedi, Tragedi dazu
Wacker versolt nach'm Baurenschuh;
Aber die Lehren und hintere G'schicht'
Hont mich sehr erbaut und ufgericht't.
Mit Wundern las ich was dort steht
Von einem Dänenprinz Amlet.

Nun ich mich sattsam ausgewühlt,
Sinnend das Werk in Händen hielt,
Dacht ich am Ende wohlgeflissen
Das wäre wohl vielleicht ein Bissen
Für den Doktor, meinen guten Freund;
Ein' ringe Gab, doch wohlgemeynt.
Ein frumm Gemüth oft sucht und ehrt
Was vor der Welt nit hellerswerth.

Schriebs, Stuttgart, am
13ten des Juni 1831.   *Eduard Mörike.*

Besides this poem and the title page supplied by Mörike, there are
no further notation in this fragmentary volume.

Mörike taught German literature and literary history to young women at the Katherinenstift in Stuttgart from Oct. 1851 to Nov. 1866. For this purpose he was using Simrock's modernized rendering of medieval texts. Mörike's notations in this work are interesting for three reasons. First, as his revisions indicate, he was dissatisfied with some of Simrock's modernizations. Second, in at least one instance we find echoes of lyric poems in Mörike's own poetry, notably in his "Ein Stündlein wohl vor Tag." Third, Mörike applied some censorship to some of the texts, which is a valuable testimony of the temper of his time.

This "censorship" must be seen in context. At the time Mörike was under the watchful eyes of the Queen of Württemberg, who once visited his classes at the Katherinenstift. Reading of erotic passages in mid-century Stuttgart to "Töchter höherer Stände" could hardly be condoned. In one instance a young lady was not allowed by her parents to attend one of Mörike's Wednesday Goethe lectures. In an unpublished letter in SNM, dated July 28, 1852, to his wife Margarete, he tells her of objections which parents had raised about *Werther*. He also tells her that thereupon he showed his copy of *Werther*, in which he had crossed out objectionable passages, to his friend and colleague Karl Wolff. (See *Eduard Mörike, Gedenkausstellung, 1975. Katalog*, p. 348.)

On the back endpaper Mörike noted only two places of the text: *387 ihm d. d. Schnüre fahren. / Heinr. v. Morungen S. 200. 4.*

In the first instance, Mörike was struck by a figure of speech in the 38th stanza of the verse story "Der gute Gerhard" by Rudolf von Ems, of which Karl Simrock includes an excerpt:

> Der Kaiser warf der Thüre
> Den Riegel vor in Hast,
> Auf daß ihm durch die Schnüre
> Nicht fuhre dieser Gast.

Mörike's second note refers to the fourth poem by Morungen, "Tagelied." Because of its striking similarity in theme, in the use of apostrophized words, which underscore the premature departure of the lover in the aubade, and in the use of the refrain to Mörike's own poems "Ein Stündlein wohl vor Tag," — I reproduce it here in its entirety:

O weh, soll mir nicht wieder je
Hell leuchten in der Nacht
So weiß wie frischer Schnee
Ihr Leib in lichter Pracht.
Der trog die Augen mein:
Ich wähnt', es sollte sein
Des lichten Mondes Schein,
Da tagt' es.

O weh, sie küßte sonder Zahl
Im Schlaf mich inniglich.
Da fielen hin zu Thal.
Die Thränen über mich.
Ich tröstete sie lang:
Sie that den Thränen zwang.
Mich in die Arme schlang,
Da tagt' es.

"O weh, daß ich ihn nimmer seh
Verweilen all den Morgen,
Wenn uns die Nacht vergeh,
Das wir nicht dürfen sorgen.
O weh, der Tag ist da!
Wie gieng es ihm so nah,
Als er den Schein ersah:
Da tagt' es."

"O weh, daß er so oft sich stahl
Zu mir beim Abendgraun,
So wollt er allemal
Meine bloßen Arme schaun.
Und fand die Bitte statt,
So sah er nie sich satt,
Daß michs gewundert hat.
Da tagt' es."

On page 214 Simrock presents his modernized version of Walter von der Vogelweide's untitled poem "Ich saz uf eime steine." Simrock entitled this poem "Gefährdetes Geleite." To this, Mörike added the note: *an Kaiser Philipp*. Mörike must have disliked Simrock's modernization so much, that he wrote his own version between the lines. Where he did not recast the wording he apparently accepted Simrock's wording. In part, Mörike returns to the original. As always, Mörike's writing is rendered in italics:

Ich saß auf einem Steine,
Und deckte Bein mit Beine
Da deckt' ich Bein mit Beine,
Darauf setzt ich den Ellebogen
Darauf der Ellenbogen stand;
Ich hatt in meine Hand geschmogen
Es schmiegte sich in meine Hand
Das Kinn und eine Wange.
Da dacht ich mir viel ange (besorglich)
Da dacht ich sorglich lange
Wie man zu Welt hier sollte leben
Dem Weltlauf nach und irdschem Heil;
Und keinen Rath ich konnte geben
Doch wurde mir kein Rath zu Theil,
Wie man drei Ding erwürbe,
Der keines nicht verdürbe.
Daß ihrer keins verdürbe.
     fährndes
Die zwei sind Ehr und zeitlich Gut,
Das oft einander Schaden thut,
  – –   *ist Gottes Hulden*
Das dritte Gottes Segen,
Der zweien Übergulde
An dem ist mehr gelegen;
  wollt'
Die hätt ich gern in einen Schrein
  das kann
Ja leider mag es nimmer sein,
Daß Gut und weltlich Ehre
Das Gottes Gnade kehre
Und Gottes Hulde mehre (jemals)
Mit Reichthum und mit Ehre
Zusammen in Ein Herze kommen

Je wieder in dasselbe Herz;
Stieg und Wege sind ihnen benommen
Sie finden Hemmung allerwärts:
Untreue ist der Sasse (Hinterhalt)
Untreu hält Hof und Leute,
auf der Strasse
Gewalt fährt aus auf Beute;
Friede und Recht sind sehre wund
So Fried als Recht sind todeswund:
(sicheres)
Die dreie haben kein Geleit, die zwei denn werden erst gesund.

In Simrock's modernized version of Walter von der Vogelweide's poem "Der Waise" Mörike's changes are less abundant:

Ich hört ein Wasser rauschen
Sah die Fischer fließen
Und gieng den Fischen lauschen,
Ich sah die Dinge dieser Welt,
Wald, Laub und Rohr und Gras und Feld,
Was kriechet oder flieget,
Was Bein zur Erde bieget,
Das sah ich und ich sag euch das:
Da lebt nicht eines ohne Haß.
Das Wild und das Gewürme,
Die streiten starke Stürme,
So auch die Vögel unter sich,
Doch thun sie eins einmüthiglich,
Sie schaffen stark Gerichte,
Sonst würden sie zu nichte,
Sie wählen Könge, ordnen Recht
Und unterscheiden Herrn und Knecht.
O weh dir deutsche Zunge
So weh dir, deutschem Lande,
Wie stets din ordenunge
Wie ziemet dir die Schande.
Mück ihren König hat
Das nun die Mücke hat ihr Haupt
Und daß dein Ehre also zergeht – bekehre dich
Und du der Ehre bist beraubt!
Die Zirkel (Diademe der kleinen Fürsten) sind
Bekehre dich! Nicht mehr zu hehre (anmaßlich)
Der Fürstenkronen Ehre.

Die armen Könge* drängen dich:
        und heiß' sie
Philippen setz den Waisen auf, so weichen sie und beugen sich.
        treten hinter sich.

        * (Bertold der Reiche v. Zähringen,
          Bernhard v. Sachsen, Otto der Welf.)

Other poems by Walter von der Vogelweide, Mörike gave special attention by marking them which a cross (in the titles supplied by Simrock): "Drückt dich heimlich Sorg und Leid," "Heißt mich froh willkommen sein," "Wunder nimmt mich nimmer, was erblickt," "Das Halmmessen," "Schönheit und Liebreiz," "Vergängliche Freude," "Das täuschende Bild," and "An die Jungfrau."

Another author whom Mörike must have found very useful for recitation in the young women's lectures was Freidank. Simrock's editorial note that Freidank was a contemporary of Walter von der Vogelweide and that Wilhelm Grimm argues that, in fact, Freidank and Walter von der Vogelweide may well have been one and the same person, was crossed by Mörike. Simrock includes over four hundred lines of Freidank's didactic poem "Bescheidenheit." Mörike used three different marks with which to indicate levels of emphasis of a given maxim. Thus, for example, the maxim "Gott dienen ohne Wank / ist aller Weisheit Anfang," Mörike marks with only one slash mark, but the couplet "Wer mit der Welt will Gedeihn / Der muß bisweilen thöricht sein," receives two slash marks, and the couplet "Wer sich selber feind ist / Der sei mein Freund zu keiner Frist," is marked with three slashes. Throughout the poem Mörike crossed at least half of the sententious maxims.

In Simrock's excerpt from Hartmann von Aue's "Der arme Heinrich," Mörike appears to have censored all passages in which the word "nackend" occurs. Mörike either put brackets around those passages, or he changed the wording. Thus, the passage in which the speaker, der arme Heinrich, tells the young virgin that she must first undress before she can be sacrificed for the afflicted Heinrich, Mörike brackets with energetic pencil strokes:

Ich zieh dich aus so nackt und bloß
Und deine Scham wird sicher groß,
Die du dann mit Recht empfähst,
Wenn du so nackend vor mir stehst.

The virgin's subsequent disrobing is also entirely bracketed, and thus also apparently eliminated from recitation:

Sie riß die Kleider aus der Nat,
Schnell fiel herab der ganze Staat
Und nackend stand sie Ganz und gar,
Sie schämte sich auch nicht ein Haar.
 Als sie der Meister angesehn
Hatte, mußte er sich gestehn,
So schönes konn auf Erden
Nicht mehr gefunden werden.

Where Mörike could not get around the plot entirely, he changed the wording, in order to avoid the fact that Heinrich sees the girl naked:

Da sah er durch die Schrunden
die Füße fest
*((*Sie nackend und*))* gebunden.

Once more, the next passage in which the virgin's physical beauty changes Heinrich's mind about the sacrifice, is bracketed by Mörike:

*((*Ihr Leib war so minniglich
Er sah sie an und sah sie auf sich
Und gewann einen neuen Muth.*))*

In Simrock's excerpt from *Parzival*, in the section "Anfortas und der Gral," Mörike adds as indicated:

Ritter saßen da genug, als man Jammer vor sie trug.
Herein zur Thür ein Knappe sprang, eine Lanze* trug er, die war lang.
(Die Sitte war zur Trauer gut), die Schneide nieder tropfte Blut.

* *dieselbe Lanze, womit Anfortas im Kampfe verwundet worden, weil er weltliche Liebe zu seinem Feldgeschrei gemacht, u. die Demuth ō geübt. Er erwartet den Ritter der fragen würde.*

On page 289 Mörike adds another clarifying note to the text of *Parzival*:

Ich greif es traun nicht aus der Luft, er war noch grauer als der Dust.*

* *der Greis – der alte Gralkönig, Titurel Urgroßvater Parzivals.*

Finally, on page 480, Mörike adds the following note to Simrock's excerpt, "Aus Salomon und Morolf." (Neu gereimt von K. Simrock. Berlin, 1839):

Auf biblischen Grundlagen ruhendes aber komb[iniertes] *Gedicht fußend auf Ca. Sal. 30. 31 die Ents*[tehung] *sehr alt, zu unterscheiden v*[on] *e*[inem] *selbst*[ständigen] *Epos in Strophen aus dem 12. Jahr*[hundert] *in Lat*[ein] *Prosabuch die Gespräche Sal. u. Morolf enth*[altend.] *Daselbe versichert zuerst im 14. Jar*[hundert] *in halb niederdeutscher Sprache.*

53 a. F.T. Vischer. *Aesthetik, erster Theil.*

Aside from commentary in the letters and in a few unpublished fragments in connection with his literary lectures in Stuttgart and aside from the corrections of manuscripts of fellow writers and poets, Mörike's marginalia in Vischer's *Aethetik* are the only source of evidence for Mörike's view on literary theory and literary criticism. Mörike was particularly interested in Vischer's discussions of the nature of tragedy, the tragic hero, the concepts of catharsis, the sublime, irony, wit and humor, as well as in his views on the contemporary novel. The most frequent illustration Vischer employs are from the works of Shakespeare and Goethe. The theoretical basis of Vischer's views are the works of Aristotle, Hegel, A.W. Schlegel, Jean Paul and others. In thie following record of Mörike's marginalia the immediate context is cited also.

On page 202 is the following discussion of proportion in the attributes of the tragic hero; to this Mörike added an illustration: "Eigen ist nun aber dem Aristoteles die Forderung einer bestimmten Größe (Poetik 7). Nicht nur die Tragödie soll eine bestimmte Größe haben, sondern alles Schöne. Es darf nicht zu klein seyn, sonst markirt es sich nicht in der Anschauung, nicht zu groß, sonst ist keine Übersicht möglich."*

wenn z.B. ein Thier 10,000 Stadien lang wäre.

Beginning with page 220 through page 340 of the section entitled "Das Erhabene," there are many passages which Mörike crossed. The following passage dealing with what Vischer calls "das tragische Subjekt," on page 287, is heavily crossed by Mörike: "Die tragische Handlung muß daher immer so beschaffen seyn, daß man sieht: der Held hat gefehlt und er konnte doch nicht anders handeln." Also, in an apparent reference to Romeo in *Romeo and Juliet* and to Iago in *Othello*, Vischer here discusses the element of guilt in the tragic hero.

The following passage, in which Vischer illustrates "das Tragische" in Shakespeare's *Kind Lear*, was also heavily crossed by Mörike on page 290: "Lears Töchter sind verdorben, wie Glosters Sohn; man erkennt einen morschen Staat im Zustande der Bösen Wildheit. In dieses alte Uebel greift Lear hinein, seine Schuld ist nur ein Wahn,

aber selbst schon ein Theil und Ausfluß der Verderbniss in einer
Umgebung, wo schöne Worte für Wahrheit wiegen, und so zieht er
sich das ganze Gewebe der Schwärze, das er an einem Faden ergrif-
fen, über das Haupt."

Vischer's concept of the sublime within tragedy occupied Mörike
further. On the endpaper there is the following notation, which
refers to Vischer's section "Das Erhabene:" *Unendliche Persp*[ecti-
ve] *S. 283.* The context is: "Wenn daher eine unendliche Perspek-
tive zum Wesen aller Schönheit gehört, so muß in dieser Form der
Schönheit der ganze Nachdruck auf dieser Unendlichkeit als einem
unabsehlichen Dunkel und Abgrund liegen, aus welchem Alles
kommt und der Alles in sich zurückschlingt."

In reference to the following context on pages 305–306, in which
Vischer discusses Aristotle's concept of catharsis, Mörike crossed the
illustrations from Shakespeare and added a comment below: "Aristoteles weist bekanntlich (Poet. 13) die überaus Schlechten und
ihren Sturz von der Tragödie völlig aus; denn dieser Sturz würde,
wie er meint, weder Mitleid noch Furcht erregen, weil wir jenes nur
dem unverdienten* . . . Sein Grund ließe sich leicht widerlegen . . .
Das tiefe Bedürfniß der Liebe, das Macbeth und Richard III vor
ihrem Untergang aussprechen, erregt die innerste Theilnahme, und
wie wir ihnen auch den Untergang gönnen, wir zittern doch mit ihnen für uns selbst, denn der Dämon, den hier die Nemesis ereilt,
schlummert auch in uns."

* *Vgl. Rob. Zimmermanns (Gesch. der Aesth.) falsche Erklärung der
Katharthis durch Einsicht der Verhältnißmäßigkeit des "großen Fehlers"
u. des daraus entspringenden Unglücks.*

On page 329 Mörike added a clarifying notation to Vischer's discussion of the tragic effect according to Aristotle; "Hier nun ist das
Wichtigste dies, was schon Par. 142, I angeführt ist: daß Aristoteles
Furcht und Mitleiden als Momente Eines Affectes scharfsinnig auf-
faßt, wozu Rhetorik 2, 5. 8. beizuziehen ist. Auch Lessing ist dort
schon genannt; er hat das Verdienst, diesen Punkt in Aristoteles
zuerst aufgehellt zu haben (Hamb. Dram. Abschn. 74ff) – Beiläufig
gesagt: schon diese Stellen der Rhetorik, ebensosehr aber alle in der

Poetik über Furcht und Mitleid widerlegen auf den ersten Anblick die von Göthe (Nachgel. W. B. 6, S. 16–21) aufgestellt, von A. Stahr (deutsche Jahrb. April 1842) aufgenommene Ansicht." –*

* *Nach Göthes Meinung wäre die Rücksicht auf den Zuschauer ein durchaus äußerlicher, der Würde der Tragödie unangemessener Zweck, Der Held soll in der "abgeschlossenen" Handlung durch Furcht und Mitleid gereinigt werden. Nur der beliebten Manier des Aristot. stets an das Nächste u. Augenfälligste anzuknüpfen sey es zuzuschreiben, daß er statt des wahren das scheinbare Subjekt der Reinigung in den Vordergrund gestellt habe.*

In his discussion of the nature of the comic, which Mörike also crossed, Vischer quotes St. Schütze on page 374, to which Mörike adds a concrete example: "Der Ausdruck strebt im Komischen nach dem Kleinsten und Speziellsten und vermeidet das Allgemeine, welches dagegen am liebsten im Erhabenen gebracht wird, weil dieses sich der sinnlichen Bedürfnisse schämt."*

Niobe in Schiller: Siegeslied.

In reference to Vischer's discussion of "Das subjectiv Komische oder der Witz," pp. 416–439, there are the following three comments in the margins:

On page 424 Mörike wrote: *Kästners?* This is in reference to Vischer's discussion of the ingredients of wit and comedy. He attributes the following witty saying to Börne; but Mörike apparently believed it should be attributed to Kästner: "Ebenso Börnes Witz: 'Als Pythagoras seinen Lehrsatz erfunden hatte, opferte er eine Hekatombe; seitdem zittert jeder Ochs, so oft eine neue Wahrheit entdeckt wird,'"

On page 435 Mörike marked a passage: *Unangenehme Vorstellung.* Here he criticzed Vischer for an indelicate illustration of the imagistic element of wit: "Es beutete Jemand den Tod einer theuren Verwandten zu mehreren Schriften aus. Einer, der um sein Urtheil darüber befragt wurde, erzählte statt aller Antwort; ein Fischer vermißte viele Tage sein Weib, endlich fand man ihren Leichnam im Wasser voll von Krebsen, die sich in ihrem Fleische füglich thaten. Diese wurden verkauft und warfen ein Hübsches ab; der Fischer beschloß nun seine Frau noch einmal in's Wasser zu werfen, und so noch mehrmals. Wird auf diese Weise das Bild umständlich ausgeführt, so wird es selbständig und man kann von der Pointe absehen." Finally, on page 439 Mörike added his own example to Vischer's discussion of "Der in seinem Gegenstand eingehende Witz oder die Ironie," p. 436ff. In the marked passage, Vischer distinguishes between two types of irony, a mild irony and a cuttingly cold one. Socrates was capable of both types depending on the circumstances according to Vischer. Vischer concludes: "Daher unterscheiden wir zunächst nur zwei Verfahrungsweisen, deren eine in der Schärfe schonend, die andere schonungslos wirkt, und decken dann den Mangel *aller* Ironie, auf, um erst zum Humor zu gelangen."*

* *Lichtenbergs ironisches Selbstlob der Physiker gegenüber v. Hamlets Wort. Es gibt mehr Dinge – als unsere Philosophie pp.*

53 b. F.T. Vischer. *Aesthetik, dritter Theil.*

The third part of Vischer's *Aesthetik* has the subtitle, "Die Kunstlehre." Here Vischer deals with genre theory and with specific literary devices in the large categories of style.

Starting on page 1220 is a discussion of personification that culminates in the method of presentation by means of adjectival use and epithet. Subsequently Vischer laments the inflation of contemporary literary language by the excessive use of adjectival, hyperbolical forms, to which Mörike added a clarification: "Wie matt muß dem, der an lauter spanischen Pfeffer gewöhnt ist, es erscheinen, wenn Göthe seinen Hermann [in Hermann und Dorothea] nur wohlgebildet, den Vater den menschlichen Hauswirth, die Mutter die zuverlässige Gattin nennt! Die letzteren zwei Prädicate sind nicht versinnlichend, sondern moralisch;* der Dichter hat ja überhaupt ebensosehr zu vergeistigen und zu verallgemeinern, als zu individualisieren.

* *dienen zugleich aber doch zur sinnlichen Vorstellung mit, verhelfen zum physiognomischen Bild der Personen.*

Judging from careful printing error corrections and other markings, Mörike was also intensely interested in Vischer's discussion of the function of the novel as a surrogate medium for the traditional function of poetry. Mörike added an illustration: "Der bedeutendere Geist wird diese Blitze der Idealität [the numinous and uncanny elements only found in poetry] aus tiefen Abgründen des Seelenlebens aufsteigen lassen, wie Göthe in den Partieen von Mignon, die* wie ein Vulkan aus den Flächen seines W. Meisters hervorsprühen."

sagt Lewes wie ein Regenbogen in den Straßen von London erscheinen.

In reference to Vischer's discussion, "Die Arten der Lyrischen Dichtung" in the subcategory "3. Ballade und Romanze," Mörike added a qualifying comment to the following passage on page 1361. "Die classische Dichtung bietet nichts für diese Stelle, im Alterthum blieb nach der Ausscheidung des Epos keine epische Form von lyrischem Charakter zurück." *Die epischem Hymnen?*

Mörike also noted an important distinction in reference to Vischer's discussion of the genre ballad: "Dagegen tritt der Unterschied der Stylprinzipien in der neueren Poesie zunächst als ein nationaler auf und lehnt sich so an die Namen Romanze und Ballade. Ballade ist zwar ein italienisches Wort und bezeichnet ein Tanzlied, das ursprünglich die bestimmte rhythmische Form von drei verschlungenen Strophen mit Refrain hatte, allein wie es in England stehend wurde als Name für das epische Lied, wie es dort und in Schottland sich ausbildete, so verband sich damit der Sinn eines bestimmten Characters der Behandlung, in dem wir ein reines Bild jener zweiten Stylrichtung haben, und die rhythmische Form bewegte sich frei in heimischen Maßen,*"

Nach Andern stammt der Name "Ballade" aus dem Altbritischen, Wallischen − gwael-awd, sprich wal-ad − d.h. Lied in der Volkssprache (siehe "Deutsche Dichter" erläutert v. Götzinger 1. Thl.) hinge also nicht mit dem ital. ballata zusammen.

In the final comment Mörike made in this volume, he criticizes Vischer's style on page 1471 in reference to a discussion under the subtitle: "Die Arten der dramatischen Poesie:" "Göthe nimmt die Wendung zum classischen Styl in seinem Egmont ... Von da an vertieft Göthe seine antik gefühlten Gestalten durch moderne Humanität und deutsches Herz, aber er setzt sie nicht in die concrete Farbe der wirklichen Individualität und Naturwahrheit, schon darum nicht, weil es mehr *Seelenbilder, als männliche Charactergestalten sind.*" [Mörike's emphasis] *Das ist richtig gedacht, ō richtig ausgedrückt.*

Conclusion

Seen individually, Mörike's note-taking in the various works in his possession, the various comments regarding such elements of the creative process as images, ideas and diction, clearly reveal his affinity for certain authors. Such writers to which he returned again and again are Shakespeare, Goethe and Lichtenberg. Such repeated readings parallel returns in his own productivity: The revision of *Maler Nolten* in the last phase of his life thus constitutes for Mörike a rereading of his first period of creativity through the years 1828–32, when his intense preoccupation with Goethe and Shakespeare leaves such resonant marks on his own work. Equally important, the record of his reading reveals once more Mörike's precision in his own poetic practice as well as his otherwise elusive literary/critical commentary as he — for example — expresses his love of the poetry of Hölty, his fascination for the ideas about the creative process expressed by the Schiller-Goethe exchange, a type of family or tribal affection for K. Mayer, but, on the other hand, out and out dislike of the poetry by Justinus Kerner. Thus the marginalia — as fragmentary as they may have come down to us — contain elements of what contemporary psychoanalytic reader-response critics would refer to as "case history", and contribute significantly to our understanding of Mörike's autobiography, especially in his role as critical reader.

Bibliography

I. Manuscript Collections:

Schiller-Nationalmuseum / Deutsches Literaturarchiv in Marbach (SNM), Mörike-Archiv, Nachlaß.

Nationale Forschungs- und Gedenkstätten der klassischen deutschen Literatur in Weimar (GSA), Goethe-Schiller Archiv, Teilnachlaß.

Württembergische Landesbibliothek Stuttgart (LBS).

Stadtarchiv Stuttgart, Mörike-Sammlung, Dr. Fritz Kauffmann.

II. Editions, Letters and Documentary Materials:
(Abbreviated titles used follow in parenthesis.)

Mörike, Eduard. *Eduard Mörike: Werke und Briefe, historisch-kritische Gesamt-ausgabe*, ed. Hans-Henrik Krummacher, Herbert Meyer, Bernhard Zeller, 19 vols. Stuttgart: Ernst Klett, 1967ff. (*Briefe, 1811–1828,* vol. X)
—————. *Mozart auf der Reise nach Prag*, ed. M.B. Benn. London: G.G. Harrap, 1970.
—————. *Sämtliche Werke*, ed. Gerhart Baumann and Siegfried Große, 3 vols. Stuttgart: Cotta, 1959. (Baumann, *Letters*)
—————. *Sämtliche Werke*, ed. Jost Perfahl and Helga Unger, 2 vols. München: Winkler, 1968.
—————. *Mörikes Werke*, ed. Harry Maync, 2nd ed., 3 vols. Leipzig and Wien: Bibliographisches Institut, 1914. (Maync, *Werke*)
—————. *Miss Jenny Harrower . . .*, [ed.] Gesellschaft der Bibliophilen. Weimar: Poeschel & Trepte, 1907.
Bauer, Ludwig Amandus. *Briefe an Eduard Mörike*, ed. Bernhard Zeller and Hans-Ulrich Simon. Marbach: Ernst Klett, 1976.
Theodor Storm – Eduard Mörike. Theodor Storm – Margarethe Mörike. Brief-wechsel, mit Storms 'Meine Erinerungen an Eduard Mörike,' ed. H. and W. Kohlschmidt. Berlin: Erich Schmidt, 1978.
Mörike, Eduard. *Eduard Mörike: Briefe an seine Braut Luise Rau*, ed. Friedhelm Kemp. München: Kösel, 1965.

225

Mörike, Eduard. *Unveröffentlichte Briefe*, ed. Friedrich Seebaß, 2nd. ed., Stuttgart: Cotta, 1945. (Seebaß, *Unpubl. Letters*)

————. *Briefe*, ed. Friedrich Seebaß. Tübingen: R. Wunderlich, 1939. (Seebaß, *Letters*)

Freundeslieb' und Treu', *250 Briefe Eduard Mörikes an Wilhelm Hartlaub*, ed. Gotthelf Renz. Tübingen & Leipzig: Leopold Klotz, 1938. (Renz, *Letters*)

Briefwechsel zwischen Eduard Mörike und Friedrich Theodor Vischer, ed. Robert Vischer. München: C.H. Beck, 1926.

"Ungedruckte Briefe Mörikes an David Friedrich Strauß," ed. Karl Walter, in *Das literarische Echo*, vol. 24 (1921—22), pp. 591—98.

Briefwechsel zwischen Eduard Mörike und Moriz v. Schwind, ed. H.W. Rath. Stuttgart: Julius Hoffmann, [1920].

Briefwechsel zwischen Th. Storm und Eduard Mörike, ed. H.W. Rath. Stuttgart: Julius Hoffmann, [1919].

Briefwechsel zwischen Hermann Kurz und Eduard Mörike, ed. Heinz Kindermann. Stuttgart: Strecker und Schröder, 1919. (Kurz, *Letters*)

Mörike, Eduard. *Eduard Mörikes Briefe*, ed. Karl Fischer and Rudolf Krauß, 2 vols. Berlin: Otto Elsner, 1903 and 1904.

"Eduard Mörike: Briefe aus seiner Sturm- und Drangperiode," ed. Rudolf Krauß, in *Deutsche Rundschau*, Heft 4 and 7 (Jan. and April 1895), pp. 59—82 and 103—120.

Eduard Mörike. 1804. 1875. 1975. Katalog der Gedenkausstellung zum 100. Todestag im Schiller-Nationalmuseum Marbach a. N., ed. Bernhard Zeller et al. Stuttgart: Ernst Klett, 1975.

Scheffler, Walter. *Die Sammlung Dr. Fritz Kauffmann . . . Gesamtverzeichnis*. Stuttgart: Ernst Klett, 1967.

Kauffmann, Fritz. *Eduard Mörike und seine Freunde. Eine Ausstellung aus der Mörike-Sammlung Dr. Fritz Kauffmann*. Stuttgart: Stadtarchiv, 1965.

Eduard Mörikes Haushaltsbuch, [ed.] Bezirksheimatmuseum Mergentheim, Bad Mergentheim: Hans Kling, 1951.

III. Works Cited and Consulted:

Adorno, Theodor. "'Lyrik und Gesellschaft," *Noten zur Literatur*, vol. 1 (Frankfurt: Suhrkamp, 1958), pp. 73—104.

Anonymous. [Review of] H. Lingg, F. Loewe, J.G. Fischer, A. Knapp in *Allgemeine Zeitung* (Augsburg), No. 300, Oct. 11 and 27, 1854.

Barnouw, Dagmar. *Entzückte Anschauung. Sprache und Realität in der Lyrik Eduard Mörikes*. München: Wilhelm Fink, 1971.

Barthel, Ludwig Friedrich. "Mörikes 'Vater Goethe'," *Goethe Kalender* (1938), pp. 101–54.

Berend, Eduard. "Mörike auf Tiecks Spuren," *Jahrbuch der deutschen Schillergesellschaft*, vol. 12 (1968), pp. 315–17.

Bloom, Harold. *The Anxiety of Influence: A Theory of Poetry*. New York: Oxford Univ. Press, 1973.

Bradley, A.C. *Shakespearean Tragedy*. New York: Fawcett, 1904, rpt. 1967.

Capps, Jack L. *Emily Dickinson's Reading. 1836–1886*. Cambridge: Harvard University Press, 1966.

Cingolani, Charles L. "Eduard Mörike: Wirklichkeit und Dichtung," Diss. Basel: Universität Basel, 1973.

Dilthey, Wilhelm. *Das Erlebnis und die Dichtung. Lessing, Goethe, Novalis, Hölderlin*, 12 ed., Göttingen: Vanderhoek & Rupprecht, 1921.

Doerksen, Victor, G. *Mörikes Elegien und Epigramme. Eine Interpretation*. Zürich: Juris, 1964.

Duncan, Bruce. "'Emilia Galotti lag auf dem Pult aufgeschlagen:' Werther as (Mis-)Reader," *Goethe Yearbook: Publication of the Goethe Society of North America*, vol. 1 (1982), pp. 42–50.

Emmersleben, August. "Das Schicksal in Mörikes Leben und Dichten," Diss. Kulmbach: Universität Würzburg, 1931.

Enzinger, Moriz. "Mörikes Gedicht 'Auf eine Lampe'," *Österreichische Akademie der Wissenschaften*, ccliv, 4. Abh. (1965), pp. 1–47.

Farrell, R.B. "Mörike and Hölty," in *Affinities: Essays in German and English Literature*, ed. R.W. Last (London: Oswald Wolf, 1971), pp. 246–55.

Gesellschaft, Literatur, Lesen: Literaturrezeption in theoretischer Sicht, ed. Manfred Naumann, et al. Berlin & Weimar: Aufbau, 1976.

Goethe, Johann Wolfgang. *Goethes Werke*, ed. Erich Trunz, 8th ed., 14 vols. Hamburg: Christian Wegner, 1967.

Goethes Briefe, ed. Karl R. Mandelkow, 4 vols. Hamburg: Christian Wegner, 1962–67.

Golther, Wolfgang. "Hans Sachs und der Chronist Albert Krantz," in *Hans Sachs Forschungen: Festschrift*, ed. A.L. Stiefel. Nürnberg, 1894.

Graevenitz, Gerhart v. *Eduard Mörike: Die Kunst der Sünde. Zur Geschichte des literarischen Individuums*. Tübingen: Max Niemeyer, 1978.

Graham-Appelbaum, Ilse. "Zu Mörikes Gedicht 'Auf eine Lampe'," *Modern Language Notes*, lxviii (1953), pp. 328–33.

Hesse, Hermann. *Nürnberger Reise*. Berlin, 1953.

————. "Beschwörungen, Rundbrief im Februar 1954." Privatdruck.

Heydebrand, Renate von. *Eduard Mörikes Gedichtwerk*. Stuttgart: J.B. Metzler, 1972.

Holthusen, Hans Egon. *Mörike in Selbstzeugnissen und Bilddokumenten*. Hamburg: Rowohlt, 1971.

Immerwahr, Raymond. "The Loves of Maler Nolten," *Rice University Studies*, vol. lvii, No. 4 (1971), pp. 73–87.

Iser, Wolfgang. *Der Akt des Lesens: Theorie ästhetischer Wirkung.* München: Fink, 1976. (*The Act of Reading: A Theory of Aesthetic Response.* Baltimore: Johns Hopkins University Press, 1978.)

Jennings, Lee B. "Suckelborst, Wispel, and Mörike's Mythopoeia," *Euphorion*, vol. 69 (1975), pp. 320–32.

———. "Mörike's Grotesquery: A Post-Romantic Phenomenon," *Journal of English and Germanic Philology*, vol. 59, No. 4 (Oct. 1960), pp. 600–16.

———. [Review of Kenzo Miyashita, Mörikes Verhältnis zu seinen Zeitgenossen], *German Quarterly* (Sept. 1974), pp. 160–1.

Jochems, Helmut. "Urne und Lampe. Vorüberlegungen zu einem textanalytischen Transformationsbegriff," *Literatur in Wissenschaft und Unterricht*, vol. 13 (1980), pp. 115–23.

Jones, Ernest. "The Oedipus Complex as an Explanation of Hamlet's Mystery," *The American Journal of Psychology*, vol. 21 (1910), pp. 1–37.

Keats, John. *The Letters of John Keats, 1814–1821*, 2 vols., ed. Hyder E. Rollins. Cambridge: Harvard Univ. Press, 1958.

Kerner, Justinus. *Die Seherin von Prevorst.* Stuttgart & Tübingen: Cotta, 1829.

Könnecker, Barbara. *Hans Sachs.* Stuttgart: J.B. Metzler, 1971.

Koschlig, Manfred. "Die Barock-Rezeption bei Mörike. Ein Bericht," *Daphnis: Zeitschrift für mittlere deutsche Literatur*, vol. 7, Heft 1–2 (1978), pp. 341–59.

Krummacher, Hans-Henrik. "Sannazaro und Venantius Fortunatus in Nachdichtungen Mörikes," *Mannheimer Hefte*, vol. 2 (1978), pp. 73–83.

———. "Zu Mörikes Gedichten, Ausgaben und Überlieferungen," *Jahrbuch der deutschen Schillergesellschaft*, vol. 5 (1961), pp. 267–344.

Lang, Wilhelm. "Rudolf Lohbauer," *Württembergische Vierteljahrshefte für Landesgeschichte*, Jahrgang 5 (1897), pp. 107–36.

Lichtenberg, C.G. *Vermischte Schriften*, 8 vols. Göttingen: Diederich, 1867.

Loewe, Feodor. *Gedichte*, 2nd ed. Stuttgart: Cotta, 1860.

Mautner, Franz H. *Lichtenberg: Geschichte seines Geistes.* Berlin: Walter de Gruyter, 1968.

Maync, Harry. *Eduard Mörike: Sein Leben und Dichten*, 5th ed. Stuttgart: Cotta, 1944.

———. "Eduard Mörike im Verkehr mit berühmten Zeitgenossen," *Westermanns Illustrierte Deutsche Monatshefte*, Nr. 556 (1903), pp. 487-502.

Miyashita, Kenzo, *Mörikes Verhältnis zu seinen Zeitgenossen.* Bern & Frankfurt: Herbert Lang, 1971.

Müller, A. *Bismark, Nietzsche, Scheffel, Mörike: Der Einfluß nervöser Zustände auf ihr Leben und Schaffen, vier Krankheitsgeschichten.* Bonn: A. Marcus & E. Wener, 1921.

Nibbrig, Hart Christiaan L. *Verlorene Unmittelbarkeit. Zeiterfahrung und Zeitgestaltung bei Mörike*. Bonn: Bouvier, 1973.

O'Swald, Harriet P. "Die Idee der Reinheit im Werk Eduard Mörikes," Diss. Seattle: University of Washington, 1969.

Partl, Kurt. "Die Spiegelung romantischer Poetik in der biedermeierlichen Dichtungsstruktur Mörikes und Platens," in *Zur Literatur der Restaurationsepoche 1815–1848* (Stuttgart: J.B. Metzler, 1970), pp. 490–560.

Plato. *The Works of Plato*. ed. Irwin Edman. New York: Random House, 1956.

Prawer, S.S. *Mörike und seine Leser: Versuch einer Wirkungsgeschichte*. Stuttgart: Ernst Klett, 1960.

————. "Mignon's Revenge: A Study of Mörike's *Maler Nolten*," *Publication of the English Goethe Society*, vol. 25 (1956), pp. 73–84.

————. *German Lyric Poetry*. London: Routledge & Paul, 1952.

Price, Lawrence M. *The Reception of English Literature in Germany*. Berkeley: Univ. of California Press, 1932.

Rehder, Helmut. "Verwandlungen des Lyrischen: Mörike und Shakespeare," in *Creative Encounter: Festschrift for Herman Salinger* (Chapel Hill: Univ. of North Carolina Press, 1978), pp. 40–44.

Rückert, Gerhard. *Mörike und Horaz*. Nürnberg: Hans Karl, 1970.

Ruppert, Hans. *Goethes Bibliothek: Katalog*. Weimar: Nationale Forschungs- und Gedenkstätten der deutschen klassischen Literatur in Weimar, 1958.

Rupprecht, Gerda. "Mörikes Leistung als Übersetzer aus den klassischen Sprachen . . ." Diss. München: Universität München, 1958.

Schlegel, August Wilhelm. *Kritische Schriften*, ed. Emil Staiger, Zürich: Artemis, 1962.

Sengle, Friedrich. "Mörike-Probleme," *Germanisch-Romanische Monatsschrift*, N.F., vol. 33 (Oct. 1951), pp. 36–47.

————. *Arbeiten zur Deutschen Literatur 1750–1850*. Stuttgart: J.B. Metzler, 1956.

————. *Biedermeierzeit: Deutsche Literatur im Spannungsfeld zwischen Restauration und Revolution 1815–1848*, 3 vol. Stuttgart: J.B. Metzler, 1971, 1972 and 1980.

Shakespeare, William. *Shakespeares Werke*, transl. A.W. Schlegel and L. Tieck, 4 vols. Berlin: Paul Franke, [no date].

————. *William Shakespeares Schauspiele*, transl. Johann Joachim Eschenburg, 11 vols. Zürich: Orell & Füßli, 1798–1804.

————. *The Words of Shakespeare, The Poems*, ed J.C. Maxwell. Cambridge: Cambridge Univ. Press, 1966.

————. *The London Shakespeare*, 6 vols., ed. John Munro. New York: Simon & Schuster, 1957.

Simon, Hans-Ulrich. *Mörike Chronik*. Stuttgart: J.B. Metzler, 1981.

229

Slessarev, Helga. "Der Abgrund der Betrachtung: Über den schöpferischen Vorgang bei Mörike," *German Quarterly*, vol. 34 (1961), 41–49.

Spitzer, Leo. "Wiederum Mörikes Gedicht 'Auf eine Lampe'," *Trivium* (1951), pp. 133–147.

Stahl, Ernst Leopold. *Shakespeare und das deutsche Theater*. Stuttgart: W. Kohlhammer, 1947.

Staiger, Emil. *Die Kunst der Interpretation*. Zürich: Atlantis, 1955.

Steig, Reinhold. "Mörikes Verehrung im Grimmschen Kreise," *16. Rechenschaftsbericht des Schwäbischen Schillervereins* (1911/1912), pp. 35–45.

Storz, Gerhard. *Eduard Mörike*. Stuttgart: Ernst Klett, 1967.

Taraba, Wolfgang. "Die Rolle der 'Zeit' und des 'Schicksals' in Eduard Mörikes *Maler Nolten*," in *Eduard Mörike*, ed. Victor Doerksen, (Darmstadt: Wissenschaftliche Buchgesellschaft, 1975), pp. 129–160.

Todorov, Tzvetan. "Reading as Construction," transl. M.A. August in *The Reader in the Text: Essays on Audience and Interpretation*, ed. Susan R. Suleiman and Inge Crosman (Princeton, New Jersey: Princeton Univ. Press, 1980), pp. 67–82.

Ulmer, Gregory. *The Legend of Herostratus: Existential Envy in Rousseau and Unamuno*. Gainesville: Univ. of Florida Press, 1977.

Unger, Helga. *Mörike Kommentar zu sämtlichen Werken*. München: Winkler, 1970.

Ungerer, Eugen. *Mörikes Aufenthalt in Wermutshausen und Schwäbisch Hall*. Schwäbisch Hall: Historischer Verein, 1950.

Vischer, Friedrich Theodor. *Über das Erhabene und Komische. Ein Beitrag zu der Philosophie des Schönen*. Stuttgart, 1837, rpt. Frankfurt, 1967.

Waiblinger, Wilhelm. *Waiblinger: Werke und Briefe*, 5 vols., ed. Hans Königer. Stuttgart: Cotta, 1980f.

———. *Die Tagebücher 1821–1826*, ed. Herbert Meyer. Stuttgart: Ernst Klett, 1956.

Weinberg, Kurt. "Mörikes 'Correctur für den Hausbrauch' am Rande eines Gedichts von Chamisso," *Euphorion*, vol. 65 (1971), pp. 429–32.

Wiese, Benno v. *Eduard Mörike: Ein Romantischer Dichter*. Tübingen: R. Wunderlich, 1950, rpt. 1978.